T0265751

How We Heal

A JOURNEY TOWARD TRUTH,
RACIAL HEALING, AND COMMUNITY
TRANSFORMATION FROM
THE INSIDE OUT

How
We
Heal

La June Montgomery Tabron

President and CEO of the W. K. Kellogg Foundation

DISRUPTION
BOOKS

New York, NY   Washington, DC

This book is memoir. It reflects the author's present recollections of experiences over time. Some names and characteristics have been changed, some events have been compressed, and some dialogue has been re-created.

Published by Disruption Books
Washington, DC
www.disruptionbooks.com

Distributed by Disruption Books

For information about special discounts for bulk purchases, please contact Disruption Books at info@disruptionbooks.com.

Cover by Liz Driesbach
Book design by Brian Phillips

Library of Congress Cataloging-in-Publication Data available

Print ISBN: 978-1-63331-101-5
eBook ISBN: 978-1-63331-102-2

First Edition

TO MY FAMILY,
THE GIANTS ON WHOSE
SHOULDERS I STAND

CONTENTS

Introduction

TOWARD HEALING AND HOPE

I T WAS A SUNDAY in late June 1963 when a young minister from
Atlanta, Georgia, visited my hometown of Detroit, Michigan. I
was eight months old, the ninth of Herbert and Mary Louise Montgomery's ten children, so I can only imagine the scene. Yet I can see
it clearly in my mind's eye.

I can picture Dr. Martin Luther King Jr. marching down Woodward Avenue with as many as 250,000 of my neighbors. Together they
comprised the Walk to Freedom, which was, at the time, the largest civil
rights protest in United States history. It commemorated, in part, one
of Detroit's most notorious race riots, fomented two decades earlier—a
riot that had claimed twenty-five Black lives, including seventeen at
the hands of police.

I can feel the righteous, hopeful demand in the summer air: that
our nation make good on its promise of democracy, of democratic
values. The demand came less than two weeks after the assassination of
civil rights activist Medgar Evers. Less than two weeks after Alabama
Governor George Wallace stood for segregation in a schoolhouse
door. One month after a group of brave students staged a sit-in at a
Woolworth's lunch counter in Jackson, Mississippi. Two months after
the start of Dr. King's Birmingham Campaign.

And I can hear, even now—amid the swirling of moral clarity and moral contradiction—Dr. King giving voice to his vision, his dream, which would define the American civil rights movement for the ages. This was an early version of the civic prayer that, through a mix of divine inspiration and improvisation, would two months later become one of the most important refrains in all American history—second only perhaps to the Declaration of Independence, to which Dr. King explicitly appealed.

"I have a dream," he said in Detroit, "that one day, little White children and little [Black] children will be able to join hands as brothers and sisters."[1]

He was talking about me.

I reflect on this moment for several reasons. First, because this dream—that every child, family, and community can thrive—came to inform and inspire my life's purpose, too. Second, because of *where* Dr. King finally shared this dream in full, and where our spirits may have met: the Motor City, Motown, the Arsenal of Democracy—but also a workshop *for* democracy.

Detroit was and is my home. It's the site of a grand but flawed experiment with multiracial pluralism, a city where hundreds of thousands of Black migrants, refugees from Jim Crow, moved for opportunity during the first half of the twentieth century. It's a city where Americans of every color and creed have always dared to dream, to build, and to push the bounds of industry, enterprise, and equality. I like to think there was a reason that Dr. King first articulated his dream at Cobo Hall in Detroit, two months before he shared it from the steps of the Lincoln Memorial in Washington, DC.

My story starts here—in this time, in this place. This is a Detroit story: one of faith and hope and love, of family and grace and generosity. A story about the ways we, as a community, fall short—but also the ways we pick ourselves up, dust ourselves off, and begin anew, time and again.

This, too, is an American story. As the poet Langston Hughes wrote, with wisdom that transcends generations:

America never was America to me,
And yet I swear this oath—
America will be!

It is a story about segregation, injustice, violence, and grief. It is a story about the power of truth—and through truth and connection, the possibility of healing.

o o o

That I have arrived here, the ninth president and CEO of one of the world's leading legacy foundations, is itself a marvel of grace and generosity—two qualities shared by a young man named Will Keith Kellogg.

In 1876, W. K. Kellogg—an accountant like me—went to work for his older brother, Dr. John Harvey Kellogg, then director of the Battle Creek Sanitarium, on the other side of the state of Michigan. In a botched attempt to make a more-digestible food than bread for Dr. J. H.'s patients, W. K. accidentally invented a new food that would change breakfast around the world: Corn Flakes. Soon after the turn of the century, he became one of the wealthiest men in the United States.

Then tragedy struck. In 1913, W. K.'s grandson, a toddler, fell from a second-story window. Thankfully, the boy survived, but he lived the rest of his life with physical disabilities. Despite his colossal riches and important personal connections, Mr. Kellogg could not find suitable immediate and long-term care nearby—a reality he found intolerable. In response to this incident, he later wrote that he "resolved to lend what aid I could to [needy] children."[2]

Mr. Kellogg began donating to good causes around Battle Creek. But he soon developed a broader vision. On June 21, 1930—about seventeen months after the birth of Dr. King—he founded and endowed the W. K. Kellogg Foundation, dedicated to "the welfare, comfort, health, education, feeding, clothing, sheltering, and safeguarding of children and youth, directly or indirectly, without regard to sex, race, creed, or nationality."

As you will see in the pages that follow, this mission has been my focus for nearly four decades. In Mr. Kellogg's calling, I have found mine: the work of serving children who are like me—and the work of serving justice. And a large part of this work has centered around racial healing, a time-tested practice that the foundation has devoted itself, over many decades, to understanding and promoting.

○ ○ ○

Right from the outset, it is important to note that the W. K. Kellogg Foundation did not *invent* racial healing. The roots of this practice reach back through millennia, to Indigenous communities across North America, Africa, and Australia.[3] We must acknowledge this fact, especially because these cultures have so often been minimized or even erased. Despite this, elements of these cultures have been passed down through history books and survived in their people, and today we all can benefit from their time-honored insights. Racial healing harnesses a deep need for connection—one that has defined human beings as a species.

It starts with truth-telling and solidarity-building. One of its most potent tools is the racial healing circle, a powerful technique I have seen at work in all kinds of settings in communities across the United States and the world. These circles are a means to share stories—which, after all, is the surest way to teach and learn. People begin to see their shared humanity. Relationships begin to congeal. And with these relationships in place, communities can begin to address the racism that has rooted itself into the many systems, structures, and institutions that give shape and meaning to our lives—locally, nationally, and globally.

In the chapters to come, I will tell you all about the racial healing process, personalizing it with my own story, in the hope that you will share yours with others in your community. I will share my own truth—the truth as I have lived and experienced it as a Black woman in the United States—in service of something bigger. My objective is never to blame or shame, but rather to illuminate the path from truth to empathy, understanding, action, and eventually repair and transformation.

I will show you how my ancestors, the Montgomery family of Mississippi, emerged from enslavement to build Mound Bayou, a Black refuge on the Delta—only to see that refuge brought to ruin.[4]

I will show you how, as a frightened little girl, I lived through the 1967 Detroit Rebellion yet lost my best friend to the white flight that followed. How I experienced a bewildering blend of solidarity, allyship, and prejudice on the campus of my alma mater—the University of Michigan—one of the world's leading public institutions of higher education, at the time still finding its way toward equity. How I secured a dream job at a major accounting firm, only to be sidelined explicitly because of my race.

I will show you what it was like to be ultimately the only full-time employee of color in a nonadministrative position at the W. K. Kellogg Foundation when I joined the organization in the late 1980s. How it felt to work in a sector where the merest mention of race was considered taboo. And how, thanks to the efforts of several courageous colleagues—largely employees of color, supported by dedicated allies across backgrounds and cultures—the foundation became the champion for racial equity and racial healing that it remains today.

Along the way, I will show how the fallacy of "colorblindness" does a disservice to us all, because it renders invisible—and allows us to ignore—the ongoing and persistent human significance of race in American life. How, alternatively, racial healing can help communities of all shapes and sizes across the United States and around the world.

5

How the methodology can change hearts and minds, creating even the unlikeliest of allies, from former segregationists to racist shock jocks. And how my husband, Avery, and I have found ourselves filled with hope for the family we have nurtured—my two sons, Justin and Jordan; my stepdaughters, Lauren and Kalynn; my three grandchildren, Marley, Avery, and Charles Jr.—and for the kind of United States that we ought to pass forward to them.

Like the poet Langston Hughes said, "America will be!"

∘ ∘ ∘

Before we go on, I offer a word of caution: Healing is hard.

Sometimes, people assume that healing is the soft stuff. Someone I know once insisted that it was "just meetings." That could not be further from the truth.

Racial healing asks us to confront uncomfortable realities about our history, our society, and our own unconscious beliefs—which is why my colleagues and I have decided to adopt a practice also utilized by others of capitalizing *White* along with the names of other races and ethnicities in this book and elsewhere. We all operate inside the same machinery of racial hierarchy—the same systems of caste, as journalist and author Isabel Wilkerson describes them—even within and among communities of color. Indeed, racial healing brings us into conversations that can make us feel defensive. It demands that we listen when we would rather turn away. Ultimately, it challenges us to commit to one another, because generations of racism—persistent bias and prejudice, born of discrimination, subjugation, and violence—cannot be reversed overnight. On the contrary.

For all these reasons and more, healing is not optional. By repairing relationships, healing enables structural and systemic change. Healing is a necessary stage in the long journey toward what Frederick Douglass called "absolute equality"—a stage that requires the hard work that, for too long, we have been trying to avoid.[5]

Despite these challenges, now we are more ready—and hungrier—for racial healing than ever. For people of all backgrounds, the brutal murders of George Floyd, Breonna Taylor, and other Americans of color represented a flashpoint: a moment when all Americans could not avoid seeing, in the harsh light of day, the painful reality of racism all around them.

No doubt, for many of us, the desire for healing is real. Across our society, amid our myriad diversity, most of us yearn for the nation of Dr. King's dream: one truly committed to equal rights, equal justice, and equal opportunity. And yet too few of us know where to start.

That is why I wrote this book: to introduce a proven model of racial healing and to offer readers the tools for putting it into practice—whether at school or work, in a neighborhood or a larger community, with people you've just met or with people you love.

We need millions of people to get involved—to start engaging in conversation—and I hope that you will be among them. The good news is that millions of people are already on this journey. Taking the next step can be as simple as turning a page.

Chapter 1
A VICIOUS CYCLE

S YCAMORES SHADED MY CHILDHOOD STREET. The great
trees provided cover as my friends and I played—running from
house to house, hitting baseballs down alleys, calling to each other
from porches under our parents' gazes. Motown music filled the air.
Laughter bounced between homes. It was a picturesque, magical life.

From some angles, it's hard to believe that this idyll was Detroit,
Michigan.

To students of urban history, the Motor City has become a cau-
tionary tale. During the closing decades of the twentieth century,
disinvestment and population decline left buildings ruined, factories
empty, and homes abandoned. By the mid-1980s, Detroit had the
highest murder rate per capita among large US cities.[1] In 2013, it
earned a dubious distinction when it became the largest US city to
declare bankruptcy.[2]

The Detroit that raised me was a different world. In the 1960s and
1970s, my neighborhood provided a haven for families like mine—part
of a thriving Black middle class in an integrated, multiracial, multi-
ethnic community.

My parents moved our family there from Clarksdale, Mississippi.
Herbert and Mary Louise Montgomery had met in elementary school
and become childhood sweethearts. But nothing they did—neither
their education nor their work ethic nor even my father's service in

the Korean War—could overcome the racism of the Jim Crow South. My father couldn't find work to support his family. So, in 1954, he and my mother joined the Great Migration.

For as long as human beings have roamed Earth, they have crossed swamps, plains, and mountains in pursuit of better lives. Black Americans are no different: The Great Migration saw my family and millions of others move from the Deep South to northern cities for better-paying jobs and a respite from the pernicious, deep-seated, and often violent racism typified by Jim Crow.

Detroit provided much of what my mother and father sought. Shortly after the move, my father earned a union job on the assembly line at the Chrysler plant in the nearby suburb of Warren. It gave him a sense of pride and dignity, which everyone deserves, and paid enough to support my mom and the first of their children, my older siblings. By the time I was two years old, in 1964, my father was doing even better: He had saved enough to move us to the cozy and quiet Cadillac Boulevard.

I spent my childhood on that street, in a big white house with red curtains. Boxwoods lined the driveway. As far as I could tell, we had everything: a finished attic, a basement big enough to ride our bikes and roller-skate in, a pool table, and enough bedrooms to hold our large, loving family. I was number nine out of ten, the second-to-last kid. My older brothers and sisters sometimes got sick of me because I stuck to them like glue. I loved it because I always had a playmate.

Rita Fay, the next-oldest sibling, took me under her wing. She was five years older and a born teacher, and she often took me upstairs to play school in the attic. Even then, I was eager to learn. Rita Fay taught me lessons she had learned in school: how to spell my name, how to write in cursive, how to read before I could even speak full sentences. Sometimes, we learned to the tunes of Sam Cooke or Ray Charles coming from our parents' record player. We pulled books from the pantry, which our mother had turned into a library from top to bottom.

Best of all, I wasn't Rita Fay's only student. Our youngest sister, Brenda—number ten—joined us as soon as she could toddle. So did our nephews and nieces and whoever else happened to be visiting at the time. And so did other kids we knew in the neighborhood, including our next-door neighbors, Ben and Jenefer.

Some people wait decades before they meet a kindred spirit. I've been lucky enough to have met a few. Jenefer was one of the first, and we quickly became best friends. She was one year younger and could have been my sister. Her brother, Ben, was my age. Her father was a preacher and a teacher, and her mother was a housewife. We practically lived together—playing every day, sleeping over at each other's houses, riding our bikes, playing baseball with the other neighborhood kids. I knew her house as well as I knew my own. She could've said the same.

It didn't matter one bit that I was Black and Jenefer was White.

As a child, I had little awareness of race. I grew up with friends like Jenefer, with trips to the local drugstore for sodas and smiles from the nice White lady who owned it. In the Jim Crow South, my parents had endured horrific racism. But they never dwelled on the past. Instead, they lived up to their motto: *If at first you don't succeed, try, try again.*

After all, this was Detroit—the East Side, the sixties, with more and more social and political freedoms written into law. In integrated neighborhoods like mine, many White and Black neighbors worked and worshipped and played together. From the big white house with red curtains on Cadillac Boulevard, it looked like the United States had finally learned from its past.

Right?

"A TIME BOMB IS TICKING"

I didn't know it, but the veil that shrouded the United States' racism beyond Cadillac Boulevard was lifting.

Over the course of the Great Migration and afterward, Detroit grew more and more segregated.[3] Black families filled homes in the inner city, making it majority-Black. White Detroiters, who had more opportunities, moved to the suburbs.[4] Despite this, the Detroit Police Department remained dominated by White personnel.[5] By 1967, the entire force of 4,700 had only around fifty Black officers working alongside White officers.[6]

Perhaps it should have been no surprise, therefore, that police brutality in Detroit had become widespread. Statistics show that during my childhood in the early 1960s—while I was playing school, riding bikes, and attending church with White neighbors and friends—Detroit police inflicted hundreds of head wounds on Black residents every year. (Tellingly, the injuries suffered by officers in these same confrontations tended to be to their hands—especially the knuckles.)[7]

Newspaper accounts revealed the brutal tactics officers deployed in the name of public safety: In one incident, a Black man chased by law enforcement for allegedly snatching a purse was shot in the back—a tragically common outcome of police interaction.[8] My neighbors and siblings, as I later learned, routinely saw cops pull up to groups of Black men on the street and harass or beat them without cause. Had circumstances been even slightly different, my loved ones could have fallen victim to these attacks themselves. By the second half of the decade, most families on my block knew someone whose rights had been violated by the police.

All of my brothers had encounters with the police. Thankfully, whether by the grace of God or by sheer luck, none of these incidents turned violent. I remember my youngest brother, Gregory, getting arrested more than once for driving with a suspended driver's license because he didn't have money to pay for the tickets he received. After constantly getting pulled over, Gregory got fed up. He declared: "I'm going to get a bike!" But even this couldn't save him from police attention. One day, he came home with his bike adorned with a brand-new ticket for a minor violation.

My brother was one of the many Black men in Detroit who were constantly subjected to these issues with police. He learned to understand it, as we all did, as simply part of the experience of being Black.

In 1961, just before I was born, Detroit elected a new mayor. For my parents and our neighbors, this change in leadership seemed to offer a glimmer of hope. Jerome P. "Jerry" Cavanagh, a White man, painted himself as a reformer in the style of President John F. Kennedy. He owed his election to robust turnout from Black Detroit; once in office, Cavanagh repaid this loyalty by hiring a number of Black Detroiters into his administration. When Dr. Martin Luther King Jr. visited Detroit in June 1963, Cavanagh marched alongside him and other civil rights leaders straight down Woodward Avenue.

Yet Cavanagh, for all his good intentions, made a profound mistake. Although he sincerely wanted to help Black Detroiters, he did not prioritize the kinds of help they asked for—and that meant he did little to combat police brutality.

Instead, like many big-city mayors before and since, Cavanagh waged an ever-escalating "war on crime," as President Lyndon Johnson would later call it, and increasingly militarized the police force to fight it. Less than two weeks after Dr. King's visit, a White police officer in Detroit shot and killed a Black woman, Cynthia Scott, after attempting to arrest her on a flimsy pretext. The officer was never charged. Worse, records suggest that some law enforcement officials conspired to suppress evidence of Scott's murder.

Meanwhile, racial tensions were rising across the United States even as the civil rights movement marched forward. In July 1964, about two weeks after President Johnson signed the Civil Rights Act—around the time my family moved to Cadillac Boulevard—New York City exploded after an off-duty White police officer in Harlem killed a Black teenager, James Powell. The following year, with Johnson's signature barely dry on the Voting Rights Act, police violence again provoked riots, this time in the Watts neighborhood of southern Los Angeles.

In the ensuing unrest, officers killed more than two dozen residents, almost all of them Black. I was too young to remember these assaults, but Black Americans across the country glued themselves to their TVs. The fear was too familiar; the instability was the status quo.

A month later, in September 1965, the Michigan Civil Rights Commission produced a report on the Watts Riots. They found the same powder-keg conditions prevailed in Detroit—chief among them being poverty, segregation, and violent policing. My family shielded me from the worst of these deprivations. But they knew Detroit could not go on like this without a similar reckoning.

As the commissioners wrote: "A 'time bomb is ticking' in Michigan."

DETROIT ERUPTS

I wish the commissioners had been wrong. But to paraphrase Langston Hughes, a dream deferred can fester like a sore—or explode.[9] In Detroit, the fuse had been lit. The aftermath would define my hometown for generations.

In August 1966, when I was just shy of four years old, police officers arrested three men for loitering near a community center run by the Afro-American Youth Movement, a local civil rights group. The center was just four blocks from my house on Cadillac Boulevard; I would walk or ride my bike by it almost every day. A growing crowd of frustrated Black residents protested the arrests, and for the next four days, clashes between police and local residents filled our neighborhood's streets. When the violence eventually died down, my family was grateful for the peace.

We didn't know something worse was coming.

Not one year later, in the early hours of July 23, 1967, the police raided an unlicensed club, known in slang terms as a "blind pig," not far west of our family home. The people inside were toasting the return of local servicemen from the war in Vietnam. The police could have told them to disperse. Instead, while my siblings and I slept, they arrested all eighty-five patrons on the spot—a process that took about an hour. A crowd gathered in the sticky heat to see what the commotion was about.

It's upsetting to see people arrested and roughly handled. When those people are members of your own community—people you know have harmed no one—it's even more disturbing. This is a truth I keep in mind whenever violence appears in the news, and whenever I recount what happened next. As the crowd watched their neighbors being tugged onto the street on that hot morning, they became more and more agitated. When policemen pushed the last of the patrons into a van, onlookers began to throw bottles. Glass shattered. And against the black predawn sky, an uprising began.

The ensuing chaos became known as the Detroit Rebellion. It transformed the city I loved into a war zone. One uprising turned into many. The disturbances converged. Looting and fires spread across one hundred city blocks. At the peak of the rebellion, twelve square miles of my city were aflame. Desperate to restore order, Mayor Cavanagh—the same man who had positioned himself as a savior of Detroit's Black citizens—asked Michigan's governor to send in state police. The National Guard soon followed.

Even then, they couldn't quell the disturbances. On July 25, President Johnson mobilized troops. Some two thousand paratroopers then descended on Detroit and mounted a military occupation of the city. They patrolled the streets in tanks, metal behemoths with long barrels of destruction, crunching concrete as they rolled past schools and churches.

The unrest came within a few blocks of our house on Cadillac Boulevard. I was not yet five years old. I remember crouching on the floor with my parents, hoping we could stay safe.[10]

In the days after the Rebellion began, my parents forbade us from leaving the sanctuary of our front porch. From there, we saw neighbors running up and down the block, carrying stolen goods. One teenager ran over to us and offered my mom an unopened box of soap powder. Stunned, my mother turned the teen away.[11] My father, incensed by the looting, took to standing guard on the porch—summoning an intimidating posture from his days in the army. When another neighbor appeared at our gate with a stolen TV, my father barked, "Nope! Don't you bring that in my house!"

After five days of disturbances, forty-three people were dead and about five thousand were left homeless. Some 1,400 buildings were burned, leaving swathes of the city in ruins. More unrest followed after the assassinations of Dr. King in April 1968 and Robert Kennedy in June of the same year.

During the next several years, parts of the city began to resemble a fortress—or a prison. Windows were barred, covered with steel plates, or bricked up completely. Building owners strung razor wire along the edges of their roofs. Inside many stores, reinforced glass shields materialized between customers and clerks.

Mercifully, my block didn't burn. Nor were our neighborhood buildings immediately bricked or boarded up. But the East Side felt the effects of the Rebellion in other ways.

For example, an apartment building near my house, at the corner of Cadillac Boulevard and Charlevoix Street, had been all-White for most of my life. After the Rebellion, every single resident moved out, and the building became entirely Black. It happened almost overnight. The drugstore with the soda fountain closed its doors during the riots and never reopened. The friendly White lady who ran it moved away, as did the White owners of the deli next door. For five-year-old me, these changes were perplexing.

Worse was yet to come. Much worse.

A few months after the Detroit Rebellion, Jenefer's mom and dad came over. This wasn't unusual; our parents were friends. But this discussion was different. I remember how sad Jenefer's parents looked.

Later, my parents told me the hard truth. Jenefer and her family had moved to a White neighborhood, where property values were better. They were afraid of losing everything.

Cadillac Boulevard without my next-door neighbors. Cadillac Boulevard without Jenefer.

My world shattered.

I didn't understand why Jenefer's parents would take my best friend away. If they loved our community, why would they leave?

It would be a long time before I learned about the decades of discriminatory policies and practices that destroyed the value of real estate in majority-Black neighborhoods and prevented many Black residents from moving elsewhere. Blockbusting—deliberate fearmongering about residents of color on the part of real estate agents and building developers—suppressed sale prices. At the same time, the federal policy of redlining denied necessary mortgage insurance to residents of Black neighborhoods. As far back as the 1930s, the Federal Housing Administration (FHA) had explicitly required segregation. As its manual read, "Incompatible racial groups should not be permitted to live in the same communities."[12]

These rules, de facto and de jure, were bad enough. And the FHA too often enforced them. For example, in 1941, in the Pembroke neighborhood of Detroit—about fifteen miles northwest of our home on Cadillac Boulevard—the agency sanctioned the construction of a concrete wall, six feet high and four inches thick, to separate the races. The Birwood Wall still stands today, a reminder of a time less than a century ago when our leaders endorsed rank inequity.

Simultaneously, restrictive covenants across the country prohibited the sale, lease, and occupation of land and houses to anyone not considered sufficiently White—not just Black people, but also Asians, Latino people, Jews, and others. Meanwhile, banks were, and still are, significantly less likely to extend mortgages to families of color.

By the late 1960s, Congress and the Supreme Court would ban

some of these more overt discriminatory tactics. But their legacy persists. Throughout the twentieth century, working-class White families were able to build up equity in the homes they owned. Many tapped into that equity to send their children to college, allowing the next generation to start higher on the socioeconomic ladder. Families of color, however, could not do the same. Redlining may have been outlawed, but racist threats and resistance re-created it in psychological form—intimidating families of color from moving into homes with higher equity. Too often, families of color watched their hard-earned investments turn to dust.

Families like mine had fewer options. Families like Jenefer's had more. Even my own family, lucky in so many respects, fell victim to this reality. In 1964, my parents had bought our house on Cadillac Boulevard for $10,000. When my mom moved out in 1988, she sold it for the same price. Accounting for inflation, though, our family lost several times that amount. Through decades of homeownership, she built zero equity—zero wealth.

Jenefer's family almost surely fared better. As the smoke cleared from the Detroit Rebellion, her parents could see their home was on the wrong side of the line—one they had no hand in creating. A racist system had backed them into a corner. They chose what they must have thought was best for Ben and Jenefer: They moved closer to Grosse Pointe, where less than 1 percent of the population were people of color.[13]

In so doing, they joined a nationwide phenomenon known as "white flight." In Detroit specifically, the departure of White residents transformed the city over just a few years. In 1966, around twenty thousand White residents left for the suburbs. In 1967, that figure doubled to over forty thousand; the following year, it doubled again to more than eighty thousand.[14] During the 1970s, more than 310,000 White Detroiters left town. In the process, my hometown went from majority-White to two-thirds Black. The relative integration that had followed the Great Migration had reversed, leaving behind broken friendships and fractured communities.

At the time, of course, none of that was clear to me. All I knew was that my best friend was gone. We'd hardly had a chance to say goodbye. For years, I felt the raw pain of this loss. I had recurring nightmares about losing Jenefer. In my sleep, I would yell, "Stop, Jenefer! Stop!" One of my sisters would have to wake me to calm me down. They'd have to hold my shoulders and insist: "Jenefer's not here."

I haven't seen Jenefer since—and her departure from my life, Cadillac Boulevard, and our beloved city remains a painful reminder of how structural inequality can tear apart even the closest-knit communities. I wish I could say I've fully healed, but I haven't. I think about Jenefer often, to this day. She was one of the first people I bonded with outside my family—and she just vanished.

While I didn't know it at the time, the forces that separated us long predated 1967—and even 1776.

TRACING THE ROOTS OF "RACE"

I probably don't need to tell you race is a social construct; it is biologically baseless. Yet if we want to understand its effects, it is worth understanding why and how "race" came to be.

Years ago, when I studied the origins of racism—a complex topic—I discovered that the concept we now call "race" has existed since the 1500s. Its role in creating a hierarchy of human value enabled European settlers and their descendants to commit two crimes against humanity on the continent of North America: genocide against Native Americans and the transatlantic slave trade.

As a nation, and as a people, we have never fully recovered. Just ask Indigenous Americans, from whom 99 percent of their ancestral land has been stolen. Just ask Black families like my own, who continue to struggle with the effects of discrimination.

Our nation's founders expressed noble aspirations: The Declaration of Independence and later the US Constitution enshrined, for some people, the fullest measure of freedom available anywhere on the planet at the time. These documents laid out a powerful case against injustice—and a promise of possibility that generations of Americans would seek to realize: All are created equal. Life, liberty, and the pursuit of happiness. We, the people. And yet the Founding Fathers reflected the social norms that had brought them to power. Instead of making these freedoms available to all, these men restricted them—in these very same founding documents.

Over the course of US history, this contradiction at the heart of our republic would come to bear on all communities of color. Indigenous Americans would be massacred, shunted off their land, and confined to reservations. Racialized restrictions would bar Asian, Latino, and Middle Eastern immigrants, among others, from the country. Japanese Americans would be forced into internment camps during World War II. Mexican, South American, and Central American immigrants would find themselves increasingly exploited for underpaid and often dangerous work. And generation after generation of Black Americans would be subjected to depredations and discrimination rooted in enslavement, one of this country's original sins.

The horrors of slavery led to the Civil War and the passage of the Thirteenth Amendment. Afterward, the federal government enacted a bundle of policies and laws that have come to be known as Reconstruction. This program's goals were ambitious: It sought to reorganize the former slaveholding states and help newly freed Black Americans assume the full rights and privileges of citizenship.

But almost from its start, Reconstruction sputtered. President Andrew Johnson neglected to enforce the more consequential and controversial aspects of the law. Organized White violence also made it difficult and often extremely dangerous for Black citizens to take advantage of available resources. The US government did not organize a serious attempt to heal racial or political wounds. Southern Whites saw Reconstruction as a punishment; Northern Whites had little incentive to support it. After a decade, the government abandoned Reconstruction—and with it, the hopes of millions.

In the aftermath, the old order reasserted its control, and Reconstruction gave way to so-called Redemption—and the emergence of what scholar and activist W. E. B. Du Bois called "the color line."[15] Through legal maneuvers and intimidation, Black citizens lost most of the rights they had earned. The legal system known as Jim Crow enforced segregation, abetted by the US Supreme Court. Sharecropping, a drastically unequal form of tenant farming, preserved White ownership of land and capital while enmeshing Black farmers in debt servitude. And this whole system was policed with vigilante justice in the form of lynchings, rapes, and other attacks carried out by terrorist groups like the Ku Klux Klan.

In the face of this relentless persecution, many Black Americans lacked hope. Yet others pushed forward. It was against this background that my ancestor, Isaiah Thornton Montgomery, and his cousin founded the all-Black town of Mound Bayou, Mississippi, in 1887.

I grew up hearing stories about Isaiah, a man who rose from oppression to autonomy. Isaiah was born into enslavement on a plantation owned by Joseph Davis, the eldest brother of Jefferson Davis—the future president of the Confederate States of America. Before the Civil War, Joseph employed Isaiah as his personal attendant; when the Union military occupied the land, Isaiah took up a similar post for its naval commander. After the war, Joseph sold the plantation for a fair price to a group of formerly enslaved Montgomery men, including Isaiah's father, Benjamin. Amid the promises of Reconstruction, the Montgomery family tried to make Davis Bend a functioning community—one where free Black folks could support themselves and live in peace.

For a while, it worked. My family's stories focused on these hard-won victories. But the fortunes of Davis Bend seemed bound to those of Reconstruction. Neglect and fighting during the Civil War had damaged the dams that kept the property dry. When the levee burst, flooding killed crops and made settlers sick. In 1877—the same year occupying federal troops vacated the South, the consequence of a corrupt compromise in Congress—Benjamin passed away, leaving Isaiah in charge. Davis Bend limped along for a few more years, but debts mounted. Eventually, he could not stay there any longer.

Isaiah looked to the Davis family for help. Unfortunately for him, Joseph had also died, and Isaiah had to deal with the new family patriarch: the unrepentant former Confederate president. In 1881, Jefferson Davis bought the land back for $75,000—one quarter of what the Montgomery family had paid for it fifteen years earlier. It is a cruel tribute to the stubbornness of racism that my mother and so many other Americans of color would face the same systemic theft over a century later.

Yet Isaiah was determined. Long before Langston Hughes decried that dream deferred, my ancestor refused to let his father's vision fade. He continued to search for the right land on which to build a self-sufficient Black community. Finally, in 1886 Isaiah found the opportunity he'd been looking for: He got a commission from a railroad company to build a town along the proposed route from Vicksburg, Mississippi, to Memphis, Tennessee.

This is where my family planted roots. This is where Mound Bayou was born.

The land Isaiah selected for Mound Bayou was part swamp and all overgrown. But Isaiah's ability to motivate people was legendary. Soon, Mound Bayou became a community of around two thousand independent Black Americans. While most Black Mississippians struggled under Jim Crow, Mound Bayou residents enjoyed a functioning local government, a thriving business community, and an effective public school system. When I heard these stories as a child, in my warm bed on Cadillac Boulevard, nothing could have seemed more natural.

Yet American apartheid was present here, too. White residents of nearby communities, jealous of Mound Bayou's prosperity, harassed residents, stole their livestock, and poisoned their wells—an all-too-common experience in Black towns. Still, Mound Bayou continued to thrive: In 1910, it received the first Carnegie Library specifically designated for African Americans. President Theodore Roosevelt even visited and declared Mound Bayou the "Jewel of the Delta."

When I think of this persistence, it's easy to see where my own parents learned to get it done and try, try again. The people of Mound Bayou were determined to do everything they did well.

Starting in 1929, however, "getting it done" became more challenging than ever before. The Great Depression hit Mound Bayou hard. President Franklin Roosevelt's New Deal policies were meant to alleviate the worst effects of this downturn, but many parts of the New Deal—like its housing policies—were explicitly racist, while others had racist effects.

Most of the job-creation programs, like the Conservation Corps and the Tennessee Valley Authority, discriminated against or were closed to Black citizens like my ancestors. Acreage reduction policies, meant to stabilize the price of agricultural produce by reducing the amount of farmland, gave White landowners more incentive to leave land vacant than to continue renting it to Black sharecroppers. As a result, in 1933 and 1934 alone, more than one hundred thousand Black farmers were evicted. All the while, Mississippi's own recovery plans—unsurprisingly—excluded Black workers and their communities.

Many residents had no choice but to move out of Mound Bayou, seeking opportunity elsewhere. Sadly, my own family—the descendants of Isaiah Montgomery himself—was among them. Decades after Montgomery realized his father's dream, his descendants were forced to leave for a safe place where they could support themselves and their families. Mound Bayou would rise and fall again over the years, but never again would it truly shine in the Delta. And never again would a Montgomery live in the community our ancestor founded.

I briefly visited Mound Bayou in 2012, after I had taken charge of the W. K. Kellogg Foundation's Mississippi programming. Originally, the town wasn't on our itinerary; we were meeting with grantees elsewhere in the Delta. But when a child walked into one of our meetings wearing a T-shirt imprinted with the words *Isaiah T. Montgomery Elementary School*, I lit up.

"That name is in my family!" I said before peppering the student with questions.

I ended up visiting the school named for my ancestor, which of course was in Mound Bayou. The long brick building filled me with pride. A sign on the front lawn read *Together we can make a difference*, next to a portrait of Isaiah himself. But as I drove through town and spoke with residents, I realized the Jewel of the Delta was in bad shape. Public and private investors perennially underfunded the town, making it difficult for residents to maintain a thriving community. The railroad had long since been torn up, erasing Mound Bayou's original reason for being. Isaiah's house was still there, but it was falling apart. Even the local hospital, which was one of the only hospitals to treat Black people in the Delta, was mostly shuttered except for a small urgent-care facility.

Since then, a group of committed citizens has been working to preserve Mound Bayou's history—and begin to build its future. But the legacy of disinvestment is hard to shed. That is a lesson I learned firsthand.

SCHOOLING AND SEGREGATION

Even after my friend Jenefer moved away, my childhood was joyful. My mom made home-cooked meals every day as well as special roast dinners on Sundays, Thanksgiving, and Christmas. Afterward, we kids took turns washing dishes according to a weekly rotation. We volunteered to keep our neighborhood clean, too, picking up trash and washing cars in programs organized by our church.

Though we missed the neighbors who had moved out after the Rebellion, my friends and I adapted to our new circumstances. We biked around the block and in nearby parks. Occasionally we ventured as far as Belle Isle, the famous island in the Detroit River with an aquarium, a giant slide, and great food—everything a curious kid like me could desire.

My family listened to music all the time. Besides Motown and the many soul and blues legends, my brother Louis introduced us to artists who spanned genres, including some of my favorites: Fleetwood Mac, Frank Zappa, Parliament-Funkadelic, the Isley Brothers. My friends and I grooved to modern artists like the Gap Band, Cameo, Chaka Khan, and Prince, too. On the radio, we all heard records spun by top DJs like Donnie Simpson and later John Mason, the announcer for the Detroit Pistons. Talk about diversity! If my family was awake, we had music playing and we were listening to it all.

We didn't just listen, either. We also sang and danced. And we knew all the trendiest moves: One day, Rita Fay and a group of friends dared me to dance the jack-in-the-box in the middle of the street. So I stood out on Cadillac Boulevard bouncing up and down, dancing my heart out. Right then, my father happened to be driving along the street, which I had turned into my stage. Seeing me from a distance, he said to himself, *Look at that fool out there, dancing in the middle of the street! Where are her parents?!* Imagine his horror when he got closer and realized it was his own daughter! I rarely got in trouble as a kid, but that day my father gave me an earful.

In those days, the schools in my neighborhood were still well funded. The education I received at Howe Elementary and Foch Junior High was on par with what my peers received in the emerging Detroit suburbs. And unlike later generations of Michigan public school students, I didn't just have stellar White teachers like Ms. Fields and Ms.

Martin; I also had teachers who looked like my friends and neighbors. My Black instructors, including Mr. Smith, Mr. Hanes, Ms. Staples, and Ms. Davis, were excellent. Ms. Chimaterro, the Latina music teacher, was another favorite of mine—even after she told me my tone was a little off. At one point when I was at Foch, my mother worked as a cleaner there, and I sometimes stayed after school to help her. My math teacher, a Black man named Mr. Stokes who saw my talent with numbers, learned that my mom was employed by the school and sought her out frequently. The two of them conspired to keep me on the straight and narrow, and fostered a love of math that has shaped my career. This kind of dedicated care and instruction from teachers of color became instrumental to my success.

In junior high, I was selected for the Sacred Heart Enrichment Program, a group modeled after the federal Upward Bound program to give kids like me experiences of the world outside inner-city Detroit. During the school year, we received extra lessons; over the summer, we went to camp. The program lasted two or three years, and at the end we did a home exchange with kids in the wealthy suburb of Grosse Pointe. My exchange family had a private pool in their backyard, a luxury I had never even considered. The whole time I spent with them, I was thinking, *Where am I?* The pool was only about five miles east of Cadillac Boulevard, but it felt like another planet.

When the time came, I tested into a venerable Detroit institution, Cass Technical High School. Founded in 1907 as one of the first four high schools in the city, Cass Tech has graduated a list of alumni as illustrious as it is varied. The legendary singer Diana Ross, the endlessly funny comedian Lily Tomlin, and jazz greats Donald Byrd and Regina Carter—all of them went to Cass Tech. I was proud to join such fine company.

Cass Tech was close to the center of Detroit, a few miles from Cadillac Boulevard, but I could take safe and reliable city buses there. The building, dating to 1922, stood eight stories tall with marble-lined hallways and bas-relief friezes around the entrances. It boasted a hardwood-floor gym with an indoor running track, as well as a three-thousand-seat auditorium with such good acoustics, the Detroit Symphony Orchestra sometimes performed there. The sports teams were elite, too.

The school was structured as an academy, meaning that students declared majors just like in college. My classmates majored in chemistry and biology, performing arts, engineering, and a range of other subjects. This created a clear pathway into higher education and prepared us for successful careers.

My own major was business, which I loved. As soon as I started taking accounting classes, I knew I wanted to be a certified public accountant (CPA)—and I was not shy about telling people. Even in ninth grade, I was giving my father tips on how to do his taxes. Cass Tech had an internship program through which, as a junior and senior, I spent afternoons working at General Motors (GM). While I was a business major, Cass Tech focused on liberal arts, and my history and civics teacher, Mr. Nelson, shaped my worldview. To honor and respect his students as human beings, Mr. Nelson referred to all of us by our surnames. I was Miss Montgomery in his class. He also drove my focus on excellence and leadership, which he expected from each student. To nobody's surprise, I focused hard on academics. I was a member of the honor society. But I also got involved in student government. When I ran for class secretary, my friends formed my campaign committee. They even composed a jingle:

L-A-J!
U-N-E!
Vote for La June
For sec-re-ta-ry!

I won by a landslide.

The combination of good schooling and encouragement from

our parents—not to mention each other—set my siblings and me up for success. We sought to embody James Brown's joyful song "Say It Loud – I'm Black and I'm Proud."[16] Of the ten of us children, eight went to college. Two got MBAs. One became an attorney. Another a social worker. Rita Fay, of course, earned a master's degree in early childhood education. Yet another sibling entered the gospel-music business, and my older sister Avaloyne followed in my father's footsteps and worked at General Motors her entire career. Every one of my siblings has enjoyed success in his or her own way. As my mom used to remind us: "Once a task has begun, do not stop until it's done. Be the labor great or small, do it well or not at all."

But the Detroit Public Schools system was living on borrowed time. While I danced and sang and studied through adolescence, white flight was devastating the city's tax base. During the economic tumult of the 1970s, capital flight compounded this damage as manufacturers sought cheaper labor outside the United States or—notwithstanding the grim irony—in the South. It was only a matter of time before the rot would catch up with Detroit's public services.

Some local leaders tried to stop this decline. Seeing a looming gulf between the inner city and the surrounding suburbs—which were quickly becoming majority-Black and majority-White, respectively— the National Association for the Advancement of Colored People (NAACP) in 1970 sued the Michigan state government, arguing that the state's housing policies had resulted in school segregation. The district court agreed and ordered schools throughout the Detroit metro area—comprising Detroit Public Schools and fifty-three outlying school districts—to desegregate through busing.

Had this program been realized, the lives of many of my friends and neighbors could have been very different. We might have chosen to walk down different college and career paths. Maybe we would have made friends with other students who didn't look like us. I'm almost certain, though, that we would have learned much earlier in life how to navigate an environment that wasn't predominantly Black. As strong as many of Detroit's schools were, studies make clear that Black students benefit meaningfully from integrated education and the diversity of resources and experiences that come with it. But instead of accepting the court's ruling, suburban Detroiters responded with fury. They sought to protect their own children—because they saw my schools, my community, as a threat.

Anti-busing demonstrations sprang up in majority-White communities across the metro area. One suburb, Pontiac, became a particular focus of unrest. Irene McCabe, a local resident who fashioned herself into a figurehead for the anti-busing movement, spoke for many of her neighbors when she said, in predictably coded language: "There are millions of little people in this country who want to preserve the neighborhood school and all it means to the American way of life."[17] Matters turned even uglier when, in August 1971, the Ku Klux Klan used dynamite to bomb a school-bus yard in Pontiac.

Three years later, during the summer between my sixth and seventh grades, the Supreme Court struck down the desegregation plan—for good. It ruled that distinct school districts could not be required to accept busing unless their intent to segregate could be proved—a test all but impossible to meet. With the stroke of a pen, the Court undid much of the progress made since *Brown v. Board of Education*, in effect reinstating the lie of "separate but equal" schools. It turned school-district boundaries into the bureaucratic equivalent of the Birwood Wall, the federally sanctioned structure dividing Black from White a few miles from Cadillac Boulevard. Justice Thurgood Marshall, dissenting, called the ruling "a giant step backwards."[18]

Detroit's decline in the years since I graduated from Cass Tech has been painful to watch. Every city service, from schools and buses to public health, has suffered from disinvestment. The racial gap that I witnessed as a teenager marveling at that backyard pool in Grosse Pointe has only widened. In the city of Detroit—nearly 78 percent

Black—the public-school graduation rate hit 74 percent in 2023.[19] In Grosse Pointe—88 percent White—the graduation rate that same year approached 96 percent.[20] Cass Tech has managed to stay strong, thanks to the generosity and activism of its remarkable alumni. But most other Detroit schools, with insufficient public funding, are shadows of their former selves.

Cadillac Boulevard, at least, retains much of its charm. Residents proudly take care of their mostly brick houses. Above them, the sycamores still spread their leaves. But the street where I used to dance now bears more potholes than before; the network of alleyways where we played behind our houses is now mostly closed off and inaccessible. In the wider neighborhood, many wood-framed houses stand abandoned, their windows boarded up. The A&P where we used to shop is now a dollar store. The former corner store is a vacant lot where brown grass peeks up from cracks in the concrete.

Detroit's highs and lows have felt like a roller coaster. When I was growing up, opportunity abounded. But then came disinvestment, and by the 1980s, Detroit's fortunes had plummeted. Businesses moved out, including much of the auto industry and its vast ecosystem of suppliers. The economy tanked. In 1999, a decades-old residency requirement for first responders and other municipal workers was abolished. Those who could move to the suburbs spared no time doing so. Before long, Detroit was a shell of itself, devoid of the investment and public goods people needed to build healthy, successful lives.

It was distressing, for a long period of time, to see my city—the one that gave me opportunity—turned into a bitter disadvantage for succeeding generations of Black Detroiters. The Renaissance City is swinging back now, thanks in part to a broad, dedicated effort to reinvest in its people and institutions. (I'll share more about the Kellogg Foundation's role in this collaborative effort in chapter 4.) But unfortunately, the decline I witnessed is all too familiar—not just in my hometown, but across the United States.

PROGRESS AND RETREAT

It's tempting for many to see 250 years of American history as an uninterrupted path of progress: slow at times, but steady. To be sure, some things have improved. My journey to the presidency of the Kellogg Foundation reflects that progress. But gains have too often been followed by backlash, retrenchment, and regression. Reconstruction was followed by Jim Crow. Mound Bayou rose and fell. The Great Migration dead-ended in urban decay and systemic disinvestment.

Recent years have witnessed yet another whiplash-inducing turn of this cycle. After Barack Obama was elected as our first Black president, pundits from mainstream media outlets like National Public Radio (NPR) hailed a new, post-racial era.[21] But white supremacy was only in hiding, concealing its ideology and iconography, biding its time. Over the past decade, hate crimes have risen, with the majority of them targeting people of color. White supremacists have become one of our biggest domestic terror risks, responsible for the vast majority of extremist murders in the United States. Communities across the country, from El Paso to Atlanta to Buffalo, have been left mourning their dead. I have had the privilege and responsibility of sharing space with these communities as they have grieved and searched for answers.

Appeals to racism and xenophobia have increasingly become part and parcel of mainstream political discourse, often tied to a conspiracy theory known as the "great replacement." This misguided concept suggests that growing numbers of Americans of color pose a threat to white dominance of society and the economy—or even presage what its proponents call "white genocide."[22] At the Unite the Right rally in Charlottesville in August 2017, crowds chanted: "You will not replace us. Jews will not replace us."[23] The rally culminated in a white supremacist terror attack that killed one peaceful counterprotestor and wounded more than a dozen others. Since then, this conspiracy theory has only continued to spread, amplified in the echo chambers of social media.

These kinds of threats to our freedom, security, and democracy are a consequence of zero-sum thinking: the false belief that one group's success comes at the cost of another's. To worry about being replaced, first you must believe there is only room for so many people to survive or thrive. And then you must convince yourself there's a reason you deserve to be among them. These are the false narratives that perpetuate segregation—which, in turn, keeps us from understanding each other and perpetuates racism itself.

In the broad arc of history, moments of violence and divisiveness, too, are part of a cycle. Periods of relative empowerment for people of color—especially economic empowerment—are often followed by renewed racist violence. Lynchings proliferated in the years after emancipation. The era of civil rights also saw egregious police violence; the 1955 murder of fourteen-year-old Emmett Till in Mississippi; and terrorist attacks like the 1963 bombing of the 16th Street Baptist Church in Birmingham, Alabama, which killed four little girls only a few years older than I was at the time.

One ugly chapter of our nation's history came in the years following World War I. During the war, many Black Americans made modest economic gains, serving their country by keeping factories humming. Yet these workers met mob violence in several cities, not just in the South. In the "Red Summer" of 1919, dozens of people died and thousands of Black families saw their homes destroyed during riots in Chicago; Omaha; Washington, DC; and other communities. Again, Black Americans had their hard-won futures ripped away. Again, White anxiety about being "replaced" proved responsible: A headline in one Arkansas newspaper read *Negroes Plan to Kill All Whites*.[24]

The violence continued for years. One of the worst incidents came in 1921 in Greenwood, the "Black Wall Street" of Tulsa, Oklahoma. Greenwood was prosperous, home to physicians, attorneys, and wealthy entrepreneurs.[25] In other words, it was like Mound Bayou: a Black economic success story thriving alongside, but not integrated with, neighboring White communities. And as with Mound Bayou, many White people—too many—begrudged Greenwood its achievements.

On May 31, 1921, a White mob descended on the neighborhood, burning more than 1,250 homes and killing around three hundred residents.[26] The mob was inspired by unsupported accusations of assault toward a White woman by a Black teenager—allegations not unlike those later used to justify the murder of Emmett Till. As with so many horrific crimes against non-White Americans, both before and since, no member of the mob was ever convicted.

The Tulsa Race Massacre erased some twenty years of Black economic achievements. It robbed future generations of Black Tulsans of inherited wealth that could have transformed their lives. And it reminded Black Americans that in a world shaped by racism, even the most dedicated work could not ensure their secure future.

RACISM'S TRAGIC TOLL

Systemic racism lies at the root of a great deal of suffering—from poisoned water pipes in Flint, Michigan, to rampant poverty among Alaska Natives, to ongoing police violence in towns and cities across America.

In 2014, a White police officer, Darren Wilson, shot and killed Michael Brown, an unarmed Black eighteen-year-old, in Ferguson, Missouri, a suburb of St. Louis. Brown's friend, who witnessed the shooting, told reporters that Brown had his hands up in surrender at the time of his death. Wilson shot a dozen rounds at Brown. Emergency services then left Brown's dead body on the road for four hours in the August heat.

As the mother of two Black sons, I can imagine the pain of Michael's mother, Lezley McSpadden, all too well. To this day, I cannot think about that beautiful boy, discarded like litter, without thinking of my own sons—particularly my oldest, Justin.

During one of his breaks from college, Justin was home in Kalamazoo, Michigan, and borrowed my car to visit a friend's house. On his way there, with Jordan tagging along, he was pulled over by the police without obvious cause. Understandably, Justin got frustrated. He asked repeatedly, "Why am I being pulled over?" But the officer who stopped him never answered. When Justin kept asking questions, the officer retaliated by arresting him.

One of my neighbors, a police officer, recognized Justin at the station and called me. "You better come get your son out of jail," he said.

In a parental panic, my husband, Avery, and I jumped in his car and drove straight there. When we arrived, the officer at the station said something that still haunts me to this day: "He's lucky we knew who he was—because of the way he was acting. If this was Los Angeles, they would kill him. He would disappear."

I told the officer I understood. Maybe Justin shouldn't have been disrespectful. But I also needed to know something. "Why was he pulled over in the first place?" I asked.

The answer was minor, borderline frivolous: One of the two tiny lights that illuminated his license plate was out. Instead of just telling him that, however, the patrol officer escalated matters. He arrested Justin, jailed him, put him in a situation that could threaten his life—all for the sake of one little light.

Both of my boys survived adolescence. They're thoughtful, conscientious, wonderful, and wildly creative people. I love them very much and count every day we spend together as a blessing. But too many Black mothers can no longer enjoy that time with their children. And there is little difference between me and them: only luck.

Our children deserve to live. Yet even today, far too often, racism cuts their lives short.

The murder of Michael Brown, along with the subsequent decision not to charge his killer, galvanized protests across the country. Their voices chorused a rallying cry: "Hands Up, Don't Shoot." These demonstrations, like the later ones following the 2020 murder of George Floyd in Minneapolis, were overwhelmingly peaceful. But too many police officers in Ferguson responded as they too often do: with violence. Their treatment of protestors reminded me of the civil rights marches I watched on TV as a child, where officers attacked peaceful activists with tear gas and rubber bullets—where protesters lay on the ground, handcuffed, as police dogs attacked them.

I watch and remember those marches every Black History Month; that abuse is never far from my mind. But the immediacy of the police brutality after Michael Brown's 2014 death brought these memories to the fore. My trauma awoke after a long sleep. This trauma would fuel my passion and drive to support this community.

Again, as countless times before, a national scandal ensued. And again, racism was the ultimate culprit. A report by the US Department of Justice found that the Ferguson Police Department, as well as the city's justice system, had for years been violently and explicitly racist.[27] Even those officers who genuinely aimed to serve their citizens with justice could not undo a racist system on their own.

This kind of brutal prejudice is by no means uncommon. In 2020, a survey by KFF found that nearly half of Black Americans have at least once felt their life was in danger because of their race; I include myself in that group. Two in five have been stopped by the police because of race—again, I am among them. One in five has suffered police violence.[28] That I've avoided such abuse speaks only to my luck.

This mistreatment of Black Americans and other minority communities has received particular attention in recent years. But we must not forget that, thanks to the pervasive legacy of racism, unequal treatment has been meted out to every racial and ethnic minority in the United States.

Alaska Natives, for example—a diverse Indigenous community comprising several distinct groups—have struggled in much the same ways as other Indigenous peoples. Government entities and private companies, especially in the oil industry, have taken their land and enforced environmental depredation. The legacy of colonization has also plunged Alaska Natives into disproportionate poverty and reliance on welfare.

Recent years have seen renewed efforts to protect the rights of Alaska Native communities, including the establishment of an official Tribal and Indigenous Advisory Council and the provision of election materials in Indigenous languages. I welcome these steps forward. But too often, even good-faith efforts like these have been followed—with depressing inevitability—by an uptick in prominent incidents of racist hate speech, discrimination, and even attacks.[29] For Indigenous Americans, as for their Black neighbors, this cycle can sometimes feel like a steel trap.

Centuries of racism have bequeathed us a society in which good health, economic success, and even freedom from physical violence continue to be distributed according to a racialized hierarchy of human value. Since the Civil War, we in the United States have made material progress. But every two steps forward have preceded at least one step back. Such is the cycle: vicious, ingrained, and often deadly.

Yet I still have hope. Even communities as marginalized as African Americans in Flint and Native populations in Alaska have achieved meaningful change through racial healing, as I'll share later in this book. These healing initiatives begin with recognition of the truth: in this case, that deep-seated segregation has stunted our ability to feel meaningful empathy across racial lines. So long as this lack of empathy persists, we will struggle to gain and maintain support for necessary change. If we are to move forward, we as Americans must start by building empathy and understanding.

Fortunately, we can.

Chapter 2

UNDERSTANDING THE
EMPATHY DEFICIT

Above us, a clock ticked. Aside from the scratching of pencils, the soft whoosh of flipped pages, and the occasional sigh, it was practically the only sound in our cinder-block study area. University of Michigan students affectionately call the Undergraduate Library, an unappealing brick-and-concrete box, "the UgLi"—and in my time there, it certainly was. But what it lacked in beauty, the UgLi made up for in tranquility. That's why my friends and I sat there, huddled over our accounting textbooks.

Cheryl, Susie, Robin, Alison, and I were among the only Black women in the undergraduate business school's class of 1984. We worked hard to keep our own grades up and to help each other do the same. It wasn't unusual for us to spend hours in the UgLi or an empty classroom, taking notes and running calculations.

Usually, the friend groups that gathered around tables in the UgLi kept to themselves, too busy studying to pay attention to anyone else. On this particular day, though, I sensed a figure approaching our table. I looked up to see a young woman from one of my accounting classes. I'd been friendly with her ever since the first time we sat next to each other in class and exchanged small talk. But today she wasn't there to make small talk. Instead, she looked at us and asked, "Why do you guys always stick together?"

It took me a moment to understand her question. I glanced at the tables around us, each crowded with furrowed faces, practically all of them White. I looked back at this classmate, at her own table across the way, also all White.

Wasn't it obvious why Cheryl, Susie, Robin, Alison, and I would stick together?

Our classmate persisted. "Why do you all sit together at lunch every day? Why do you do *everything* together?" This time, her tone was confrontational.

I realized that this classmate didn't see my friends and me the way she saw her own friend group: Her friends were the in-group, so of course they sat together. No one would question it. But when a group of Black women came together, we stuck out like a sore thumb.

This exchange was the first time I noticed a deficit that exists across the United States, one much longer lasting and more insidious than any fiscal shortfall: the empathy deficit. Put simply, we struggle to understand each other across racial lines. We fail to see things from other people's perspectives. And this causes all kinds of pain, from large-scale violence to minor, everyday cruelties that pass quickly but leave a lasting scar.

My classmate's question might have originated, at one time, from a place of genuine curiosity. But her doubts and confusion had hardened into skepticism and distrust, which happens in our society all too quickly and all too often. Sitting in the UgLi with my girlfriends, I had just experienced the empathy deficit in full force. It was not the first time, and it definitely would not be the last.

CODE-SWITCHING ON CAMPUS

My family and I had never questioned whether I would go to college. Cass Tech existed to build a better Detroit by empowering students across communities. Funneling students into higher education was one way to fulfill that mission, and a path I was more than prepared to walk down. Learning was also one of the most important values in the Montgomery family, and it didn't end with Rita Fay's attic classroom or our mom's pantry full of books. I was at the top of my graduating class and, without a doubt, headed for college. *Where* I should go, however—that was a different question.

At GM, where I interned during my junior and senior years of high school, the managers were impressed with my work. Knowing that graduation was right around the corner, one of them wanted to recommend me for a place at the General Motors Institute (GMI), a four-year engineering and management college now called Kettering University.

"I want you to go to GMI because you've been a great worker," he said. "We'll support you, and you'll have a whole career waiting for you afterward. What do you say?"

I was thrilled. At the end of my shift, I hurried home, burst through the front door, and announced to everyone: "Guess what? I'm going to GMI!"

I didn't get the enthusiastic reception I had expected. Instead, my siblings jumped in: It turned out they *all* had thoughts on where I should go to college. My brother Sylvester—nicknamed Sonny—was the first one to urge me to reconsider. "If you go to GMI," he said, "you'll do well and you'll get a great job at General Motors. But La June, you can go to any college you want. College opens up all kinds of opportunities. And you can always go back and work at GM if that's what you want to do."

Sonny's advice made sense, so I set my sights on the same college he had attended: Michigan State University. But when I told my older sister Marian that I was going to apply, her response was swift and determined: "Oh, no you're not!"

Marian, who also went to Cass Tech, was convinced I belonged at her alma mater, the University of Michigan, one of the world's foremost public academic institutions (both then and now). U of M had an excellent undergraduate business program—a big draw for a girl who'd always wanted to be an accountant. It was a temptation I simply could not resist.

I had stalwart support in my family and in Cass Tech. Marian helped me prepare my application, and Cass Tech had given me one of the best educations Detroit could offer. When I received my acceptance letter, I rejoiced. Within a few months, I was traveling to Ann Arbor for orientation week.

I didn't know what to expect at U of M, but reality took no time catching up with me. As I toured the campus, with its monumental buildings and lush summer foliage, my eyes scanned the landscape looking for one—just one—face like mine. I came up empty.

Coming from a neighborhood and high school that were nearly all Black, this stunned me. While other students milled around, I kept staring. The truth is, I had never seen so many White people in one place.

In Detroit, I had spent just enough time in racially mixed spaces like concerts, fast food joints, and department stores—not to mention my internship at General Motors—to learn how to code-switch: to adapt my vocabulary and syntax from African American Vernacular English, the dialect many Black Americans speak, when communicating across racial lines. So talking to other students didn't concern me. What really got to me was the wildly disproportionate makeup of our campus: Of the thirty-two thousand students on campus, more than 80 percent were White. Fewer than two thousand were Black, and even fewer students than that—*combined*—were Asian, Latino, or Indigenous American.[1] Never in my life had I felt so small. And never in my life had I realized that sanctuary and community were things I had to seek out and build in order to find comfort in unfamiliar environments.

At last, as I stood in line to pick up my ID, I found what I was looking for: the face of a fellow Black woman. Cheryl and I became friends immediately. We shared a love of dancing, intelligent conversation, and the universal U of M obsession: sports—especially basketball and football. We wound up rooming together our sophomore year, and we've been close friends ever since.

I met the other members of our group in much the same way. Whenever we saw each other around campus, we gravitated toward one another. Soon, the five of us were fast friends: all of us type-A women, high achievers, and independent thinkers. We would talk all the time, about all kinds of topics. Sometimes, our political discussions could get heated. One day, Cheryl and I were debating the welfare system in our dorm room when our neighbor knocked on the door to say we were getting too loud. She was finding it hard to study.

"But by the way," she added, "I agree with La June." Through the wall, she had followed every word of our conversation. Cheryl and I doubled over laughing.

For all five of us, our first priority was getting good grades. We hunted high and low for silent spots to hit the books, and soon set our sights on the reading room under U of M's Gothic cathedral of a law library. Here, we found a low-ceilinged maze of individual study carrels, quiet as a crypt. It was meant to be only for law students, but we discovered that if you arrived early enough, nobody would check your ID.

When we weren't studying individually, we would hold group revision sessions in an empty classroom, writing problems on the board and discussing the solutions. If one of us was struggling, the rest would rally around her. "Come on," we'd say. "Let's do an extra session." We'd go through the material together and bring our friend up to speed. Whereas other students may have had different and university-provided support systems, we kept each other's spirits up. We encouraged each other. And ultimately, we got each other through.

That was no small feat. Outside of class, my friends and I had fun at some classic Ann Arbor institutions. We played arcade games at Pinball Pete's, attended concerts at Hill Auditorium (where I saw

Prince and Morris Day and The Time for the first time), and of course, hailed the victors at the Big House, U of M's enormous stadium. But even in those settings, our experiences could be isolating. Despite the joy we took in each other's company, it was hard to be five of very few Black women on campus.

Our saving grace was Mary Markley Hall, the huge dorm complex east of the main campus where Cheryl and I roomed together. There, we had a built-in sanctuary—a lounge set aside for students of color, particularly Black students. It was named in honor of Angela Davis, the legendary Black academic and activist. To this day, the walls of the lounge are decorated with paintings featuring Davis and other Black American icons.

Some critics have charged that safe spaces like the Davis Lounge promote resegregation. But that couldn't be further from the truth. For my fellow Black students and me, safe spaces allowed us to express the parts of ourselves that weren't always welcomed in our everyday, integrated environments. We could be ourselves—and process our emotions—without worrying about what people unfamiliar with our cultures would think of us. The founding of dedicated spaces for Asian, Latinx, Arab, and other students of color wouldn't begin until 1985, the year after I graduated, and in this way, we Black students were the fortunate ones. The Davis Lounge helped us find comfort and community, which allowed us to recharge and prepare for tough conversations later in our day—the kinds of intellectual and emotional exchanges that college is all about.[2]

So it was no wonder that all the Black students in Markley Hall hung out in the Davis Lounge. It was there that we created the vibrant communal space so many of us craved. My friends and I played card games and board games there during the week and held parties on the weekends. Sometimes, impromptu talent shows would break out, fueled by sheer exuberance. Within the lounge's walls, I recaptured some of the happiness I felt while growing up on Cadillac Boulevard.

Above all, the Angela Davis Minority Lounge was a place where we could be ourselves without code-switching, without putting on airs, without worrying about what our classmates would think of us. It was our own Mound Bayou—a refuge.

MENTORSHIP AND ROADBLOCKS

In the early 1980s, Ann Arbor was a relatively progressive town when it came to racial equity, and U of M, a key theater in the fight for affirmative action, was a more welcoming place for people of color than many other college campuses. The university offered a platform to some iconic civil rights activists: During my junior year, much to my delight, Rosa Parks and Kwame Ture (formerly known as Stokely Carmichael) spoke at a forum held on campus.

To this day, I'm grateful I attended U of M—where I received a top-notch education, made lasting connections with mentors, and met some of my best friends. I love the community, from the "Diag" in the center of campus—the large diagonal green where we would gather outdoors in the days before cell phones—to the student and alumni chapters around the world. I cherish the values that the university represents and to which it aspires. And I cheer loudly for the Wolverines on Saturdays.

Yet I must say, when I was a student there, the school's progress on issues of race remained, at best, a work in progress. Usually, incidents were relatively small-scale, like the classmate in the UgLi confronting me and my friends for "always sticking together." Today, we call those kinds of incidents "microaggressions"—subtle, perhaps even unconscious, moments of othering or discrimination against marginalized people. But although we were more accustomed to them back then, they stung, and they still do.

One day during freshman year, I was taking an accounting exam in a big lecture hall. The test was designed to be challenging, and all of us in the class were sweating a little. I was sitting in front, alongside an acquaintance of mine, a young woman with whom I had chatted now and then. We were both working hard, silent but for the sounds of writing.

Suddenly, our teaching assistant (TA) appeared, his voice and presence breaking the silence. My classmate hadn't asked for him. No one else in our row seemed to expect him either. Yet he approached my classmate and bent down to her desk. "You know this," I heard him whisper as he pointed at her paper. "It's . . ." And he helped her figure out the answers.

Is that how it works? I asked myself. *She gets the answers while I sit here struggling?*

I like to joke that, as a Libra, I'm always noticing things that aren't fair. My parents and siblings have tried to break me out of this habit. Even now, I can hear them telling me, "Life isn't fair, La June. So quit looking for fairness!" Well, I knew I wouldn't find fairness that day. Instead, as I watched our TA help my classmate on her test, I thought, *I'll show them what I can do.*

A few weeks later, the same TA walked to the front of our lecture hall and called for our attention. With four hundred students looking at him, he asked, "Who is La June Montgomery?"

"I am," I called out, putting up my hand.

"Oh," the TA said, sounding surprised. He paused. "You scored the highest on the test."

I felt a flush of triumph. A part of me was still frustrated that I had to work harder than many of my peers to prove my worth. But I *had* worked hard for that grade—and in that moment, I was glad to be seen. Frankly, it was a refreshing change. If I was going to stand out, I wanted it to be for what I held inside my brain, not on the surface of my skin.

My friends and I weren't totally on our own. Other teachers were more supportive—including one economics professor who offered us extra mentorship to counteract the double standards he knew we all faced. But our most important supporter was another economics professor, one to whom my sister Marian introduced us: Dr. Alfred L. Edwards.

Dr. Edwards was an impressive and inspiring man. He had fought in World War II and earned his PhD before being appointed by President Kennedy to the post of deputy assistant secretary of agriculture—making him one of the first Black Americans to serve in that department's leadership. After a decade of government service under administrations of both political parties, Dr. Edwards had joined the U of M business school and made a name for himself as a leading academic in political economics.

But to my sister, my friends, and so many other Black students, Dr. Edwards also became known as the business school's number-one mentor. He championed the Consortium for Graduate Study in Management, the premier organization for promoting Black, Latino, and Indigenous inclusion in business education. He also supported the Black Business Students Association, which I wasted no time in joining. (Fittingly, the association's annual conference is now named in Dr. Edwards's honor.)

By the time my friends and I arrived at U of M, Dr. Edwards had set his office up at the business school, and it became a haven for stressed-out students of color. We would gather there to seek friendly advice or just to decompress among friends. During exam season, his office door was practically a turnstile, with students bustling in and out. And his support extended well beyond his office. Dr. Edwards hosted us at his home for dinner, threw us cookouts, and offered us work-study assignments. The kind of encouragement Dr. Edwards offered was rare and invaluable.

Thanks to Cass Tech, I already knew I wanted to major in accounting. At U of M, there were two ways of doing so: You could either declare a regular major in the College of Literature, Science, and the

Arts or take the more unusual route of applying to complete your junior and senior years in the business school—one of the most prestigious in the country. U of M was already competitive, but the undergraduate business school was on another level. Of the thousands of undergrads on campus, only a couple hundred were accepted each year. Once you were in, the challenges didn't stop: Many of the courses administered to undergraduates were already MBA-level.

Seeing my enthusiasm and aptitude, Dr. Edwards told me right off the bat, "Do whatever you can to get into the business school." He talked me through all the classes I would need to take and helped me map out how to tackle the prerequisites. With his encouragement, I became all the more determined to get in and set about the task with my usual resolve.

By the middle of my sophomore year, I had taken almost every course I needed. The final three prerequisites were statistics, economics, and calculus classes, and I had all three on my schedule for the spring semester. I just needed a sign-off from my guidance counselor, and I would be good to go.

I went to see my counselor, who happened to be a Black woman. I assumed my experience with her would be much like the support I received at Cass Tech: We would talk about why I wanted to take the classes, and she'd approve my academic goals without hesitation, eager to see a young Black woman like herself thrive. But to my shock, she kept her pen on the table. She told me, point-blank, "I'm not signing off on this schedule."

I tried to find my voice. "What are you talking about?"

"You'll never pass all these classes in one semester," she replied.

"But if I don't take these classes now, I can't get into the business school."

"I know that," the counselor said. "But I'm not signing off on it, because you're setting yourself up for failure. You can't do it."

I wielded every argument I could think of: that I'd already taken the classes at Cass Tech, that I'd been at the top of my class in high school, that I was still excelling here at U of M. I rolled out a list of my academic achievements, the milestones I'd worked so hard to pass ever since my pint-sized desk in Rita Fay's attic classroom. But my arguments were futile. I couldn't persuade this guidance counselor that I had any chance of success. She wouldn't sign.

Coming from a high school—not to mention a family—where everyone encouraged me, I was stunned by the guidance counselor's obstinance. She was judging me as less-than: less capable, less deserving of the benefit of the doubt. She wouldn't give me a chance to prove myself. It was one of my first times encountering somebody face-to-face who didn't believe in me, plain and simple. It was devastating.

I knew that the support I had received up to that point was a rare privilege in the lives of young people. But for me, sitting in that counselor's bland office, the discrepancy was jarring.

I thought back to an incident Rita Fay had told me about years before. Thanks to her lessons, I had arrived in kindergarten already able to write cursive. I wowed the other kids in the class by signing my name—and theirs. My kindergarten teacher was less impressed. She sought out Rita Fay, who was all of ten years old, and told her: "You need to stop teaching La June so much. You're taking her too fast." But Rita Fay, wise beyond her years, hadn't listened. She kept teaching me, and I kept learning.

Now, I faced a type of discouragement that was unfamiliar to me, though it was all too common on campus. At U of M, my friends of color had told me about expressing their ambitions and meeting disbelief, even derision, in return. Many more simply selected themselves out, thinking it would be fruitless even to try to pursue their dreams. I remember one Black classmate who said, again and again, "We'll never get into the business school. They'll never let us into the business school." She wound up dropping out after sophomore year.

Even Susie, one of my five closest friends at U of M, had a crisis of confidence about her chances of being admitted to the business school. But true to form, my friend group rallied around her and convinced her—reminded her—that she could do it. We were right: Susie got in.

And so would I.

I was a daughter of Herbert and M. L. Montgomery; a sister of Rita Fay and Marian Montgomery; a mentee of Dr. Alfred L. Edwards. The guidance counselor was wrong. I could do anything.

After leaving the counselor's office, I told Dr. Edwards what had happened, and he helped me bypass her approval. I took those three tough classes all in the same semester, and I didn't just pass; I got excellent grades, high enough to earn myself a place in the business school.

Later, I went back to that guidance counselor to let her know her advice had been wrong. To her credit, she apologized. But neither of us acknowledged the undercurrent of her disbelief. To this day, I wonder whether she would have expressed the same doubt about a White student. Although the counselor was also a Black woman, it's hard for any of us to avoid the judgments that are so common around us. Had she deemed me less capable because of the way I looked, the way I spoke, the neighborhood I called home? I'll never know for sure.

But often, when I consider the pervasiveness of prejudice, I think of that counselor. In a racist system, bias entraps us all. It exists within, between, and among us. As the poet and activist Kyle "Guante" Tran Myhre puts it: "White supremacy is not a shark; it's the water."

It was precisely because of these sorts of attitudes that we encountered at U of M—many well intentioned, or at least unexamined—that my friends and I chose to stick together. It was the reason students of color tended to room together, the reason we preferred to enjoy each other's company in the sanctuary of the Angela Davis Minority Lounge, the reason that Dr. Edwards reached out to support students of color. But many of our classmates didn't—and maybe couldn't—understand.

That is the empathy deficit.

"THE CLIENT KNOWS BEST"

In April 1984, I graduated from U of M with a bachelor's degree in business administration. The following month, to my delight, I started work in the profession I had long dreamed of joining: public accounting. I was hired into the audit department at a prestigious national accounting firm. I became the third Black woman in the entire audit group, one of very few people of color among a staff of hundreds. I expected to persevere and flourish, just like I had at U of M. But I couldn't have anticipated the challenges ahead.

From day one of my new career, I was advancing through the firm at what felt like a blistering pace. Within a few months, I was leading audits for nonprofit clients and had a team reporting to me. For an ambitious young woman in her early twenties, this was exactly the kind of experience I had been preparing for. But I knew I was capable of doing more. I knew that the real source of prestige within the firm was to work on audits not just for nonprofits but also for big corporate clients. So, when the opportunity to join a corporate account came, at around my one-year mark, I seized it. I was assigned to work for a major real estate company. I was thrilled.

Unfortunately, it didn't take long for this opportunity to become an obstacle. During my first week working for the real estate client, I called up my designated point of contact. "I need to come and ask you a question," I said. I pronounced the word *ask* as a homophone of *axe*, which I had done for years without causing confusion.

"What?" said the client representative, barely suppressing a sneer. "You're going to 'axe' me a question? Don't you know how to say 'ask'?"

At first, I found his response puzzling. Until that point, no one had called me out for how I pronounced words. As long as I was making myself clear, I was sure it shouldn't matter. I didn't yet recognize this incident for what it was: a comment designed to humiliate and belittle me.

At the end of the first year on the assignment, the partner who had hired me called me into her office. She and I had always gotten along. She was one of the first women leaders at the firm, dedicated to bringing more women up the ladder behind her. I held her in high esteem. I trusted her.

In this conversation, though, she took me by surprise. The partner told me I would no longer be assigned to the real estate company. The firm was moving me onto a different account. I found this reassignment strange, but I didn't question it at the time; I was too busy to give it much more thought.

As time wore on, though, it started to bug me. Surely, I thought, the move couldn't have come from my performance. The logic simply didn't make sense: I was excelling. I was leading audits. I'd earned nothing but praise from my bosses. So when it came time for my next six-month review, I finally asked the partner why I had been moved off the account.

She told me that the client "axed" that I be switched out. Then came the whole truth: "They didn't want any Black people on their audit."

My jaw almost hit the floor. I hadn't even considered that possibility. As I stared in disbelief, I wondered, *Is this really happening in 1984?* After I took a deep breath, I asked the partner if she felt that removing me had been the right thing to do. She uttered some platitudes about how we "had to do it" and "the client knows best."

I could tell that she thought she was doing me a favor—even protecting me, just as the U of M guidance counselor had thought she was saving me from bad grades. But this wasn't the Jim Crow South. This was Detroit in the mid-1980s. I didn't need their protection. I needed their empathy. I needed them to believe in me the way Rita Fay and Mr. Stokes, Mr. Nelson, and Cheryl and Dr. Edwards had.

Imagine if, instead of agreeing to a bigoted client's demands, this partner had taken the opportunity to tell the client they were wrong. What good might have come from that act of bravery—for me, for the partner, for the firm, and for the client himself, who would have kept a top-performing auditor on his team? I'm not suggesting this would have been easy; speaking truth to power rarely is. But empathy—had this partner built some with me or others like me—might have steeled her spine. I've seen it happen.

The partner could have turned this injustice into an opportunity for learning and growth. She could have built trust and community with a hardworking colleague. Instead, she denied me what should have been a valuable assignment—not to mention my sense of safety and support at work.

Once again, I felt the injustice of a senseless double standard that had been deemed illegal two decades earlier when the landmark Civil Rights Act of 1964 was enacted to end segregation and ban discrimination on the basis of race, color, religion, sex, or national origin. But this time, there was no equivalent of Dr. Edwards to offer support. In college, I had worked hard to make sure my race didn't overshadow my intelligence or achievements. But in the real world—the working world—I realized this was sometimes out of my control. People could and would take opportunities from me because of my identity. And until they understood my experience, they could never understand my pain.

NARRATIVES AND COUNTERNARRATIVES

The empathy deficit often emerges in individual interactions like the ones I have described, but its roots go far deeper. In fact, the empathy deficit exists because of the stubborn belief in a racialized hierarchy of human value. It reorganizes our social systems according to that hierarchy. And—as we've seen during the periods of backlash and violence that follow progress—it encourages us to see prosperity, opportunity, and even basic good health as zero-sum games in which members of different groups compete for resources.

I think, for instance, about how many White people with limited income opposed the Affordable Care Act (ACA)—despite it being a piece of health care legislation that benefitted all demographics tremendously. Why would they oppose a law that was intended to help them? Well, as it turns out, some of the most powerful anti-ACA messaging is rooted in the empathy deficit. Advocacy groups effectively advertised against the ACA by painting the bill as a handout to people of color.

Dr. Jonathan Metzl, a psychiatrist and sociology professor, was carrying out research in Tennessee as the ACA was taking shape. The White people he spoke to were largely in favor of the measure—until racialized rhetoric took hold. One of Metzl's interviewees, a man named Trevor, said that because the ACA helped immigrants and people of color, he would rather die than sign up for it. Dr. Metzl later wrote a best-selling book on the subject, poignantly titled *Dying of Whiteness*.

I've encountered that zero-sum mentality firsthand. It was on full display during the debate over Proposal 2, the 2006 ballot initiative that would eventually ban affirmative action in Michigan. One acquaintance of mine, a White man, openly campaigned for it. "Vote for Prop 2," he would tell his White colleagues. "That's your seat at the table they're taking." It didn't occur to him that through inclusivity, we could make the table bigger.

As Heather McGhee, an expert in economic and social policy and former president of the think tank Demos, wrote in her 2021 book *The Sum of Us*: "The narrative that White people should see the well-being of people of color as a threat to their own is one of the most powerful subterranean stories in America. Until we destroy the idea, opponents of progress can always unearth it, and use it to block any collective action that benefits us all."[3]

That mindset—with deep roots in US history—has proved hard to move. I've had the great fortune to travel across the country and the world, meeting people of all backgrounds, which is an ideal scenario for cultivating empathy. But travel, too, is a rare privilege. For most people, strangers remain separate from us. This distance allows the empathy deficit to self-perpetuate, until it becomes a chronic inability to recognize the essential humanity of those different from us.

The empathy deficit breeds fears and false beliefs, which keep people apart physically, psychologically, and even emotionally. Segregation feeds this deficit, which then continues to force people apart and keep them there. White families flee cities for the suburbs. People of color are underrepresented in colleges and professions. Faced with a paucity of non-White faces in their daily lives, White people learn to hold negative views of people of color and vice versa. And the cycle continues.

In ways both large and small, I have seen the empathy deficit at work in my own life. It was this deficit that spurred my classmate to ask, "Why do you guys always stick together?" It was this deficit that led a Black guidance counselor to view a Black student as less capable. It was this deficit that allowed a feminist audit partner to tell me that our racist client "knew best." It is this deficit that continues to rob otherwise intelligent, compassionate people of their ability to understand, believe, and sometimes even see the experiences of communities of color.

And the consequences of this deficit can be deadly.

During the pandemic, a Minnesotan executive I know told me a story about a friend of his, a fellow businessman, who had chosen to take a much-needed break from the rat race. This businessman, Vikas Narula, decided that what he wanted above all was to forge meaningful connections with his fellow human beings from all walks of life.[4] He had recently taken up sailing as a hobby, and started walking around his local lake on foot, just asking people how they were feeling; Vikas asked about their days, their dreams, what brought them joy, and so on. If the conversation went well, he would invite them to come fishing with him on his boat.

Most people turned down his offer, not convinced that they could trust this stranger with his unusual, probing questions. (In their position,

I probably would have hesitated too!) But finally, Vikas found some takers: two Black men, one a very tall man in his mid-forties named George. Neither of them had been out on a boat before, and George was particularly enthusiastic about the idea. They agreed to meet back up and go out on the lake. Vikas taught his guests how to fish. For hours, they just talked, caught bass and pike and bluegills, got to know one another, and took photographs together. Vikas felt more than comfortable in the company of his guests, and the feeling seemed mutual. At the end of the day, the businessman docked his boat and thanked his new friends for the experience before the three went their separate ways.

The tall man on the boat that day was George Floyd. A few months later, Floyd was dead, murdered by Derek Chauvin, a White police officer bound by oath to protect him.

Chauvin's pretext for the violent arrest was a flimsy allegation: Floyd had allegedly tried to pay a nineteen-year-old convenience store clerk with a possibly counterfeit $20 bill. Yet Chauvin's reaction was anything but mild. Chauvin chose to subdue Floyd not with department-approved de-escalation tactics but with brute force. With a knee on Floyd's neck, Chauvin pinned his victim to the pavement outside of the convenience store. Witnesses later described the panic and pain in Floyd's eyes and voice as he repeatedly told Chauvin that he couldn't breathe.

For nine minutes and twenty-nine seconds, Chauvin knelt on George Floyd's neck, ignoring his pleas. When Floyd called out for his mother, Chauvin's expression remained impassive. Finally, Floyd lost consciousness. He was dying. My heart ached when I heard him call for his mother, and I thought of my two sons. How hopeless I would feel in that moment. I still hurt every time I think of it.

While an ambulance took George Floyd's limp body to the hospital, an eyewitness approached Chauvin and objected to the way he had treated Floyd.

"That's one person's opinion," Chauvin said. He kept filling out his paperwork.[5]

The dehumanizing and unwarranted violence Chauvin doled out to George Floyd that day is now burned into our collective memory. Floyd's murder, and the disproportionate number of murders of other people of color by police, represents the depths of depravity. This extreme, fatal violence fills the darkest chasm of the empathy deficit.

One would think that highlighting these deaths would make a difference. But it's not that simple—especially because of the way police brutality is reported by the media.

Through her *Counternarratives* project, the award-winning artist Alexandra Bell has detected—and attempted to correct—structural racism in *The New York Times'* coverage of racist events. The urgency of her work is epitomized in a front-page spread that ran on August 25, 2014: the day of eighteen-year-old Michael Brown's funeral. The publication chose to assign equal column inches to side-by-side profiles of Brown and of Darren Wilson, the White Missouri police officer who fatally shot him. The very layout of those pieces seems purpose-built to minimize the radically different challenges that confronted these two human beings—the vast gap in their experiences simply because of the color of their skin.[6]

This false equivalence brings to mind one common response to the Black Lives Matter movement: an insistence that "all lives matter"—or even, in reference to police, "blue lives matter." Statements like these, which ignore the unique hazards of being a person of color in the United States, are just another way the empathy deficit shows up in our lives.

The problematic layout was just one of the racial discrepancies published in that day's *Times* spread. The photos chosen for the two profiles were the most obvious double standard: While Wilson was shown in his police uniform, Brown's photo showed him in a baseball hat with store labels still stuck to the brim, despite the widespread availability of a better-quality image of Brown in his high school graduation cap and gown.

When Michael Brown's death, and the death of George Floyd six years later, sparked mass demonstrations, that coverage, too, was often tainted by the empathy deficit. All protests depend on media coverage to effectively carry their message. Yet news and other media organizations might offer White protestors the benefit of the doubt, publishing profiles, attractive photos, even interviews to better understand their opinions. When Black people protest, by contrast, the footage tends to focus instead on more fringe incidents: masked individuals moving in the shadows, throwing Molotov cocktails, and smashing windows. Because of this focus on property damage, news outlets are more likely to mischaracterize the meaning of the demonstration by framing Black protests as "riots."[7]

Similar bias seems to apply in reverse, when "protests" by White people turn violent. In 2016, for example, a group of armed White extremists in Oregon forcibly occupied the headquarters of the Malheur National Wildlife Refuge and demanded that the federal government hand over protected land for their private interests. The media company Vox analyzed news coverage of the standoff and concluded that news organizations had overwhelmingly covered it as a "peaceful protest," relegated it to the sidebars of their websites, and limited any mention of the militiamen's repeated threats of force.[8]

I used to notice this type of bias on the local news in Michigan and elsewhere. When TV journalists reported on a Black male suspect of a crime, they always seemed to identify him as "a Black man." When the suspect was White, however, the reporter would only call him "a man," as if somehow his race was not relevant. National news outlets often repeat this treatment in coverage of mass shootings. A 2018 study showed that the news media was most likely to attribute White shooting suspects' crimes to isolated incidents of mental illness. Black and Latino suspects, by contrast, were most often depicted in far less sympathetic terms: as persistent and violent threats to the public.[9]

Academic literature confirms the broad scale of this bias. A 2019 study by scholars from Indiana University and the University of Houston found that reports of protests in newspapers across the country followed "a hierarchy of social struggle, in which certain topics are given precedence and legitimacy, and others are delegitimized, trivialized, or ignored altogether."[10] That hierarchy, of course, closely mirrors the racialized hierarchy of human value—with protests supporting the needs of White people at the top, and anti-racist and pro-Indigenous rights protests at the bottom.

The title of another study sums up this phenomenon in four words: "White Protests, Black Riots."[11] Labeling of this kind leaves little room to consider the roots of Black political unrest—and puts little pressure on policymakers to address those issues. Even the signer of the Civil Rights Act, Lyndon Johnson, suffered from this lack of discernment. In the aftermath of the Detroit Rebellion, Johnson appointed commissioners to look into its cause. Their diagnosis was conclusive: Racism had provoked Black Detroiters. Or as they put it: "What the rioters appeared to be seeking was fuller participation in the social order and the material benefits enjoyed by the majority of American citizens."[12] But rather than grapple with racism, Johnson denounced his own commission. In doing so, he robbed his administration of the chance to enact critical policies that could have given Black Americans what they were crying out for: autonomy and dignity.

THE COSTS OF BIAS

Such dramatic expressions of the empathy deficit have long-standing and far-reaching consequences. But the deficit also manifests in other ways—ways that can be disturbingly intimate.

When we see another human being experiencing pain, our brains are wired to undergo a sympathetic response: In essence, we feel a gentler version of the same discomfort we notice in the other person. But studies suggest that the strength of that response depends on the race of the person harmed. In one experiment, participants were shown images of skin being pierced. When the skin shown was Black, the sympathetic response became muted.[13] The researchers behind a similar study reported: "People assume that, relative to Whites, Blacks feel less pain because they have faced more hardship."[14]

In this latter study, the empathy deficit seemed to apply even to participants who were nurses—whose jobs require them to care for all patients equally.[15] Another study confirms that medical professionals are by no means immune to the empathy deficit. For example, on visits to the emergency room, people of color are less likely than White patients to receive painkillers.[16] Why? Because the empathy deficit exists in medical school too. In 2016, the National Academy of Sciences surveyed first-year medical students and found that 21 percent believed that Black people have stronger immune systems, while 29 percent thought that Black people's blood coagulated more quickly than that of White people.[17]

The data on perceived pain thresholds for non-Black people of color aren't as clear. But over the years, studies have consistently shown that medical professionals treat patients differently based on their race. Indigenous Americans, for instance, report being denied pain medication, or released from the hospital without treatment, because of untrue and hurtful "drug-seeking" stereotypes.[18] Asian Americans have now become the only racial group in the United States with cancer as a leading cause of death due to misdiagnoses, delayed care, and cultural and language barriers.[19] And one-third of Hispanic Americans report having to advocate strongly for themselves in the doctor's office to receive the care they deserve.[20]

I should emphasize that I am not accusing any of these medical professionals of conscious racism. I am confident that every person reflected in those studies acted with the best intent and all the knowledge available to them in difficult moments. Instead, I am observing that they, like all of us, have lived their entire lives inside racist systems. That is especially true of the medical profession, whose roots go back through the "scientific" racism of the nineteenth century and include such progenitors of modern US medicine as Samuel Morton, who compared Black and White skull volume and concluded that Black people were genetically less intelligent, and Samuel Cartwright, who attributed the escape efforts of enslaved Americans to a mental illness and prescribed whipping as the cure.

Empathy deficits have also been observed in other professions centered around caring. Teachers, for example, tend to rate Black students' academic abilities lower than those of their White classmates, even when their grades are identical.[21] Infrastructure problems that threaten students' health are more likely to be unaddressed in schools with majority-Black, Indigenous, and Latinx populations.[22]

Against this backdrop, it will surprise nobody that—across the board—outcomes in health, education, economics, and criminal justice, among other areas, are worse for people of color.

The disparities begin at birth. Compared with White babies, Black babies are more than twice as likely to die in infancy. Native Hawaiian, Pacific Islander, and Indigenous Americans have similarly high rates of infant mortality.[23] But the hazards of being a person of color do not end there. During the Covid-19 pandemic, for example, people from Black, Latino, and Indigenous communities were all more likely than White Americans to be hospitalized[24] and to die[25]—in no small part because inequitable health care experiences in the past made them less likely to trust medical advice that could have kept them healthy and alive.

Children of color are less likely to graduate high school, attend college,[26] or enter the middle class.[27] And they are much *more* likely to be suspended or expelled, becoming easy fodder for the infamous "school-to-prison pipeline."[28] Native Hawaiians, for example, make up just one-third of the state's youth population yet comprise a majority of all youth imprisoned.[29] Since Angela Davis began warning of the United States' culture of mass incarceration in the 1960s, the problem has only gotten worse, with wildly unequal rates of imprisonment among Latino and especially Black people. I confronted this fear firsthand when the Kalamazoo police officer arrested my son Justin over a broken license-plate light. Thank God I was able to go get him out: Not every young Black man regains his freedom so easily. For some, the empathy deficit costs them their lives.

At the other end of the criminal justice system, the scale of police violence in the United States is a horror disproportionate to that of any other developed nation. To take just one example: The Prison Policy Initiative found that police in the United States killed about 1,100 people in 2019. That same year, in Canada—the democracy with the next-highest number of police killings—the equivalent number was thirty-six.[30] In the United States, of course, the victims were disproportionately Black and Latino. It is no surprise given that organized American law enforcement has roots in racism, tracing its beginnings in part to the slave-catching posses organized in prerevolutionary Virginia.

Policing and medicine have particularly egregious histories. But in truth, few individuals, organizations, or coalitions of any kind are entirely free of racism. Even the women's movement, one of the noblest campaigns in US history, was tainted by prejudice: In the wake of emancipation, many of the campaign's leaders argued that White women should get to vote before Black Americans. In 2017, I saw more evidence of this view when I visited the Civil Rights Museum adjoining the Museum of Mississippi History in Jackson, two institutions that the Kellogg Foundation is proud to support. The museum displays a Reconstruction-era open letter from suffragists arguing that women should receive the franchise so that White voters would outnumber

Black voters. Faced with the possibility of standing up for *all* women, these activists reserved their cause for *some*.

Today, the racist history of feminism is less overt. But it is still there—if you know where to look. Indeed, the feminist movement has tended to promote the success of elite women within existing power structures; I think about the partner at the accounting firm, who, despite her advocacy for women, saw no contradiction in acceding to a client's racist demands. Meanwhile, too many feminist leaders have done little to question the status quo or seek broader empowerment for women with limited incomes or women of color. Again, the lack of empathy here is largely unconscious. And again, the hurt it causes is real.

Breaking down the emotional barriers raised by racism is no simple task. But another experience of mine suggests how we can begin to tackle this steep, uphill challenge.

Once, at a moment of heightened emotions, I calmly advocated for myself and pointed out unfair practices and unproductive behaviors in the workplace. I was met with a response that so many Black professionals have heard throughout their career: *Stop being so angry.* I felt the sting of this familiar and pernicious stereotype. Like many Black women who express themselves clearly and directly in uncomfortable circumstances, I've been labeled an "angry Black woman" more than once.

Labels like this come from the empathy deficit: When genuine understanding is in short supply, people fall back on the stereotypes drummed into them by the dominant culture. It's not easy to call out microaggressions like this—especially when you're aware of how the empathy deficit works behind the scenes. It's even harder when you know there is a fundamentally good person on the other side of the conversation who likely misspoke and caused unintentional harm.

But instead of bottling up the hurt like I did when I was overlooked academically in college, and again when I was pulled from the real estate account at my first job, I chose to approach this moment of mischaracterization with hope. My hope that the other person would recognize the impact of their words—and my hope that we could heal our relationship and move forward.

Fortunately, we could. I pointed out the label, the stereotype it invoked, and the way it made me feel. This allowed me to begin a dialogue with the person who had used it. Speaking up about micro-aggressions can be difficult, and it's not easy for people to hear when they've made a misstep. But what makes those conversations possible is the belief that by calling attention to the empathy deficit we can push past the awkwardness into mutual understanding and repair.

The significance of this experience is clear: Healing can begin only when we share uncomfortable truths. One of those truths is that we are all implicated in a reality indelibly shaped by structural racism. Fortunately, each of us can begin to change that reality—and close the empathy gap—when we commit to fearless truth-telling.

That is how healing must start.

Chapter 3

SPEAKING THE TRUTH

DESPITE THE INCIDENT with the real estate client at the accounting firm—or maybe because of it—I still wanted to prove myself as a CPA. I buried my lingering hurt and rededicated myself to the work, all the more determined to show my bosses what I could do. I stayed with the firm for a couple more years, never forgetting how quickly opportunities could slip out of my grasp for reasons beyond my control. Then, in 1987, I received a phone call out of the blue.

"This is Dr. Peter Ellis," said a commanding voice. "I'm calling from the W. K. Kellogg Foundation in Battle Creek." He told me bluntly that they were looking for a new financial controller. Somehow, my name had come up, and he wondered: Would I be willing to interview for the role?

At this point, I was only twenty-four years old. The foundation was a big deal, with billions of dollars in assets. And controller was an important job, with responsibility for gathering data for all of the organization's major financial reports. I probably should have been flattered. But all I could think of was location, location, location. Battle Creek is a two-hour drive from Detroit. How could I leave the hometown I loved so much?

Nevertheless, I was curious. "Who gave you my name?" I asked Dr. Ellis. I thought maybe I had audited one of the foundation's grantees. Or perhaps a friend of my sister Marian had passed on my details?

Dr. Ellis chuckled. "Sorry, I don't divulge my sources." He was true to his word: To this day, I still don't know for sure who told him about me.

Politely, I declined an interview. But over the weeks that followed, Dr. Ellis kept calling. And I kept avoiding him. At one point, he called and asked to meet.

"No, I'm too busy—I can't," I told him. His voice boomed back through the phone: "Oh, yes, you can!"

After that, I agreed to meet Dr. Ellis for lunch, hoping it would scare him off. Nope. He kept calling in the hope of wearing me down. Each call sounded more authoritative than the last.

After a few more rounds of phone tag, I decided to do some research on this W. K. Kellogg Foundation. I already knew about Kellogg's cereals, of course. The foundation, created by Mr. Kellogg's generosity but independent of the Kellogg Company, was less familiar to me. But over time, I pieced together a picture of its history, its mission, and some of its current grants. And I appreciated what I learned.

A COMMITMENT TO EQUITY

I read, for example, about one of the foundation's earliest efforts, the groundbreaking Michigan Community Health Project, through which it invested in K–12 education, helped create local public health departments, and modernized basic care in rural areas of the state—helping children thrive even during the bleak years of the Great Depression.

In the 1940s, '50s, and '60s, the foundation expanded its work, investing in the nursing profession and training a new workforce to use postwar medical technologies. Its grantees established several professional nursing education programs, with particular attention to the needs of local communities, making a major dent in a nationwide nursing shortage.[1] In the 1970s and early 1980s, the foundation's grantees even helped create the field of palliative care.

Given this impressive history, I was surprised to learn that from the beginning, Mr. Kellogg harbored no delusions of grandeur.[2] He donated substantial sums to get the foundation off the ground, but he refused to endow his own creation permanently until he had proof it was making a difference. This was true to Mr. Kellogg's character: He wanted to do whatever would generate the most impact, regardless of how it reflected on him.

Thankfully, the foundation did indeed prove its worth—and quickly. Mr. Kellogg wound up establishing a trust for the foundation's benefit, giving it almost all of his shares in the Kellogg Company, a 54 percent stake that brought his total contribution at the time to $66 million—which would be worth well over $1 billion today. The seed that Mr. Kellogg planted has since grown into a multibillion-dollar organization stewarded by generations of inspired, dedicated professionals. Indeed, it is one of the largest philanthropic entities in the world.

Reading about the foundation's first half century, I was struck by the idea of helping people "without regard to sex, race, creed, or nationality."[3] Even in 1987, this commitment was not shared across philanthropy. In 1930, it was nothing short of extraordinary. In those days, people of color were often denied their right to vote, relegated to "separate but equal" schools, and redlined into segregated neighborhoods. Yet Mr. Kellogg, a White man, wanted to help children of every race.

From the beginning, the story of the foundation was one of racial equity. The foundation didn't use that language yet, but for me—a young Black woman considering the significance of its work—this was a seismic shift. It was a story that spoke to me.

I learned something else important in my research, too: Long after Mr. Kellogg's passing, the foundation had made meaningful investments in a number of historically Black colleges and universities (HBCUs). At that time, the mid-1980s, computers were becoming ubiquitous in university libraries, but many HBCUs lacked the funds to buy them.[4] The foundation's grants were designed to make up this deficiency and help HBCUs compete with better-funded, majority-White institutions like my own alma mater, the University of Michigan.

This commitment to Black education spoke to me in a way I hadn't expected when I began researching the foundation. I had learned enough, and I finally agreed to make the 240-mile round trip to Battle Creek for an interview.

Dr. Ellis was thrilled. He told me I should plan to come for a few days and bring my husband at the time: Dr. Ellis and his colleagues wanted to meet him too. The foundation booked us a deluxe room at the one big hotel in town, a sixteen-story building called Stouffer's. We checked in at the front desk, settled into our room, and went to sleep in the big, comfortable bed. I wanted to be well rested so I could make a good impression at the next morning's round of interviews.

Between midnight and one a.m., however, we were startled awake by the sound of banging on our door. "What's going on?" I yelled, panicked. Was the building on fire? Were we in danger? My heart was going a hundred miles an hour. I didn't want to open the door in case whoever was on the other side meant us harm.

A key turned in the lock.

The door burst open.

On the other side of the threshold stood several members of the hotel staff, their faces burning with indignation.

"What are you doing in this room?" they demanded. "You're not supposed to be here."

My husband and I could only gape at them. "What are you talking about?" I asked. "We checked in at the front desk. They gave us this room. I don't understand."

"No, no," said the staff. "Our records show this room is supposed to be empty."

I was baffled. Why would their records show that? And why had the night staff felt such a pressing need to check, especially after we'd given them a legitimate explanation?

Of course, I can't say for sure what was going through their heads. But I can make an educated guess: There was no way these two young Black people were in this nice room for legitimate reasons.

My husband and I had checked in like everyone else. We'd been given room keys and told about the checkout time the following day. And yet because of implicit bias, these staff members simply couldn't fathom that we belonged in their hotel.

My mind raced as I pieced together what was happening. In the moment, though, my husband and I had a more immediate priority: handling the crisis at our door. After a few more minutes of back-and-forth, we convinced the hotel staff that we were in their establishment legitimately. They returned to their duties. We went back to bed and tried our best to sleep.

The next morning, when I arrived at the foundation, I found a beautiful breakfast spread laid out on the table. A number of executives were there to greet me, all of them White. As I walked into the room, they welcomed me warmly. The CEO at the time, Dr. Russ Mawby—a bespectacled man with graying hair and a quick grin—was the first to speak. "How was your evening?" he asked, clearly hoping to make me feel at home.

Another person in that situation might have glossed over the previous night's incident to keep the peace. But if there was one thing everyone present would soon learn about me, it was this: If you ask me a question, I am going to answer fully and honestly. It wouldn't have crossed my mind to do otherwise.

"Well," I said, "it wasn't that great." And I shared the whole story.

The executives' faces froze, turning red with embarrassment. They paused, unsure of what to say. I couldn't blame them.

My experience at the Stouffer Hotel might have soured my interest in working for the foundation, were it not for one of the executives who interviewed me that day: Dr. Norm Brown.

Norm rose from humble beginnings. A White man born in rural Michigan at the tail end of the Great Depression, he had attended elementary school in a series of one-room schoolhouses.[5] Thanks to his hard work and empathetic spirit, Norm had climbed the ranks through government service and academia to become executive vice president at the foundation. Soon after I joined, he would be named president, and subsequently he became chief operating officer.

I didn't know it yet, but Norm Brown would become one of the most important allies in my life.

Norm made a big impression on me because of how honest he was. In one of my interviews, he shared a story about a conversation he'd had recently. He had invited representatives of several important grantees to the foundation and taken them on a tour of the building, showing them all the staff hard at work. But instead of smiling at this display of support, their faces had been grave. Back in the meeting room afterward, Norm had asked the grantees what they thought.

"I am shocked," one had said, "that an organization that talks about inclusivity is not itself inclusive. I expected to see people from different communities among your staff. But all the people you talk about, all the people you support—they're not here."

When Norm recounted this story, his own smile faded. "I promised, there and then, to fix it," Norm told me. "And I intend to. When people show up here, I want them to see the people we serve."

The sincerity of his commitment impressed me. Decades before our present focus on racial equity, Norm had made it his mission. In doing so, he followed in the footsteps of Mr. Kellogg, who had made equity part of the foundation's mission from the beginning.

All right, I told myself. *I'm going to give this five years. Then I'll go do whatever I'm supposed to be doing with the rest of my life.*

Decades later, I'm still here.

And I am immensely proud of the foundation's work to advance racial healing, in service of supporting children, families, and communities—inside of our walls and out. But it hasn't always been an easy journey.

A TRUE ALLY

In his quest for diversity, Norm had his work cut out for him.

I was one of the only full-time employees of color at the foundation. The others were women too: a receptionist and two secretaries. They were considered "support staff" and in those days were treated very differently from "professional staff" like me. Their benefits were not as good, and their voices were almost never heard in meetings.

Moreover, while my hiring marked meaningful progress toward representing African Americans, the foundation had made only a few inroads with other communities of color. Despite its thriving public health programs in Latin America, dating back to World War II, the organization took much longer to work with Latino professionals in the United States, engaging them only through time-limited initiatives such as fellowships. Indigenous and Asian Americans served as fellows as well, although initially not in great numbers, and outreach programs to Native communities were in their infancy when I started working at my new job.

Many African Americans had a similar experience with my new employer. The foundation had hired Black professionals before me, but only on short-term contracts with no guarantee of renewal. Their tenures had been short-lived—not because their contracts didn't get renewed, but in many cases because the environment wasn't supportive. When I joined, I encountered one such professional: Dr. Dan

Godfrey, a food and agriculture scholar from a prominent HBCU, North Carolina A&T State University. Over dinner, Dan told me he wouldn't be staying beyond his one-year contract. He and his wife hadn't found a cultural fit, either at the foundation or in Battle Creek. About a month later, he was gone.

I understood why he felt that way. At the start, I didn't feel like I belonged there either, though I certainly admired my colleagues and their dedication. In fact, I didn't feel like I belonged in philanthropy, period. When I went to big meetings of the Foundation Financial Officers Group, our professional affinity organization, I would see maybe three faces of color among the hundreds in attendance.

Once, a colleague at the foundation asked me straight up: "So, when are you due to leave?"

"Well, that's an odd question!" I replied. But I knew what they were getting at. If you were a person of color, the expectation was that you wouldn't stay long at the Kellogg Foundation. And with attitudes like that, was it any wonder that many colleagues of color chose not to stick around?

Nowadays, it has become well known that a lack of diversity in any setting tends to suppress creativity and innovation, and there is evidence that it also can negatively impact the bottom line.[6] In the nonprofit world of the 1980s and 1990s, I saw that phenomenon first-hand. Not only did almost everybody look alike; they thought alike, too. They ran their organizations in the same old ways, regardless of how effective or ineffective they were. Throughout the field, homogeneity had bred stodginess. By contrast, I noticed that I would usually be the one to challenge the status quo, to suggest new or different ways of doing things.

This sometimes made me unpopular.

Early in my career—it would have been the early 1990s—my immediate boss, in the finance department, tasked me with creating a new budget process. I did as she asked, coming up with a set of procedures that would be effective, efficient, and ready to present to senior staff. But whenever leadership meetings popped up on our schedules, my boss found an excuse to go without me. Eventually, I found out that she was presenting my work as her own.

Finally, she let me accompany her to one meeting. My boss began a presentation to the senior staff about how our new budget process worked. She was composed and confident, but she was getting it all wrong. I knew because I had designed it!

In what could fairly be called an outburst, I took the floor and told everyone that my boss had her facts wrong. For a few seconds, you could have heard a pin drop. Around the table, the mouths of senior executives hung open. Staff members at my level were barely expected to speak at meetings, let alone talk over their superiors or contradict them. But I persevered through the palpable awkwardness, explaining how the budget process *really* worked.

The meeting went on. When it ended, my boss left without a word to me. Afterward, Norm Brown pulled me aside. He told me that while I had been correct in what I had said, there was a more effective way to get my point across. And he gave me an impromptu coaching session on speaking truth to power. He did this in his characteristically kind and generous way. I knew, in part because of the trust we had already built, that he wanted to help me, not patronize me. That brief conversation would prove invaluable in the coming years as I continued to push for change in the way we approached our mission at the foundation.

Norm would soon show the depth of his allyship in an even more dramatic way.

My boss's understanding of budgetary procedures may have been imperfect, but I was still pleased to be reporting to one of the few high-ranking women in the organization. And I was doubly pleased to be responsible for preparing the foundation's tax return, having been fascinated by that process ever since Cass Tech. I knew what information needed to be collected, and I went about gathering the data with my usual zeal for detail.

For the most part, my boss left me to my own devices. Every so often, though, she said something that rubbed me the wrong way. One morning, for instance, she interrupted a conversation about Detroit to question the way I pronounced the word *police*.

In the moment, I was stunned: She had turned me, and anyone else who said *POH-lice* instead of *po-LICE*, into a monolith. And she pronounced the word the same way I did! What exactly was wrong with the way some people said *police*? And why was my boss speaking to me about it?

Her comment reminded me of the put-down I had received a few years before over the word *ask*. It made me uncomfortable. But once again, I chose to focus on my work and made sure my performance spoke for itself. That seemed to work, and my immediate boss did appear to trust me. She let me do my job with minimal supervision, and I appreciated her apparent confidence in my performance.

One day toward the end of the tax return process, I was meeting with my boss's boss to give him an update. I was excited to tell him about all the work I'd done. But instead of listening to my presentation or asking questions, he brought up allegations he had heard from my boss. It turned out, she had told him that I hadn't been working on the tax return, that it wouldn't be done in time, that I had gathered incorrect information, and that my work would need to be redone by someone else.

None of this was true. In fact, some of it was contradictory. How could I have gathered incorrect information if I wasn't working on the tax return? Even worse, this was the first time I was hearing these allegations. My boss had been making them behind my back.

I tried to endure the accusations, but I wasn't given the opportunity to defend myself and speak the truth. Finally, it became too much to bear. "Wait a minute," I said. "You don't know what you're talking about. And neither does she!"

The man sat there, blinking at me. I guess he wasn't used to anyone talking to him like that, let alone a subordinate two levels down.

And I wasn't finished yet.

"You know what?" I continued. "I'm done. I quit." And that's exactly what I did.

After months of enduring snide comments, alleged theft of my work, and now these baseless accusations, I walked straight downstairs to human resources and told them I was resigning. I had reached my breaking point.

HR must have known how close I was to Norm Brown, because instead of giving me a piece of paper to sign, they called him. By that time, Norm had become president of the foundation. It turned out he was stuck in a meeting, but nevertheless he found a way to intervene: He asked Dr. Tyrone Baines, a Black colleague and friend, to keep me in the building until he could meet with me in person.

Tyrone came down and spoke to me plainly. "Look, it's going to be all right," he said. "Stand your ground. If you're right, you're right." His words were balm enough that I didn't storm out right away. But I was still mad, and I still thought this was the wildest place I'd ever seen or worked at.

Finally, Norm appeared. "I will fix things," he said, echoing his words about diversity in our very first meeting, the day after the incident at Stouffer's. For starters, he told me he would immediately reshuffle my responsibilities so that I would no longer have to report to my boss or my boss's boss. And he would give me an office in HR that was physically distanced from them, so I could focus on my work.

All right, I told myself. *I'll stay to finish the tax return.* That was my job. Everything they were saying about my work was untrue, and

I didn't want to lend any credence to their lies. So I committed to finishing the return—and then I fully intended to quit.

Norm could have made those changes and left it at that, hoping the problem would fade away as passions cooled. Instead, he went out of his way to make sure I didn't face this situation alone. After the allegations about my work were proved untrue, Norm acted as a true ally—finding a solution that not only encouraged me to remain at the foundation, but also to enjoy the career path that has ultimately led to my becoming CEO.

It was Norm's commitment to diversity that had persuaded me to join the foundation. Now, his commitment to allyship helped persuade me to stay.

There were deeper reasons to stay, too. In the aftermath of the tax return incident, I realized that what I was doing at the foundation was not just my work; it was my purpose. And I enjoyed many friendships with the colleagues and peers I worked alongside—all dedicated to the children, families, and communities at the heart of our mission.

These realizations came at just the right time. It was the late 1980s and early 1990s, a time when it felt like the gains of previous decades were being erased—an era of renewed unrest. In 1992, Los Angeles erupted following the brutal beating of a Black man, Rodney King, and the acquittal of the White police officers responsible. Meanwhile, urban segregation continued. Gaps in wealth, employment, and postsecondary educational attainment were widening. Staying at the foundation seemed like my best chance at helping to change this reality.

TALKING IN CODE

I still had a long road ahead of me. For alongside the implicit ban on speaking "out of turn," there was another taboo at the foundation in my early days, equally tenacious: We did not explicitly talk about race. Mr. Kellogg had wanted his foundation to benefit children "without regard to sex, race, creed, or nationality." And the foundation's dominant culture at the time took the phrase *without regard* literally, despite decades of visionary grantmaking in support of children and families of color.

When talking to trustees, for example, we couldn't say that we needed to hear the views of people of color, however true that might be. Instead, we had to use code words. We would say things like, "We want to get the right people at the table."

Program directors could talk all day about how their projects addressed economic or educational differences within communities. But those who dared to suggest that they were tackling *racial* disparities were likely to find their requests for funds stalled and their portfolios under increased scrutiny.

One of my first Black colleagues on the grant-making side of the organization, Dr. Henrie Monteith Treadwell, found that she often struggled to obtain funding for causes that would specifically help people of color. When she began to speak about the need to support Black men and boys, she was told, "You don't need to touch that. That's not going anywhere." (This was many years before President Obama brought the issue into the national spotlight with his My Brother's Keeper initiative, which we at the foundation were proud to help fund.)

Similarly, Henrie drew attention to the gulf between the piecemeal support we offered to HBCUs—like those library computers I had read about while researching the foundation—and the vastly greater funding we provided to the state's flagship institutions, the University of Michigan and Michigan State. When she suggested leveling the playing field, one of the senior administrators told her, "Well, the HBCUs don't get the money because perhaps they don't deserve it." That shut down the conversation, because Henrie knew that it would only turn into an argument—one she would lose. The attitude was: *They already got their investments. They should be grateful. Don't ask for more.*

We quickly learned how to talk our way around these taboos. On another occasion, while Henrie was advocating for projects in

Alabama, a trustee asked her a loaded question: "Why are they having these problems down there? What's it all about?" Both Henrie and the trustee knew the answer, of course: structural racism. But saying anything about race could have put these projects in jeopardy. So Henrie was forced to reach for yet another code phrase.

"I think it's for historical reasons," she said.

Finally, through a blend of determination and guile, Henrie got her projects in the Deep South funded. And one day, when driving down to visit them, she received a shocking reminder of why they were so necessary: By the side of the road, she saw crosses burning—a white-supremacist warning of the violence that awaited any Black person who stepped out of line. When Henrie returned from her trip, however, many of our White colleagues simply refused to believe what she had seen. They thought she was exaggerating or being oversensitive. After that, Henrie had to keep quiet about it.

This attitude of avoidance and denial was part of the reason professionals of color tended not to stay long at the foundation. In any organization, simply hiring more people of color is the easy part. To give them an incentive to stay, you need an atmosphere that helps them feel they belong. And attempting to ignore—or even erase—racial differences is the opposite of a warm welcome. That's why I have spent my career at the foundation taking control of the narrative of race: I know that the only way to be more expansive is to acknowledge racial differences and celebrate all they bring to our organization and the people we serve.

Back in my early days, however, there was no getting around it: If you wanted to make an impact at the foundation—if you wanted to get the money out the door and into the hands of the grantees we knew needed it so badly—you had to play ball. If obscuring the impact of race was what we had to do, so be it.

That didn't make our maneuvers less frustrating. Day after day, year after year, we had to grit our teeth in response to questions like, "Why can't we talk about all children, not about Black or White or Hispanic children?" Well, because of white supremacy, and the harmful effects of an inequitable system on children of color. But that answer wouldn't have flown back in the 1980s or 1990s. Instead, we were supposed to pretend that the preceding four hundred years of history hadn't happened—and didn't have any impact on our work.

This reluctance to talk about race wasn't confined to the foundation, of course. It was a symptom of a widespread fallacy—one that still holds today. I am talking about the idea that we can, and should, choose to be "colorblind." If only people stop paying attention to race, the thinking goes, racism will go away.

Most people who hold this view do so with the best of intentions. And I understand why it is so tempting to believe. The trouble is, as we have seen, racism is not that simple. It has seeped not just into our subconscious minds but into all of the systems and institutions that make up our society. Refusing to talk or think about race will not make racism go away. In fact, ignoring racism will make it worse.

The mythology of "colorblindness" is intoxicating. In 2023, even the US Supreme Court fell victim to this thinking when six of the nine justices decided to end affirmative action in college admissions. The majority opinion centered around a forceful statement of "colorblind" logic. Decrying the notion that race has anything to say about a person's identity, it called the idea that students of color and White students bring different experiences to campus a "pernicious stereotype."[7]

In his concurrence, Justice Clarence Thomas went even further, describing on-campus havens like my beloved Angela Davis Minority Lounge as a form of "segregation." He recoiled at any acknowledgement of race as an important factor: "Far from advancing the cause of improved race relations in our Nation, affirmative action highlights our racial differences with pernicious effect," he wrote. "These trends increasingly encourage our Nation's youth to view racial differences as important."[8]

By now, we know the problem built into this worldview: We might not like it, but racial differences *are* important. They have been important since before our country was founded. They remain critical today. Pretending otherwise is willful ignorance. Justice Ketanji Brown Jackson summed it up: "If the colleges of this country are required to ignore a thing that matters," she wrote, "it will not just go away. It will take *longer* for racism to leave us."[9]

The truth is ugly. The truth is distasteful. But to make any progress at all, we need to face it head-on.

FACING THE TRUTH

At the foundation, the process of finally confronting that truth was a long one. It began with Norm Brown's quest for representation. I may have been the first person of color among the full-time, noncontract professional staff, but I was not to be the last. Norm made certain of that.

Colleagues of color arrived in a trickle at first. I took on the role of field recruiter. I had many dinners with promising candidates. And when I say promising, I really mean it. We hired the cream of the crop—some amazing leaders. With support from Norm Brown and other allies, we gradually pushed the foundation to recognize the role race plays in the lives of the children we serve and to fund more race-conscious projects.

I have already mentioned one of the earliest additions—a woman who was destined to become a close friend. Dr. Henrie Monteith Treadwell came from a well-known family of civil rights activists.[10] In her late teens, Henrie had already become famous for desegregating the University of South Carolina in 1963. She was the lead plaintiff in a lawsuit that struck down the university's segregationist admissions policies. Less than a year had passed since a white-supremacist mob, two thousand strong, had rioted against integration at the University of Mississippi, causing the deaths of two people. Just before Henrie was due to matriculate, the home of her uncle—also an activist—was bombed in retaliation for the court case. But Henrie strode proudly onto campus that fall, destined to become the University of South Carolina's first Black graduate since Reconstruction.

In the years that followed, Henrie went on to earn a PhD in biochemistry and make a name for herself as an outstanding public health expert. Among other things, she led a major effort to increase access to health care in underserved communities, called Community Voices. She also designed an academic fellowship program for Black, Latino, and Indigenous Americans. True to the spirit of a woman who had stood against Jim Crow, Henrie was ever the rebel. At the foundation, she never met a troublesome policy she couldn't bend or circumvent. She always pushed the envelope and did what was right to support children.

Dr. Tyrone Baines, the colleague who made sure I didn't follow through with my plan to resign from the foundation, arrived around the same time.[11] A selective integration program in Tyrone's hometown of Dover, Delaware, had made him the only Black kid in his class all the way through high school graduation. Some of the other kids would throw apples and pencils at him. They yelled out hateful names at anyone willing to be seen with him. But Tyrone's friends stood by him, as true allies must. These experiences would go on to shape Tyrone's views around—and his practice of—racial healing.

When Tyrone appeared on our radar as a potential new director for our youth initiatives, he was simultaneously being considered for another big job: president of North Carolina Central University. I was still only twenty-five or twenty-six years old, but it fell to me to persuade him to come work for the foundation instead. To this day, he says it was my enthusiasm that convinced him to join.

As program director for youth initiatives—the first full-time Black program director in the foundation's history—Tyrone secured grants for NAACP chapters and worked directly with the Black community in Detroit as well as Indigenous communities in Michigan's Upper Peninsula. He was instrumental in shaping the Kellogg Youth Initiatives Program (KYIP), an important step toward making our programming more relevant to the communities it served.

Another early recruit was Dr. Bobby Austin. The son of a railroad porter from Kentucky, Bobby had obtained a PhD in sociology before going on to become a power player in Washington, DC. He was as warm and friendly as he was accomplished, and he quickly became our unofficial social secretary, invaluable for his ability to bring colleagues together to talk, unwind, and get to know one another. Among other achievements, Bobby founded and edited the academic journal *Urban League Review*; started his own consultancy firm; and worked for other prominent Black Americans, including Patricia Roberts Harris (the future secretary of housing and urban development) and Ron Brown (the future secretary of commerce).

At the foundation, Bobby worked hard to highlight the barriers facing men and boys of color, a demographic that has too often been unfairly maligned. He designed innovative programming to serve them and cowrote a landmark report on the issue: *Repairing the Breach*, which William Raspberry, a Pulitzer Prize-winning columnist for the *Washington Post*, called "*the* plan to save America."

Dr. Valora Washington started her career at the foundation shortly after me as well. When she was eleven years old, her life had been forever changed by tragedy: One of her classmates and his three younger siblings died in a fire that began in a bar beneath their apartment. The sight of their four small coffins made young Valora commit her life to empowering and protecting children—a perfect fit for the Kellogg Foundation. By the 1980s, she was already a recognized expert in early childhood care and education.

The foundation didn't recruit just outstanding Black professionals, either. In the 1990s and early 2000s, a number of Latino, Asian, and Indigenous professionals took full-time positions. Luz Benitez Delgado initially helped support the foundation's programming in Latin America and the Caribbean before rising through the ranks and joining more community-focused, domestic efforts. Dr. Valorie Johnson, a member of the Seneca–Cayuga Nation and the Eastern Band of Cherokee Indians, worked to build the foundation's investment in Indigenous leaders and communities. Eliana Vera expanded the foundation's work in Mexico and throughout Latin America, with a special focus on fellowships and youth exchanges. Dr. Albert Yee, who was Asian American and a doctor by training, worked to expand an Alaska Native dental therapy program in the continental United States. And Dr. Marcos Kisil became the director of the foundation's Latin American and Caribbean program, leading the office from São Paolo, Brazil.

These were just a few of the colleagues of color I was thrilled to see joining us in Battle Creek. And in 1991, the foundation pulled off yet another coup: recruiting the one and only Dr. Gloria Smith, who would become one of my greatest mentors and a dear friend. Gloria had started her career in public health as a nurse in 1955, at a time when the city of Detroit was booming. She rose to become dean of Wayne State University College of Nursing and a member of the National Academy of Sciences, among a roster of other honors.

Gloria came in as coordinator of health programming, but she was soon promoted to vice president for the foundation's health programs. She was just that good. Gloria spearheaded the foundation's programs on community health, improving access to health care for medically underserved communities. She worked to ensure that the care people received would be culturally sensitive as well as affordable and high quality.

If Henrie was forthright, Gloria was on another level. She would tell people off, up one side and down the other, with the spirit of a nurse who had been around the block and seen it all. In meetings, if she heard something wrong or wishy-washy, she'd call it out, saying, "What are you talking about? Are you a fool? This is ridiculous!"

Talk about telling the truth.

With Gloria's formidable presence at such a high level, the issue of race couldn't stay hidden for long. Racial equity was at the core of how Gloria operated, and she was not about to change that—not for the foundation, and not for anyone. When the foundation added a focus area called "capitalizing on diversity" in the early 2000s, she took issue with the vagueness of the language.

"The word 'diversity' is too weak, too broad," she said. "You have to focus on *race*. That's the underlying cause of all the issues we're dealing with." Remember, this was more than twenty years ago; Gloria's instinct—and bravery in sharing it—was before her time.

Gloria was the first high-ranking foundation leader to talk about race so openly with leadership. More than anyone else, she forced open the doors to allow more programs that considered the impact of racial disparities—a huge step forward for the foundation and for philanthropy in general. Thanks to her example, other colleagues of color began to obtain leadership positions as well.

The presence of more leaders of color had yet another positive effect, related but distinct: It brought the foundation closer to the communities it served.

When I joined, the foundation was making its grants according to an old-school philanthropic method called "institutional investment." What this meant, in essence, was that we would give money mainly to universities, which would then carry out social research and, down the line—if they thought it appropriate—pass the funds on to the communities they deemed most in need. The benefit of this methodology, at least in the minds of those who followed it, was scale. By working with big institutions, they believed they could have a broader, more systemic impact. The drawback was that it put us two or even three levels away from the people we intended to serve.

Tyrone Baines was among the first at the foundation to advocate for changing this system. When I was trying to recruit him, he made it clear that he believed the foundation was minimizing its impact by failing to fund the right grantees on the ground. I assured Tyrone that we were serious about moving toward more community-based grant-making, and Norm Brown backed me up.

With more professionals of color at the foundation, we were even better positioned to carry out our mission. Many of us had come from communities like the ones the foundation sought to reach—in neighbor-hoods like mine in Detroit, towns like Mound Bayou, and Indigenous spaces across the country. We could help the foundation engage these communities. We felt comfortable physically being there, meeting local leaders and activists face-to-face, asking them the right questions to determine their needs. We could confront their issues head-on in a way that most traditional philanthropic executives would not have been comfortable doing. In the process, we were able to find smaller, more grassroots grantees that had not been on the foundation's radar before.

Internally, although the taboo on talking about race was beginning to lift, we still had to be strategic about channeling support to these community grantees. And here was where we exercised our skill in navigating spaces where we were the first, or only, representatives from our communities.

My young-adult years had taught me an important lesson: To succeed in the workplace—almost any workplace—people of color must understand the dominant culture at play. The reasons are not hard to fathom. That's where the power is. That's where the jobs are. My colleagues of color and I knew well how to navigate largely White spaces. Most of us had learned this skill in college, having graduated from predominantly White institutions like U of M. Tyrone Baines, who had attended an HBCU, Morgan State University, was a rare exception. But prior to that, remember, he had been the only Black kid in his K–12 classes. So, we all knew how to play the game.

I think some of us had hoped it might be different at the foundation. But it wasn't, at least not to begin with. The Kellogg Foundation had made sincere commitments to racial equity. Yet for more than half a century, its founders, its leaders, and the vast majority of its employees had been White. To be sure, they were laser focused on the mission—and on impact. They did great, inspiring work. And yet they couldn't help but at the same time infuse into our organizational culture a dominant worldview and vernacular. As a result, my colleagues of color and I had to figure out how to make ourselves heard and understood when it came to advancing the foundation's next generation of goals at the community level.

Although I did what I could to help move resources in the right direction, I was on the finance side rather than the program side. The difference in supporting communities of color really came down to the diligent work of program officers and directors of color, including people like Tyrone, Al Yee, Val Johnson, Luz Benitez Delgado, and Francisco Tancredi and Marcos Kisil in São Paolo, Brazil. These officers would talk to individual trustees before taking their proposals to the full Board of Trustees. They would listen to each trustee's concerns and iron things out if possible, or at the very least ensure that the trustees were not blindsided by the upcoming project.

If a trustee was worried about accountability, for example, someone like Tyrone or Henrie could say, "All right, this is going to be a partnership. This group you already know is going to handle the finances, but the grantee on the ground will deliver the program." Once a grant was established, we were able to stay in touch with grantees, listen to their feedback, and implement their suggestions to make the grants as effective as possible. In doing so, we achieved optimal outcomes while avoiding the old elitist philanthropic trap of assuming we knew it all.

Over time, we shifted the foundation away from monolithic "institutional investment" and toward an approach grounded in communities—a change I have continued to advance as CEO.

REPRESENTATION MATTERS

As the years went on, more professionals of color joined the foundation. Marvin McKinney converted his contract into a permanent position as program director, bringing with him a background as a scholar and experience working in communities as diverse as Greenwood, Mississippi; Fort Walton Beach, Florida; and the South Side of Chicago. At the foundation, Marvin led Joining Forces and Zero to Three, two programs aimed at early development and well-being among young children. Tyrone Baines continued pushing the Kellogg Youth Initiatives Program to new heights.[12]

Gloria Smith hired Barbara Sabol to work alongside Henrie Treadwell on the Health Team, as it was then called.[13] Like Gloria, Barbara was a registered nurse with a wealth of government experience, but in temperament, she couldn't have been more different. Whereas Gloria and Henrie got people fired up, Barbara could perform the equally important task of calming passions in moments that called for a cooler, more analytical approach.

Barbara was responsible for Turning Point, a program that aimed to build greater community public health participation, in partnership with the Robert Wood Johnson Foundation. The leaders of Turning Point theorized that diverse groups working together could better identify and influence the social determinants of health: the environmental conditions that affect a wide range of economic and quality-of-life outcomes for individuals. They were right. A 2002 study found that the program had revealed landmark implications for national public health policy.[14] Like Tyrone with KYIP, Marvin with Zero to Three, and Henrie with Community Voices, Barbara took Turning Point to the next level. These programs helped communities build up leadership to advocate for change.

In 2001, we took another important step forward when Joe Stewart joined the foundation's Board of Trustees. Joe hailed from a small town outside Baton Rouge, Louisiana. In the late 1960s and into the 1970s, he was director of child nutrition for Washington, DC's public schools—"right under the eyeballs of Congress," as Joe puts it. Knowing how impossible it is to teach a hungry child, Joe advocated fiercely for breakfast programs in DC's schools—work that earned him national acclaim.[15, 16]

In 1980—my freshman year at U of M—Joe moved to Battle Creek to become director of child nutrition programs at the Kellogg Company, which has its own operations, is legally separate from the foundation, and has since split into two entities: Kellanova and W. K. Kellogg Co. By the time Joe retired, twenty years later, he had become Kellogg's senior vice president of corporate affairs and chief ethics officer. That's when he joined the Kellogg Foundation's board.

Joe made an instant splash at the foundation. One of his first presentations to his fellow trustees argued, in so many words, that no amount of philanthropic money would make a real difference for young people until we tackled the racism holding them back. Some trustees bristled at this, resenting the feeling, however misplaced, that Joe was calling *them* racists. But Joe persevered. To paraphrase Joe in his inimitable style, "Either work to fulfill the dreams of everyone in this nation or tear down the Statue of Liberty."

Like Gloria Smith before him, Joe told the Board of Trustees the unvarnished truth, no matter how uncomfortable it made them feel. But unlike Gloria, Joe was a member of the board.

By the mid-2000s, it was clear that momentum was building around the idea that the foundation should be tackling racism head-on. Dr. Bill Richardson, the generous former president of Johns Hopkins University, who served as the foundation's CEO from 1995 until 2005—and who was another mentor of mine—instituted Healing Modern Racism workshops for all foundation staff and board members. The workshops were led by Dr. Valerie Batts, cofounder of Visions, Inc., a groundbreaking firm in the field of diversity, equity, and inclusion.

Gloria, the first senior leader at the foundation to insist openly and forcefully that we had to face up to racism, retired in 2001. Leadership appointed me to take her place as chair of the Diversity Advisory Committee. In my periodic reports to the foundation's Executive Committee, I did my best to carry on Gloria's legacy of speaking truth to power.

This often made me unpopular. As Joe had found with the trustees, senior leadership tended to get defensive when confronted with the truth about racist systems in which they (like everybody else) were implicated. I understood why they felt uncomfortable: Racism is a tough topic to address. But I wasn't interested in running a diversity effort just for show, the way too many organizations do, even today. I kept pushing race and racism into focus—no matter how many times I had to be the bearer of bad news.

By 2006, the board had transformed—and so had the way trustees viewed the world and the foundation's work. Half of our trustees were people of color; half were women. The women on the board were outstanding champions for women and people of color. Dottie Johnson, Shirley Bowser, and Wenda Weekes Moore raised the bar of consciousness at the foundation. That year, a new CEO, Sterling Speirn, took office.[17]

Arriving with a wide grin and a lot of experience running nonprofits, Sterling could see how passionate the foundation's staff had become about tackling racism. What was missing, he realized, was an "authorizing environment": one in which staff were empowered to act on this passion. For that to happen, the organization's highest authority would finally have to name racism as one of the primary underlying causes of the challenges facing American children.

Sterling called in Valerie, the architect of the Healing Modern Racism workshops, to address the board directly. Valerie invited the trustees to reflect on how racism affected the foundation's ultimate beneficiaries: children. She described the problem in stark terms: As Americans, we think that each generation should have a better life than the one before. But racism was one problem that was not getting better. In fact, in some ways, we seemed to have gone into reverse since the 1960s. Valerie asked the trustees to think about their own lives, across the many categories of their identities, and the different ways in which they had been affected by racist systems.

Finally, after years of hard work, the board was ready to hear this message. One trustee, speaking to Sterling around this time, invoked an ideological debate from the civil rights era—between integration and nonviolent resistance on one hand, and Black nationalism and racial justice "by any means necessary" on the other. "Boy," the trustee said, "I thought my kids wouldn't grow up in a racist society the way I did. But here we are. Maybe I should have gone with Malcolm X instead of Dr. King." Just a decade prior, it would have been hard to imagine trustees speaking this urgently and directly about race and racism, let alone invoking a wing of the civil rights movement that many have considered radical.

After Valerie's presentation, Sterling asked the trustees, "What do you want to tell the staff, now that you have reflected on this?"

Their conclusion was unanimous: The foundation should declare itself explicitly anti-racist. In fact, it should strive to be the most effective anti-racist organization in the United States.

At last, in December 2007, the Board of Trustees of the W. K. Kellogg Foundation named publicly and forthrightly the problem that lay at the root of most of the issues the foundation had been trying to address since its establishment: systemic racism.

The Kellogg Foundation is committed to being an effective anti-racist organization . . . Our commitment to anti-racism paves the way for funding work to dismantle structural racism and to heal and reconcile racial attitudes, beliefs, and misunderstandings that constrain the lives and futures of vulnerable children.[18]

I could scarcely believe how much the organization had changed since I had joined exactly twenty years before. Back then, the foundation had been traditional, a corporate-like environment. Norm Brown's work to bring greater representation was the exception, not the rule. Now, we were breaking new ground. At a time when major foundations on the coasts and across the country had yet to call out racism in such stark terms, it was our children-focused foundation in Battle Creek, Michigan, that had the courage to lead.

I was proud of the role I had played in this transformation. At the same time, I was also relieved. For twenty years, my colleagues of color and I had felt like we were carrying the racial equity work—*embodying* it—almost by ourselves, with the help of White allies. Now, the Board of Trustees had decided to own the issue. We had spoken the truth—and with representation, resilience, and relentless commitment, our truth had become too urgent to ignore.

This was progress. Today we have a staff of 51 percent people of color and a board that's 50 percent people of color, two historic milestones. But by itself, it was nowhere near enough.

Now it was time for the real work to begin.

Chapter 4

CLARIFYING OUR COMMITMENT

DECLARING AN ORGANIZATION ANTI-RACIST is one thing. Delivering on such a sweeping promise is another. Thankfully, by 2007, the foundation realized we would need help figuring out how to live up to our new commitment. So, we went looking for someone who could guide us: a new vice president for program strategy to lead our anti-racism efforts.

That was when I first encountered the transformative work of Dr. Gail C. Christopher.

It was Barbara Sabol who recommended Gail, a Black woman and a leader in the field of holistic health (and mother of the aforementioned brilliant author and advocate Heather McGhee). From the moment I sat down with a panel of interviewers to discuss the job with Gail, I knew she was somebody I wanted as a partner. She told our interviewing team not just about her health practice, but about her dreams of turning her Maryland home into a healing center—even though she would have to move to Battle Creek for the job. Gail's candor surprised and intrigued me. By the end of the interview, I was thinking to myself, *I've got to get to know this woman.*

Get to know her I did, both professionally and personally. In the office, Gail was always passionate about her work. She and I had the same no-nonsense attitude: We'd do whatever it took to get the job done. Our connection over values quickly evolved into long, strategic conversations about how to advance racial healing at the foundation. When Gail and I weren't strategizing, we were talking about health—my health, to be exact.

A healer through and through, Gail would often tell me, "You need to take more vitamins." She was determined to make sure I got the nutrients I needed—so much so that she wrote up a list of vitamins for me at least fifteen times! One time when I visited her home in Maryland, I noticed she had added a beautiful new wine fridge to her kitchen. Imagine my surprise when I opened the fridge and found it full of vitamins! Only a well-prepared, lifelong healer like Gail would think to turn a wine fridge into a vitamin fridge. She lives her values in every part of her life.

Like Mr. Kellogg decades before, Gail had found her life's purpose through a family tragedy. In 1972, she gave birth to her first child, a daughter named Ntianu. Just six weeks into her life, Ntianu was diagnosed with congenital heart disease. The doctors told Gail and her husband that there was nothing they could do until Ntianu was five years old—assuming she survived infancy.[1]

That advice was flat-out wrong. In fact, the necessary cardiovascular procedure had been developed as early as the 1940s. Its inventor was Dr. Vivien Thomas, a Black American who rose from humble roots in the Jim Crow South to become director of Surgical Research Laboratories at Johns Hopkins University and a trailblazer in pediatric heart surgery. Had Ntianu received Dr. Thomas's procedure, her little life might have been saved. Instead, at only three months of age, Ntianu passed away.

From that moment, Gail knew that she would be a healer. She moved from Cleveland to Chicago to study naprapathy—a form of holistic medicine that seeks to relieve pain by focusing on the connective tissues binding the body together. Naprapathy changed Gail's whole outlook on life. As she wrote years later: "I view connective tissue as a metaphor for universal love. Love is the force that connects and pervades all things. This holistic understanding evolved into an optimistic and deeply appreciative view of life and of people."[2]

At the same time, Gail's naprapathy practice also pointed her toward a more unsettling truth. She realized that most of the factors influencing people's health are not medical but social: elements such as education, housing, food insecurity, and access to quality health care.[3]

As we have seen, all these goods are still distributed according to implicit racial hierarchies of value. The lower a person is on this hierarchy, the fewer resources they are likely to have available to them—making upward social mobility more difficult to obtain and sustain.

Another key tenet of naprapathy describes the physical consequences of this uphill battle: The more stress a person faces, the more vulnerable to illness their body becomes. And just as stress poisons a body, Gail realized, so too does racism poison society.[4]

Propelled by this realization, Gail became an early expert in the social determinants of health and well-being. She began working to steer public policy toward addressing these challenges, amassing experience as a scholar, an advocate, and a leader at institutions like Howard University, the National Academy of Public Administration, Harvard's Kennedy School of Government, and the Joint Center for Political and Economic Studies.

Faced with the monumental challenge of overcoming structural racism, it would be easy to become cynical. But Gail's outlook remains optimistic to this day—inspired, once again, by her knowledge of holistic medicine. When asked, she points out that all human beings crave connection, belonging, and self-expression. These desires are not just emotional; they exist on a chemical level. We see this with oxytocin, the human hormone of love and personal relationships. When we forge meaningful connections with our fellow human beings, our oxytocin levels rise. We heal in body as well as in soul.

Since the 1970s, Gail has worked to apply this logic to the healing of society's most persistent chronic disease: racism. By the time she and I first met in 2007, she had organized countless healing circles—small groups specifically designed to confront difficult issues and build bridges between people across the chasms that divide us. These circles have roots in Indigenous cultures around the world, particularly the Americas, Africa, and Australia. Though Gail has told me she wasn't aware of this rich history when she began her clinical practice, she has always felt a personal, ancestral pull to these kinds of collective healing practices—no wonder, since she has Indigenous heritage herself.

From the foundation's perspective, our choice was clear: Gail was perfect. The vice president for program strategy job—and the work of leading our organization toward anti-racism—was hers.

As we worked side by side, Gail and I quickly bonded over our shared experiences as Black women navigating majority-White spaces. We sensed in each other a similar kind of hurt. For example, at her overwhelmingly White alma mater, Hofstra University (just outside New York City), Gail had at first intended to pursue her passion for theater. But when she started drama classes, her professors told her she could only play maids. Discouraged, she soon switched to African Studies.[5]

Like me, Gail also knew how it felt to lose a friend to structural racism. During high school, she was selected to attend an arts camp in upstate New York. At one point, Gail and her classmates opened for none other than Broadway legend and Black American icon Paul Robeson. As the summer wore on, Gail became friends with her assigned roommate, a White girl.

Toward the end of camp, Gail's roommate suddenly attempted suicide. After she was taken away in an ambulance, Gail found her note: *I don't want to go home. My father has taught me to hate Black people. I now know that is a lie. I don't want to live like that anymore.* Gail never saw her again.

I didn't hear that story until years later. But when I did, it brought back the pain of losing my friend Jenefer when her family fled Detroit. Our society's divisions have all too many ways of driving people apart. However, with Gail's leadership, the foundation could begin to bring people together in more meaningful ways.

"FOCUS ON WHAT YOU ARE *FOR*"

Early in her tenure as vice president for program strategy, Gail gave a presentation to the foundation's trustees, who were seated around a table in the boardroom. Just as Dr. Gloria Smith had challenged the word *diversity*, Gail took issue with the term *anti-racism*.

"This declaration is a major milestone," she told us from the front of the room. "No doubt about it. But 'anti-racism' is not a good handle for this work."

Once again, I was surprised. It had taken decades for the foundation to declare its anti-racism. My colleagues and I had worked hard to get to this point. Why shouldn't we shout it from the rooftops?

"You're focusing on what you're *against*," Gail continued. "That's a mistake. Being against things will drive people away. If you're going to bring about change, you must focus on what you are *for*. You need to call people into the work, not just call them out."

Gail had our attention. What did she recommend?

"It's not about destroying racism," she said. "It's about healing."

The trustees and I sat back in our chairs, absorbing what Gail had just told us. None of us disagreed with her. In fact, we all understood the power of racial healing.

Foundation leaders had been interested in the idea for years. Dr. Tyrone Baines, who had gone through racial healing workshops at his HBCU alma mater, Morgan State, brought the practice into the foundation before leaving in 2003. Specifically, Tyrone had become fond of a method developed by Nathan Rutstein, an American reporter and educator who had founded Institutes for the Healing of Racism around the world—and whose 1993 book *Healing Racism in America* had become a cornerstone of literature in the field.

As Tyrone told me later, he was impressed by Nathan's ability to get diverse groups of people talking about race without making anyone feel guilty. Instead, Tyrone noted, Nathan's methodology worked to build relationships and get people fired up to take action in their own lives and communities.

Through a foundation program called Experts in Residence, Tyrone brought Nathan in to lead racial healing circles. These circles would start with a talk from Nathan likening racism to a chronic disease— one we all catch, but one that can be healed. Then, participants would divide into smaller groups, sharing with one another their experiences with the symptoms of this ailment. In this way, they built empathy. People became inspired.

Together with people like future foundation board chair Joe Stewart, then still an executive at the Kellogg Company, Tyrone and Nathan put together Calhoun County's Institute for the Healing of Racism in Battle Creek. Participants included local leaders such as the super-intendent of schools, the presidents of the Kellogg Company and the foundation, and prominent businesspeople from the community. Tyrone and Joe held sessions at their homes—Tyrone in his basement, Joe on the patio in his backyard.[6]

Around the same time, I began to encounter my first healing circles through my work with Starr Commonwealth, a Michigan-based social services organization and all-boys residential school that has been dedicated to changing the lives of boys across the state for nearly a century. Joe and Tyrone worked with the organization and with john a. powell, a civil rights expert who spells his name in lowercase as a gesture of humility, to scale up racial healing. The trio's collaboration resulted in circles hosted in hotel ballrooms for leaders across Battle Creek. I used to call these gatherings "works in progress": The leaders, mostly White men, often didn't understand why the circles were necessary. But everybody came together. It was a start.

And in their basement and backyard, Joe and Tyrone went even further.

Despite sharp distinctions in participants' backgrounds and politics—and the occasional display of irritation or awkwardness—the conversations in these circles remained constructive. Participants told each other the naked truth and respected each other for it. As Joe said later, "That's what healing is all about. It's people putting the truth on the table. . . . You tell your story, and nobody's got a right to say, 'I don't believe you.'"[7]

Racial healing turned out to be powerful medicine. Tyrone remembers even seasoned leaders openly crying as they revealed their experiences to one another. After sharing those deep truths, their relationships were never the same: They approached every issue after that conversation with a sense of unity—a kind of trust that could only come from knowing a piece of another person's true self.

By the time Gail Christopher joined the foundation in 2007, efforts toward racial healing like those pursued by Joe and Tyrone (under the guidance of Nathan Rutstein) had been going on for years. Both Tyrone and Joe continue to participate in racial healing circles today: Tyrone attends one every Tuesday in his retirement community, while Joe helps run a large-scale healing effort alongside Jesuit priests and the descendants of people enslaved by their order. Indeed, Gail herself had used similar methods. What she proposed next was a step up in terms of scale and organization.

First and foremost, Gail wanted to create space to host a community of practitioners, where experts from all over the United States could share knowledge and practical experience, learn from one another, and ultimately strengthen the whole field of racial healing. In this way, Gail hoped to bring the practice in the United States to the next level.

Fittingly, she called the project America Healing.

The foundation's leadership was ready to bet big. CEO Sterling Speirn, having been instrumental in building support for the anti-racism declaration, now championed racial healing as the best means of making good on this landmark commitment. Equally important, to no one's surprise, was Joe Stewart. By this time, Joe was not just on the Board of Trustees; he was now its chair. Joe brought to this movement his authority and decades-long passion for racial healing, paving the way for the foundation to back racial healing on a grand scale.

With Joe and Sterling's guidance, the board wound up committing no less than $75 million over five years, making America Healing the largest single program in the foundation's history at that time. I had followed in Norm's footsteps and was chief operating officer by this time, so it fell to me to find the money. I could not have been more delighted to do so.

By May 2010, we were ready to launch America Healing. Sterling made the announcement at an event in Washington attended by an icon of the civil rights movement: Congressman John Lewis. Congressman Lewis's presence was a dazzling endorsement. But Sterling's visible commitment to America Healing was also important. It demonstrated to the world that America Healing was not some pet project pursued just by people of color: Our CEO, a White man, was firmly on board too. Once again, Sterling embodied the value of public allyship.

Despite enthusiastic support from the top of the organization, not everyone in the foundation shared our commitment to racial healing right away. Internally, I encountered skepticism from some colleagues who, steeped in traditional philanthropy, didn't yet understand how we would calculate the return on investment from such a broad program.

"Why are you all spending money on that?" they would ask me. "That's soft stuff. It's just about meetings and chitchat." These colleagues may have assumed they would find me in agreement—after all, I'm an accountant with a master of business administration. But if so, they were disappointed. My invariable reply was that healing is not "soft stuff" but, in fact, one of the hardest jobs we have as a nation and a world. If it weren't so difficult, we would be healed already.

More than once, I had to use my accounting and business acumen to make the case for funding our partner organizations that pursued racial equity at the grassroots level. I strongly believed that this was the investment we had to make if we were going to achieve anything further down the line. It would take years—maybe decades—to see major progress. But I was determined to help steer us through the course.

To no one's surprise, external opposition soon surfaced, too. An op-ed in the *Wall Street Journal* called America Healing a "boondoggle" and predicted that "nothing good is likely to come from this."[8]

Yet the evidence was undeniable: Nothing would do more to further the charge Mr. Kellogg gave the foundation to "use the money as you please so long as it promotes the health, happiness, and well-being of children" than ending racial inequity. We were *for* the children. And that meant we were also against racism.

A NATIONAL PLATFORM FOR IMPACT

True to Gail Christopher's vision, America Healing started bringing her fellow racial healing practitioners together in national convenings. Over time they developed, strengthened, and standardized the practice of racial healing—and strategized its wider deployment.

These convenings also provided a prominent platform for truth-telling about race, directed toward the wider American public. In New Orleans in April 2012, for example, we held the Healing for Democracy conference. The conference brought together almost five hundred leaders from activism, academia, and the news media, not to mention a legendary headliner: the great singer and civil rights leader Harry Belafonte. I remember his presentation like it was yesterday. He described all of the activist movements he had joined or led over the course of his life. Vividly, he told us about his journey with Dr. Martin Luther King Jr. during the civil rights movement. He recounted how he had used his career as an artist and entertainer to help advocate for change. Like everyone else in the audience, I was in awe.

Another memorable presentation in New Orleans was the panel on unconscious bias. In keeping with the practice of racial healing, the panelists started from a place of compassion. Respected journalist Maria Hinojosa spoke about the need to allay anxiety among White communities about what a version of the United States that is no longer majority-White might mean for them. john a. powell, who helped organize some of the first racial healing circles I had participated in, said that implicit bias "doesn't make us racist. It makes us human. And if we're going to address it, we have to acknowledge that."[9]

In parallel, the foundation issued a nationwide request for racial healing proposals. We received almost one thousand responses, from nearly every state—further evidence that Americans were ready for this big idea. We funded grantees in all kinds of communities. In Oakland, California, the People's Grocery brought the city's diverse racial groups together to correct historical imbalances in access to healthy food. In New Mexico, Texas, and Mississippi, Centro por la Justicia created ties between Black and Latinx youth, empowering both. In Minnesota, the Saint Paul Foundation facilitated frank conversations about race issues and built relationships across racial lines. And from coast to coast, the National Indian Child Welfare Association helped communities begin to heal the wounds caused by the long, painful history of removing Indigenous children from their families.

These are just a fraction of the new projects we funded. All told, the foundation received so much interest in America Healing that, even with $75 million, we could not fund every proposal. But we did put together a catalog including the projects we couldn't back. We were glad to see this catalog help many of those organizations attract much-needed and well-deserved funds from elsewhere.

America Healing also funded landmark research into the effects of racist structures on our society. A study by the Kirwan Institute at The Ohio State University documented sharp racial disparities in school discipline, alongside a worrying rise in referrals of students of color to the criminal justice system. Turning to potential remedies, the researchers encouraged educators to consider how their own implicit bias might play into their decisions.[10]

Meanwhile, research by the Altarum Institute, a nonprofit founded by professors at the University of Michigan, explored the economic upsides of ending structural inequity. The study found that closing the earnings gap between White people and people of color would raise US gross domestic product (GDP) by trillions of dollars.[11] By 2050, in fact, we could increase the GDP by $8 trillion[12]—more than the entire federal budget in 2023.[13] I was proud to see such a transformative report had a connection to my own alma mater—and I know that my mentor, Dr. Alfred Edwards, who advocated with such determination for Black students at U of M, would have felt the same.

Over its five years of addressing racial issues, America Healing raised awareness across the country. It began to change the narrative on race. It pushed new concepts into the mainstream. This is no exaggeration: The foundation's evaluators confirmed these effects empirically by analyzing fluctuations in online traffic and content. For example, whenever Gail Christopher published a commentary to add to the growing national conversation about structural racism, we would see a big upward spike in media mentions of the terms she used.[14]

At last, we were moving the needle. We were speaking the truth and shrinking the empathy deficit, one circle at a time.

OWNING THE SPACE

By 2012—the year of our star-studded conference in New Orleans—America Healing was reaching its climax. Later that year, Sterling

Speirn announced his retirement as president and CEO, effective at the end of 2013.

Sterling told me in advance that he planned to leave. I urged him not to. I felt that, finally, our racial equity work was gaining traction, and he was an important champion for it. Within the foundation, too, he had pursued deeper diversity, equity, and inclusion via trainings and culture change. Indeed, Sterling had achieved a great deal as CEO.

Perhaps most significantly, Sterling had targeted half of the foundation's resources toward a place-based strategy focused on children, families, and communities in six distinct locations: Michigan, Mississippi, Louisiana, and New Mexico in the United States, and Haiti and Mexico internationally. While each of these named places was and is unique, all were also places where the foundation could build from strong existing partner relationships and community-driven investments could have a profound impact on the well-being of children, especially within growing communities of color. And he made sure our commitment to each community would be generational. Having previously led a community foundation for many years, Sterling knew how much more powerful a grant could become when the grant-maker really understood the people it was trying to help and invested in the long term. By focusing on a handful of areas without a time limit, alongside our systems change grant-making portfolio at a national and international level, Sterling brought us still closer to the communities we served.

After eight years, however, Sterling was determined to move on. Try as I might, I couldn't persuade him to do otherwise. So, the Board of Trustees began to search for his replacement.

One glance at the portraits of past foundation leaders, all the way back to Mr. Kellogg himself, suggested how the new CEO would look: a dignified White man with thinning hair and glasses. And to be fair, these men had achieved a great deal of impact for children and families—starting with Russ Mawby, who had served in the CEO role for twenty-five years. Bill Richardson had implemented workshops on healing modern racism and advocated for employees of color, including me. Sterling had championed racial healing and brought us closer to the communities we served. Norm Brown was never CEO, but as executive vice president of operations, and then president, he had worked his darndest to ensure better representation for people of color—and had succeeded in changing the faces of our staff.

There was a good chance the next CEO would look like all the others. But as board chair, Joe Stewart was determined to challenge that assumption, knowing firsthand the importance of visible representation at the highest levels. What Joe sought to create was an opportunity for something new at the foundation: a leader of color. Serving in this capacity would come with heavy expectations. And after a quarter century at the Kellogg Foundation, I realized that the task might fall to me.

Over the previous few years, I had earned two significant promotions: first to executive vice president of operations—the job Norm Brown had held when he first interviewed me in 1987—and then, a few years later, to chief operating officer. In effect, I had become one of Sterling's top deputies. At the same time, Sterling had sought to tee me up for even higher office by putting me in charge of the foundation's programming in Mississippi and New Orleans. By the time he announced his retirement, I had experience in finance, HR, and now programming.

Frankly, however, I wasn't sure I could work effectively with the board. Some trustees, like Joe Stewart, were mentors and shared my vision for the organization. But others told me I lacked the "gravitas" to serve as CEO.

What does "gravitas" really mean? I wondered. *How is it measured?* This coded scrutiny was an unwelcome reminder of the guidance counselor who had tried to keep me from the business school at the University of Michigan. For some of the trustees, no matter what I had achieved, I could not convince them I would be successful.

Thankfully, these individuals were outnumbered by trustees who believed in me, so they weren't my main obstacle. Rather, I hesitated even to seek the CEO position—because I had concerns about the way the board operated.

Like most other philanthropic organizations that disburse hundreds of millions of dollars each year, our board still insisted on approving every grant over $400,000, in an astonishing twelve meetings per year. Moreover, the trustees had a habit of issuing guidance individually instead of collectively, leading to confusion among the staff when information or instructions seemed to contradict. I worried that this level of micromanagement and the lack of unity would hamper my ability to lead.

But my hesitation did not last. About six months after Sterling's announcement, the search firm came to me. With encouragement from Joe and others, I finally applied—knowing that when my interview came, I would have to share a harsh truth with the board: If I were CEO, I'd need to make some changes to the way we operated. The trustees might not like it, but I have never been one to sugarcoat.

Luckily, I had a few aces in the hole.

My greatest asset, as ever, was my family. My youngest sister, Brenda, after graduating from the University of Michigan a few years behind me, had made her career in corporate management. By 2013, she was running her own strategic consulting firm out in California. We worked together to craft position statements on all the major topics I might want to speak about—including the management changes I sought. We created questions for me to ask the trustees. We even picked out a wardrobe, so that I would enter the room looking every inch a CEO.

My longtime professional coach, Jo Ann Morris, also got me fired up. Jo Ann is one of the cofounders of White Men as Full Diversity Partners, a consultancy that was working with the foundation internally on race issues. In other words, she was an expert on difficult conversations. I still remember what Jo Ann told me: "You need to own this space," she said. "You know how to do this job. You've *been* doing it. You need to walk in there *telling* them it's your job, not begging them to choose you." Good advice.

Finally, I sought guidance from the ultimate authority on the Kellogg Foundation: Mr. Kellogg himself. I was always telling people to let our founder's example guide their work, so this was an opportunity to take my own advice and reconnect with the foundation's DNA. Besides, Mr. Kellogg was a meticulous and determined man. If I got it wrong, he would surely haunt me!

In preparation for my interview, I reread *The First Eleven Years*, the foundation's 1941 progress report, cover to cover—three times. With each read, different passages jumped out at me. What struck me the most was our founder's unyielding compassion coupled with his focus on communities. In his foreword, Mr. Kellogg lauded the foundation's "programs designed to help people to help themselves . . . utilizing our experience as a means of assisting other communities throughout the country in their efforts at self-improvement." He concluded: "It is only through cooperative planning, intelligent study, and group action—activities on the part of the entire community—that lasting results can be achieved."[15]

Reading and rereading Mr. Kellogg's prescient words, I realized something important: I might look different from the foundation's previous leaders. I might come from a different place, geographically and socially. But what really mattered was the mission in my heart. And in that regard, Mr. Kellogg and I were one.

With support from Brenda and the rest of my family, from Jo Ann, and from Mr. Kellogg, I was ready to face the challenge head-on.

MOVING BOLDLY FORWARD

The unlikely setting for my interview with the full Board of Trustees was a beige conference room in a hotel at the Detroit airport. Thanks to my prep sessions with Brenda, I entered the room thoroughly prepared—not to mention immaculately dressed. I scanned the dozen faces of the trustees. Despite my nerves, I was struck by the progress we had made toward diversity since I had joined the foundation. White men were now in the minority on the board. Half the trustees were people of color. One-third were women. If what I said next ended my career at the foundation, I could still be proud that I'd helped usher in that level of representation at the top.

Our meeting began with a few minutes of innocuous back-and-forth as we sat smiling around a long, wooden table. The fluorescent lights hummed. We sipped hotel coffee and my drink of choice, tea. Then we got to the hard part: One of the trustees stared at me intensely. "If you were CEO," the trustee asked, "how would you manage the parking lot?"

I took a deep breath. I had expected this question.

At the foundation, the "parking lot" was an endless list of tabled items that the board maintained. Every time a question arose about a grantee that someone couldn't immediately answer, the board added the question to the parking lot. Years into this habit, the list practically stretched for miles. And although I understood the good impulse behind it, addressing the parking lot usually devolved into micromanagement. Between board meetings, trustees would press for action on specific items, even though staff could manage perfectly well without them.

I had spent a lot of time thinking about the parking lot, even before I considered what I might do as CEO. And I knew exactly how I would handle it.

"If I'm the CEO," I said, "that list will disappear."

The room went silent except for the muffled sound of jets taking off and landing outside the hotel. For a different person, this would have been the perfect moment to move quickly on to easier topics. But I knew that speaking the truth, uncomfortable as it was, would help the foundation in the long run.

"The parking lot is dysfunctional," I said. "It's not helpful. The board can't keep micromanaging." Now I was gaining momentum.

"That's not the only thing that needs to be fixed," I continued. "You should also know that when the board offers twelve different points of view, you give no direction at all. It's hard to run an organization when people can pick and choose which guidance to follow."

The silence broke as audible gasps escaped from some of the trustees. In my head, I ran through the résumé I had been polishing, just in case this meeting didn't go my way. For a few moments, I stared at the trustees, trying to guess what they were thinking.

At last, Fred Keller—chair of the CEO search committee—spoke. "She's absolutely right," he said. "We shouldn't have that list, nor should we be managing from it."

What? Was I hearing him correctly?

My heart skipped a beat when Joe Stewart piped up too. "La June," he said, his face serious. He took a breath. "I never thought about things that way, but you're right. We're not giving you the guidance you need."

I couldn't believe it. I was so relieved, I nearly fell out of my chair. "Joe," I said, "if I'm CEO, I'm going to need the authority to fix it." Joe nodded. "I know. You've given us a lot to consider."

The board spent a few more months interviewing candidates. Then, right before a board meeting in Grand Rapids, Fred pulled me aside to break the news: "You have been selected as CEO." He swore me to secrecy while we ironed out the details.

Somehow, I made it through that trip without spilling the beans. As soon as I got home, though, my husband, Avery, and I celebrated. I was over the moon.

Our trustees could have chosen another CEO who looked like all the ones who had come before. They certainly could have picked an external candidate, which was what typically happened in philanthropy. Instead, they had decided to promote from within—and to invest in the potential for deep, long-lasting change.

The importance of this inflection point for the foundation wasn't lost on me. When I joined the organization, people of color were scarce, talk of race was frowned upon, and hierarchies ruled. Now, the board had appointed its first woman and first Black president and CEO. What's more, the trustees had heard an uncomfortable truth from me, listened to it, and agreed to change the way they operated.

I will never forget the day the staff at the foundation was told I would be their next CEO. It was a powerful moment: People erupted, stood, applauded, and even cried. I did too. As I looked around the room, I caught the equally tearful eyes of several people who had helped make my journey at the foundation possible: former CEO Russ Mawby, who had wanted to be in the room that day; board chair Rod Gillum, who had never seen staff at any organization react so strongly and positively to a CEO announcement; and the finance and HR staff, many of whom I had worked alongside since my start at the foundation more than twenty-five years earlier.

The experience was surreal. I remember thinking later, *What was that applause about, that explosion of gratitude and celebration?* Looking back, I don't think that outpouring of emotion was just for me. It was also for the Board of Trustees and its courage to do something different and meaningful—and for the foundation and its capacity to change and move boldly forward.

The board's decision was yet another landmark for representation and for the foundation's relationships with the communities we serve. As I noted when the foundation announced my appointment in October 2013, having grown up in a family of ten children in inner-city Detroit, I understood the challenges facing the families we sought to help—just as I understood the powerful journey those families could take with the right support. Here I was, the ninth child in my family, becoming the ninth president—and the first woman and first Black president—of the W. K. Kellogg Foundation.

"IT'S NOT ABOUT ME. IT'S NOT ABOUT YOU . . ."

Following the October announcement, one of the first outside emails I received came from the chambers of Judge Gerald Rosen, who at that moment was busy overseeing Detroit's municipal bankruptcy. As it turned out, my hometown was to figure prominently in the early months of my tenure. In fact, it began to loom large even before I stepped into the new role.

The city was in dire straits: Detroit was—and remains—the largest US city ever to file for bankruptcy. When filing, the state-appointed city manager revealed that Detroit's debts had reached $18 billion.[16] Needless to say, Judge Rosen wasn't reaching out to congratulate me on my promotion; he wanted my help. He was putting together a broad coalition to help with the assistance package that would eventually become known as the Grand Bargain.

The Kellogg Foundation already had a history of investment in Detroit, so from that point of view, it made sense for us to participate. Nevertheless, some felt it was unfair for us to do this for Detroit and not for other cities. Others thought, in essence, that it was not philanthropy's job to save a destitute city from itself.

I disagreed. To me, this was an opportunity for more healing. Specifically, it was a chance to lift up a community laid low by decades of segregation and disinvestment. And in that respect, it aligned precisely with the foundation's mission: to prioritize serving the children.

Still, it took me a beat to decide whether we would be part of the Grand Bargain. Initially, I worried that the city was too focused on protecting the Detroit Institute of Arts, whose world-class collection was at risk of being sold to pay off the city's creditors. The loss of the art would have been devastating—a further blow to the city I love. But there was another imperative in play: City workers stood to lose their pensions. These were the people who had helped keep Detroit going through the most difficult period in its history. They had stood by Detroit while everyone around them was leaving, in much the same way my family had stayed following the 1967 Rebellion. Now, a promise made to them and their families was about to be broken. I felt strongly that those families should not be abandoned.

As many community members and even people outside of the city debated whether to sacrifice Detroit's art and culture or sell out its pensioners—both unthinkable options—I added my voice to a growing chorus pointing out that this was, in fact, a false choice. It was another example of zero-sum logic at work. We didn't have to choose between a treasured cultural institution and the people and communities around it. We could find a way to serve both.

Throughout the process, I met multiple times with Judge Rosen and the other funders he had assembled. Collectively, we ensured that the community's best interests would factor into the Grand Bargain. And for our part, the Kellogg Foundation would ultimately invest $40 million to help save the city for Detroiters. This was the third-largest investment made by any philanthropy as part of the Grand Bargain.

This was also the first big investment of my tenure. Technically, we put together most of the deal before I even officially took the reins. To this day, I wish we could have done even more for Detroit's retirees. But the foundation's support for the Grand Bargain remains one of the most personally meaningful investments I have overseen.

Boosted by this early success, I officially started as CEO on January 1, 2014, stepping into my new role with a powerful sense of gratitude toward the leaders who had come before me. I learned from their successes and challenges—just as I had learned from my siblings. And the main lesson I took was that the most powerful leadership is not built on a command-and-control approach. It's built on mutual respect and shared ownership of the mission. I might sit on top of the pyramid now, but I didn't want anyone catering to me.

"Forget about me," I told the senior staff in my first speech as CEO. "Don't try to make me happy. Get out there and work every day to make those kids happy."

I wasn't content just to say it: I even had T-shirts printed. The front of the shirts read, *It's not about me. It's not about you* . . . The back said, *It's all about the children.* I wore that shirt myself in internal meetings. I also gave one to each of the dozen trustees, as a reminder that our work wasn't about *them* either! And I have made sure that, to this day, new employees still receive those shirts in whatever language they prefer to speak: English, Spanish, even Haitian Creole.

This, too, came right out of Mr. Kellogg's own playbook: He wasn't interested in the limelight, and he certainly didn't want anyone appealing to his ego. That was why he would sit nine or ten rows back in every meeting—even in the auditorium that bore his name. That was why he refused to endow his own foundation until it had proved its worth. That was why he told his staff: "Use the money as you please so long as it promotes the health, happiness, and well-being of children."[17]

I was excited to roll up my sleeves and get to work. Little did I know, my ideas about compassion and community were about to be put to the test.

"YOU GUYS FAILED US"

I heard about Michael Brown's death on August 9, 2014, the same way millions of Americans did: by watching the news. Shot at least six times in his hometown, the eighteen-year-old became the latest victim of the United States' pandemic of police violence. The moment of his death was not captured on camera—that shock would come later, with the murders of George Floyd and others. But pictures did surface of Michael Brown's body, lying face down in a public street in a pool of his own blood. It was sickening—like seeing the aftermath of a lynching. Protests erupted across the country, spearheaded by a new generation of young activists shocked by those images.

At that point, I had been CEO for just over eight months. The foundation's semiannual meeting of our big racial equity grantees was coming up, and I decided that we should hold it in Ferguson—and that we should invite community members, to give them a space where they could process their pain.

In addition to members of the public, the heads of ten big-name nonprofits attended. These were all organizations the foundation had worked closely with, in part to facilitate greater cross-community solidarity—among them, the Advancement Project, Faith in Action, the NAACP, the National Congress of American Indians, National Council of Asian Pacific Americans, UnidosUS, and the National Urban League. As representatives of our respective organizations, we were all frequently quoted in the news, and our names and faces would have been familiar to anyone following the outpouring of media commentary. Our discussion that day was all about bureaucracy: process, governance, the kind of things that big-league philanthropists worry about.

The wrong things.

As we ran through our agenda, a group of young activists entered the room, shepherded by a young pastor from a nearby church. They had been invited by Starsky Wilson, a longtime activist and another local pastor, who later became president and CEO of the Children's Defense Fund. A young man spoke up—a rapper whose stage name was T-Dubb-O. He leveled his gaze at the assembled leaders and spoke calmly.

"You guys failed us," he said. "You let us all down. We're here because of your failures."

His words were so sharp, they seemed to pierce my heart. But I forced myself to keep listening.

"You were supposed to dismantle racist systems and structures,"

T-Dubb-O said. "You sit in those seats. You're on TV all the time. But nothing has changed. In fact, it's gotten worse. And now we have to bear that burden. We're out here marching and risking our lives to fix your mistakes."

To my left and right, the big-name leaders went silent. The mood was solemn. What could we possibly say to these young people?

A year before, when I had faced the Board of Trustees, I had spoken truth to power. I knew how much courage that takes. Now, these young people were speaking their truth to me and my peers. We had to listen.

More than that: We had to act.

Once T-Dubb-O was done, I raised my voice—and made sure he and the other activists, still standing in the room, could hear me. "He's right," I said. "Our only hope is to support these young people. That's where our money needs to go."

In short order, my fellow leaders and I rallied around those young activists. We made space for them on our agenda. We agreed with their message and were eager to help them and their fellow emerging leaders—young people who were stepping up, and standing up, all over the country.

This convening redirected the foundation's work at a crucial moment for our country. But it also reminded me of a core belief I shared with Mr. Kellogg: that the best way to change systems takes place at the community level.

America Healing was a vital step forward. It had brought hundreds of racial healing practitioners together in a community of practice. It had helped codify their work. It had given Americans new communication tools with which to discuss racial inequity. But America Healing, a national initiative, could not be the end of the story. The death of Michael Brown, and its painful aftermath, showed us that if healing was to happen at all, it would have to happen locally—person to person.

That was our next step.

Chapter 5

HOW WE HEAL

W HEN WE SAW THE POLICE CRUISER following us, at first we were confused.

This was an ordinary evening in Battle Creek, and I was driving home with my husband, Avery. I had just begun my tenure as president and CEO of the Kellogg Foundation.

At first, the patrol car behind us didn't seem like a big deal. But as we drove south out of downtown and toward our neighborhood, we realized that the officer at the wheel was matching us turn for turn. Eventually, he followed us all the way home. When we pulled into our driveway, he stopped right outside our house and peered at us long and hard through his driver-side window.

A Black couple, driving through a quiet residential neighborhood, tailed by a cop. How do you think this story ends?

If you watch the news, sadly you might already have an image in mind. Maybe it is an image of injustice. Maybe even violence.

This story *does* end with me face-to-face with a cop: a square-jawed White man who also served as a lieutenant colonel in the Michigan National Guard. But that confrontation wasn't with the officer tailing us—it was with Jim Blocker, the Battle Creek chief of police. And what started as a confrontation ended in conversation.

But before we get there, let me rewind.

In 1987, when I started at the foundation, I opted not to move to Battle Creek right away. It had been only a few months since some staff members at the Stouffer Hotel had tried to make us leave in the middle of the night. My then-husband and I wanted to join a community that looked like us, a community that was diverse and inclusive. Worried that Battle Creek might not be a good fit based on that first impression and experience at the hotel, we made our home in Kalamazoo, about twenty-five miles west along Interstate 94.

Kalamazoo extended us the warm welcome we had hoped for. We built friendships with neighbors from a range of backgrounds. My sons were happy at the local schools. For twenty-seven years, Kalamazoo was our home. Still, I liked working in Battle Creek. I liked socializing with friends and colleagues there. And I served the community on the boards of multiple nonprofit organizations, including the Art Center, the United Way, and the Family Health Center.

Over the course of almost three decades, I witnessed a change in Battle Creek. With every year that passed, I saw more and more Black and Brown faces—not just around the foundation's offices but in the city's streets, stores, and cafes. By 2014, Battle Creek's population was about one-third people of color,[1] around the same proportion as Kalamazoo—even though, as in many American cities, redlining and segregation had concentrated residents of color in a handful of neighborhoods. In Battle Creek, these were the districts toward the north, center, and south of the city.[2]

When I became president and CEO of the Kellogg Foundation, I decided it was finally time to move to Battle Creek. No other CEO had lived in the city during their tenure, and I felt a special responsibility to show my commitment to the community. In spite of the demographic trend, my husband and I decided to buy a house southwest of the city center.

I was familiar with the area: It was one of my favorite neighborhoods in which to run or walk during my lunch break and after the workday had ended. Along my running route, one particularly beautiful street adjacent to a golf course always caught my eye. It was so stunning, in fact, that I took Avery there one afternoon to see it. As we turned onto the street, I was surprised to find that one of the houses had a brand-new for-sale sign. I spared no time calling the listed number, and the realtor drove up about five minutes later. We talked, we toured the house, and just like that, Avery and I had found our Battle Creek home.

The neighborhood was just as tranquil to live in as it was to run in. Our new home backed onto a beautiful lake, a popular spot for boating, fishing, and open-water swimming. In this idyllic setting, we felt at home. We grew close to our neighbors. We often waved at friends as they played golf.

This was the house to which we were returning, shortly after the move, when we noticed a patrol car behind us. What had we done wrong? As far as we knew, nothing. Our license plates were up to date. Our car's lights were working. Our seat belts were on. We hadn't been drinking. We hadn't parked illegally. We hadn't so much as rolled through a stop sign.

Knowing all this, we wondered: What should we do? What *could* we do—besides keep driving, keep following the rules?

We were lucky. After we pulled into our driveway, the police officer drove off. That night, we felt relieved. But the more I thought about the incident, the more chilling it became for me.

We have known for decades that drivers of color are more likely to attract police attention, often on a flimsy pretext. President Lyndon B. Johnson's Kerner Commission, established following the Detroit Rebellion and similar disturbances elsewhere, found that one of the main complaints precipitating the unrest in July 1967 was police stopping Black Detroiters without good reason. Three decades later, a report by the ACLU showed that the threat had not abated:

Americans of color were likely to be stopped more frequently than Whites, no matter their social standing or how closely they followed the law.[3]

As people of color often say, we're constantly under suspicion for an imaginary offense: "driving while Black." This harassment is traumatic enough in itself. But all too often, it leads to escalation, to life-destroying encounters with the criminal justice system, or even to deadly violence.

Between 2014 and 2016—during which time this cop followed me and my husband to our home—the United States was shocked by a spate of police killings of drivers of color. In Bridgeton, New Jersey, two police officers shot Jerame Reid as he was getting out of his vehicle with his hands up. In Charleston, South Carolina, a cop killed Walter Scott after pulling him over for a broken taillight. In Ohio, a University of Cincinnati officer shot Samuel DuBose in the head during a stop for a missing front license plate. In Falcon Heights, Minnesota, police killed Philando Castile in front of his partner and her four-year-old daughter.

In 2015, the same year Scott and DuBose were killed, police in Hempstead, Texas, stopped Sandra Bland for failing to signal a lane change. They proceeded to keep her in jail for several days while her family worked to scrape together bail money. Traumatized by her ordeal, Bland was found dead in her jail cell three days after she was pulled over. Shortly before her death, Bland had been posting on her YouTube channel about racial profiling in her hometown of Chicago. There and elsewhere, she had experienced at least ten encounters with police, which she had attributed to racial profiling.

In my own case, it just so happened that I had a meeting scheduled for the very next day with many local leaders, including Battle Creek's top career official, city manager Rebecca Fleury. Thanks to all the civic engagement I had done over the years, Rebecca and I enjoyed a good working relationship. Of course, my tendency to tell people the whole truth had not diminished over the years. So, in the same matter-of-fact way I had told the foundation executives all those years ago about the incident at the Stouffer Hotel, I mentioned to everyone at the meeting that a police car had followed me home the previous evening.

The color drained from Rebecca's face. "Oh my God," she said, her voice shaking. "I can't believe they did that." She shook her head as she made a note of my story.

A few days later, Rebecca called me. "I told the police chief what happened," she said. "He wants to talk to you."

I hadn't asked her to tell the chief, but I agreed that the conversation could be useful. So we set up a meeting at my office.

Like me, Chief Jim Blocker had been in the top job for less than a year. Unlike me, he looked exactly the way most Americans expect someone in his position to look: tall, lean, his gray hair clipped into a conservative cut. If he hadn't been a lawman in real life, he could have played one on TV.

Chief Blocker had gotten into policing as a young man when he chased down a drunk driver who narrowly missed hitting a four-year-old boy. The arresting officers invited him for a ride-along. Since then, he had spent his whole career in law enforcement, serving with the Battle Creek Police Department since 1997. He'd been a detective and a SWAT team member, and on top of his position as police chief, he was serving as a lieutenant colonel in the Michigan National Guard.

Blocker was tough, no doubt about it. But he was by no means heartless. In 2014, the same year he became chief, he created a Fusion Center with the goal of bringing police together with local nonprofits. The ultimate aim was to ensure that people suffering from mental illness and substance abuse would get the help they needed and avoid becoming trapped in the criminal justice system. The chief openly encouraged his officers to feel compassion for the suspects they pursued.

But he was just as susceptible to the empathy deficit as anyone else.

After we introduced ourselves and I told him what had happened that evening with the patrol car, Chief Blocker thought for a moment. "The car you drove wasn't suspicious. The officer was on routine patrol," he said. "You could have just pulled him over and told him to stop following you."

I breathed in sharply. This was one of those *Wait, what?!* moments. "Are you serious?" I asked him. "You think an African American male and I are going to flag down a police officer and tell them not to follow us anymore?"

"Sure," he said. "People do it all the time."

I frowned at him, but he looked perplexed. To Chief Blocker, a straitlaced White man, it must have seemed like a reasonable suggestion. "In your experience," I said, keeping my voice level, "how often do Black people do that?"

At this point, the discussion became heated. Chief Blocker, who considered himself progressive when it came to policing, resented the implication that his force had a race problem. He remained adamant that his officers did not intentionally discriminate.

We didn't agree on the matter at hand, but we did promise to keep up a dialogue about the issue. That was important, because as luck would have it, the foundation was at that very moment working to crystallize a method for building empathy and understanding.

GOING LOCAL

My experience in Ferguson had shown that America Healing, a national movement, was only the first step: We now needed to go local. We needed to build movements for healing in individual communities, focused on their specific issues and challenges. Mr. Kellogg had come to this same conclusion seventy years earlier: "In all of our work," he wrote in 1942, "we have had in mind the possibility of utilizing our experience as a means of assisting other communities throughout the country in their efforts at self-improvement."[4]

So, in that spirit, we decided to incorporate healing methodologies and frameworks advanced by others into a strategy that could be rolled out to communities of all shapes and sizes. We dubbed this new framework "Truth, Racial Healing, and Transformation"—or TRHT for short. Where America Healing had strengthened the field of racial healing nationwide, TRHT would implement those learnings in communities, putting the insights of leading experts into action.

Again, Gail Christopher stepped up to lead this work, and she drew on two vital inspirations. First, she employed the practices of truth and reconciliation commissions—bodies set up to help heal divided societies by documenting historical human rights abuses. Perhaps the most famous of these was the commission set up in postapartheid South Africa under the leadership of Bishop Desmond Tutu. But similar processes had been created in other countries. For example, commissions in Guatemala, Sierra Leone, and Timor-Leste investigated government repression, while those in Canada and Australia addressed the trauma caused by forced separation of Indigenous children from their families.[5]

At least two truth and reconciliation commissions have been created in the United States: one in Greensboro, North Carolina, and one across the state of Maine. In 2013, that Maine commission began to examine the multigenerational trauma of the Wabanaki Nations, with a special focus on the impact on Indigenous children.

Lessons from such commissions have helped shape TRHT, with one major caveat: *Reconciliation*, a priority for many divided societies, cannot apply to the United States. That word implies the *restoration* of unity. Unfortunately, as we have seen, our country was born divided: The poisonous idea of a hierarchy of human value, initially imported from Europe, was written into the US Constitution itself. So, despite our country's name, there never was a time when the whole American people were truly "united." This truth is important to recognize at the outset because it shapes the strategies we must use to address the problem. Instead of reconciliation, TRHT points toward *transformation*. It's a radical notion for a country with our history—full of hope and promise, contradiction and hypocrisy. We were never united. But we *can* be.

Second, and even more fundamentally, Gail drew inspiration from the practices of Indigenous peoples around the world. In Australia, Aboriginal people resolve disputes and try offenses in restorative justice circles involving everyone with a stake in the outcome: not just the "plaintiff" and "defendant," but also representatives of the wider community. Many Native American tribes follow similar practices, as do some Indigenous African peoples.[6]

TRHT would share with Indigenous practice a fundamental assumption: If we want transformation, we first need healing. We must uproot our society's entrenched belief in a hierarchy of human value. We must plant in its place the seeds of interracial empathy. Only then can equity prevail.

In keeping with its healing mindset, TRHT would explicitly reject adversarial approaches to racial equity. At first glance, this might seem counterintuitive. Given the hurt that racism has caused over the centuries, it is only natural to want to confront and punish those we see as holding racist beliefs. But in Gail Christopher's words, TRHT would not be about "making people wrong." Why? Because an attitude of anger tends to provoke anger in return—or at least defensiveness. If your aim is healing, trying to name, blame, and shame is counterproductive.

That was why Gail, right from the start of her tenure with the foundation, had recommended against placing too much emphasis on the term *anti-racism*. Opposing a set of beliefs can too often imply opposing the people who (however unconsciously) hold them. Besides, as we have seen, racist systems harm *everyone*. Progress can only come from making everyone feel that they belong in the healing work. So, in the hope of reaching as many people as possible from as many backgrounds as possible, TRHT would focus on compassion.

It would start with an earnest effort to build connections across cultures and races—to break down the walls that divide us, creating trust and allowing genuine relationships to form. Repeat this process of empathy-building enough times, the thinking goes, and you leave no room for even implicit belief in a hierarchy of value. You create, in the aggregate, a truth and transformation commission for the United States. And in turn, you build long-term, broad-based support for measures to dismantle structural racism—but locally, community by community, away from the divisive national discourse.

Still, the United States is a big country. To practice healing at sufficient scale, we would need to reach a lot of people—millions, in fact. Luckily, we enjoyed the support of more than a few friends.

To help design and implement the new methodology, the foundation brought together more than 170 partner organizations from around the country. These organizations represented all sectors and affinity groups, from faith to business and everything in between, and ranged from community-focused to national in scope. Some were already practicing racial healing; others focused on related equity concerns, like education and housing. Still others, like Sojourners, the YWCA, and the American Library Association, could offer venues for dialogue.

Collectively, these partners had the potential to reach 289 million Americans with hope and healing. That was almost 90 percent of the population.

CIRCLES, TOUCHSTONES, AND TRUTH

What would that healing process look like at the ground level? As advanced and adapted by Gail, our staff, and our partners, a racial healing circle is beautiful in its simplicity. Facilitators typically work in pairs. They first seek to understand the specific challenges facing a community—be it a neighborhood, a city, a business, a school, or any other group of people—as well as any measures that have been suggested already to address those challenges.

Based on this local knowledge, the facilitators select a small number of willing individuals, usually no more than about thirty, to participate in racial healing. When selecting participants, the facilitators seek to maximize diversity in terms of background, perspective, industry, and politics. The circle itself might last anywhere from half a day to three or four days. Everyone sits in a literal circle, with no barriers between people, so all are equal and can look each other in the eye.

At the outset, the cofacilitators establish "touchstones"—another concept honoring Indigenous practice. These ground rules are designed to guide the conversation along productive paths. For example, the racial healing effort established in Flint, Michigan, includes the following from the Center for Courage & Renewal among its touchstones: "Listen intently to what is said [and] listen to the feelings beneath the words. . . . Suspend judgment. . . . Speak your truth. . . . If you find yourself disagreeing with another, becoming judgmental, shutting down in defense, try turning to wonder: 'I wonder what brought her to this place?' 'I wonder what my reaction teaches me?' 'I wonder what he's feeling right now?'"[7]

Next, the facilitators will initiate a version of what Latino equity activists have long called *conocimiento*—which means "knowledge," to know or be aware. It also means "wisdom," to be conscious or to become aware. Conocimiento is an intentional process of getting to know another person by acknowledging their common humanity and seeing them as full people.

For those just starting out, the prompts are intentionally light-hearted: Participants might be asked to tell the circle about a place that's special to them or talk about the origin of their name. These are designed to be easy to answer: If we were in a circle together, I could describe riding my bike to Belle Isle with my friends or how my mother chose my name. *La June*, as she told me, is an homage to our family's military background and inspired by Camp Lejeune, a Marine Corps base in North Carolina.

Once everyone is comfortable sharing, the conversation turns to weightier issues: matters of safety, self-expression, and personal agency. But the focus is still on telling personal stories, not making value judgments. For example, the facilitators might invite participants to share stories about situations where they were perceived as a "minority" and someone went out of their way to make them feel welcome, or about a time when they had to face up to their own unconscious bias and the effect it had on another person.

As they discuss these questions and share their stories, participants alternate between the full group and pairs chosen in advance to emphasize diversity. There are essentially only two rules for these conversations: When you speak, speak from the heart. And when you listen, listen with all your heart. Allow yourself to feel the impact of other people's stories. Allow them to affect you. This is listening with intent: the intent to unearth unconscious bias and learn how it affects people.

In keeping with the nonadversarial nature of a racial healing circle, participation is always voluntary. Nobody is forced to participate, nor is anyone allowed to just observe. Everyone who chooses to be involved is a willing and active participant. That is vital: No participant should see the process as a chore, let alone a punishment. And people do volunteer to take part, in numbers that grow with each passing year. Across communities, across cultures, across political ideologies, millions of Americans are crying out to have these conversations; they just don't always know how to do so in a way that won't devolve into finger-pointing. Racial healing circles provide a structure and a method to make sure the discussion stays civil and productive.

Still, that's not to say everyone comes to the exercise with the same level of enthusiasm. To quote one of the world's leading racial healing practitioners, my friend Monica Haslip: "Some people are there because they feel like they have to be or it's the right thing to do. When you say, 'racial healing circles,' everybody gets a stomachache because they feel like they're going to be called out."

Knowing of this potential stumbling block, facilitators go out of their way to make clear that racial healing is not an exercise in blame. Instead, they try to establish and instill collective goals that everyone in the community can get behind. But when tense moments do arise, facilitators don't shy away from them. On the contrary, they lean in, seeking to turn these flashpoints into opportunities to see a fraught issue from a different perspective.

I've had the privilege of seeing this aspect of racial healing circles in action—particularly in the circles we hosted during our America Healing meetings. Our facilitators were incredibly skilled and able to prevent tension from building into bigger conflicts. I remember participants crying after powerful questions prompted them to do some soul-searching. The mood was heavy, but at the same time, it was tender and open—creating a safe space for people to process their emotions and grow closer to one another.

As a healing circle draws to a close, facilitators invite participants to imagine a better, more equitable society—and what they might do to help bring it about, whether alone or in collaboration with other group members.

Racial healing circles are designed to raise up seldom-heard voices and highlight untold stories. Participants feel connected. They grow more conscious of how other people experience racist structures. They see that equity is possible, and they resolve to take action. And gradually, but with gathering pace, the society around us begins to change.

To quote the Reverend Alvin Herring, a former director of racial equity and community engagement at the foundation: "History is not just constructed by those who have the capacity to write great books and great treaties and great letters. History is constructed every day by everyday people saying, in their own voice, with authenticity, 'This is who I am.'"[8]

"LA JUNE, I NEEDED THAT"

In December 2016, we launched our Truth, Racial Healing, and Transformation program with a five-day summit amid the sun-soaked palm trees and mission-style architecture of Carlsbad, California. The summit arrived on the heels of a divisive presidential election, and I could not imagine a more eloquent testament to the need for healing. By contrast, our event was joyful, full of hope and compassion. After a post-programming dinner, I even got the chance to show off my dance moves.

The summit agenda, naturally, included many racial healing circles, and there was one attendee I was especially eager to invite: Battle Creek's own Chief Jim Blocker.

True to our word, Chief Blocker and I had stayed in touch following the tense discussion in my office. We had come to understand each other's point of view. Gradually, Chief Blocker had come to terms with the fact that his force—like most organizations in the United States—had issues with unconscious bias. Better yet, he was ready to do something about it. The foundation gave the Battle Creek Police Department a grant to conduct racial healing circles among its officers.[9]

The results have shown real progress. Since they began racial healing efforts, police in Battle Creek have become more comfortable and skilled at de-escalating situations. With the foundation's support, the department brought in experts on unconscious bias. This work was a success. More than once, Chief Blocker called me after a news report, his voice filled with gentle pride. "Did you see what happened last night?" he would ask. "You see nobody died. We got him to the hospital. We made sure that it was treated as a mental health issue, and we didn't overreact."

The Battle Creek police department's efforts would eventually lead to national recognition. In 2019, the National Civic League gave Battle Creek an All-America City Award—a prestigious honor recognizing the success of the city's de-escalation and mental health initiatives.

With this history, I thought Chief Blocker would bring to the Carlsbad summit a heartening success story: He was a White, male authority figure who had embraced the work of racial healing. But a couple days into the summit, I received a call.

"We've got a problem," said the voice on the other end. "Chief Blocker just walked out of his healing circle."

Uh-oh.

It seemed that the discussion had turned to police shootings. Chief Blocker had shared a cop's perspective, saying that the young men shot in these circumstances were sometimes culpable.

When I heard this, my toes curled a little. I thought back to the moment he had asked me why I didn't flag down the officer who was following us. I worried that once again, in trying to be helpful, he'd unintentionally come across as insensitive.

Predictably, some of the other participants had reacted negatively. The representatives from community organizations, in particular, had spoken out as one enraged chorus. Feeling attacked, Chief Blocker had left—maybe, I thought, out of embarrassment or frustration, or maybe because, as a police chief and high-ranking National Guard officer, he was unused to being contradicted with such directness. It became readily apparent to me the biases we all battle were very much in the room.

I was busy with the summit, so I couldn't address the issue right away. That turned out to be a blessing: By the time I got a chance to talk to Chief Blocker on our campus in California, his mood had cooled. He explained what had happened from his point of view: Chief Blocker felt that the rules of the circle had been broken. He had been attacked because other circle participants held strong feelings surrounding his job. Their anger had nothing to do with who he was as a person and everything to do with their perceptions of the police.

"We're all on the same side," he said. "So why are we fighting?"

He had committed to attend another session at the conference, I reminded him. Would he agree to go back, despite the confrontation?

He met my gaze, calm and determined, and explained that after the first disastrous attempt, a few people from the circle had sought him out to apologize. The olive branches they'd extended had made all the difference.

"La June," he said, "I needed that. They encouraged me to listen, and now I understand. That's what these circles are all about. I see this as a crossroads, just like with the mental health work. I have to ask myself, what do we do? So yes, I'm going back."

Just as before, Chief Blocker kept his word. He went back the next day. We caught up later, and he was full of gratitude. He described the healing circle in Carlsbad as one of the most meaningful experiences of his life.

"All of this allowed me to reflect. Truth-telling is real and it's powerful," he told me. "I understand that now, and I want to be part of that journey."

Chief Blocker's experience is by no means unique. Indeed, it's emblematic of our innate ability to empathize with one another, if given the right opportunity. It also shows that healing is not all rosy. It's messy. It's hard. Sometimes deep-seated trauma reemerges. Sometimes participants leave agreeing to disagree on certain topics. But the rewards, each time, are life-changing. Around the country, racial healing has produced cathartic change—often from people who might initially seem the least receptive to it.

Racism has deeply hurt generations of Alaska Natives, for example. Today, overt hostility toward Indigenous people remains all too common. One ugly incident took place in May 2010, when Bob Lester and Mark Colavecchio, two Anchorage radio hosts well known locally as wannabe shock jocks, aired a skit mocking Tlingit (pronounced like "clink-it") people—even going so far as to imply that they would sell each other for quick cash.

In response, instead of anger, Liz Medicine Crow of the First Alaskans Institute offered empathy. She convened healing circles that included the DJs and members of the Alaska Native community. Over the course of three months, these circles addressed the hurt produced by stereotypes and the role of the media in perpetuating them. Liz gave the radio hosts their say too: They spoke about the racist beliefs they had grown up with and the difficulty of letting go of such ingrained prejudice.

Asked why she was so eager to forgive, Liz said, "It's the Native way of trying to work forward. It's so easy to go negative. We're going in the right direction."

The DJs agreed. At the end of the healing process, Bob Lester said he felt "so blessed that this opportunity has happened," while Mark Colavecchio said, "Everything I've heard in the last three months has made me a better human being."

Since then, with help from a 2017 grant from the foundation, the First Alaskans Institute's racial healing efforts have broadened to include a network of accountability partners: government officials, business leaders, and others with the power to influence the systems that need to change in order for Alaska Natives to achieve equity.

Speaking at a foundation event in 2021, Liz Medicine Crow, by then president and CEO of the First Alaskans Institute, summed up this work in eloquent terms. "We need to speak our truth to power, and we need to be able to have each other bear witness to our stories," she said. "At the heart of what we ask our accountability partners to do is to be there to listen to these testimonies, and to then look back at the legacy of their work, of their presence, of their place in Alaska, and tell the story about that legacy . . . and then to sit again in that circle with all of us ... to create the transformation, the solutions, and the policy work that we want to see moving forward."[10]

Meanwhile, healing has found purchase in another racially troubled region of the country: the Deep South. Selma, Alabama, was the setting for three landmark voting rights marches in 1965—and for violence against the marchers at the hands of state troopers, sheriffs' deputies, and members of the Ku Klux Klan. Today, Selma is one of the poorest cities in the United States—and still one of the most deeply segregated.[11]

In the spring of 2017, Selma became one of the first communities in the nation to receive TRHT funding. Our grantee, the Black Belt Community Foundation, set about confronting the ugly truth of Selma's past and present. They created a project in 2020 called Know Your Roots, allowing residents from across Selma to uncover their ancestors' role in slavery and segregation. This led to frank discussions about history and possible avenues to address persistent inequity. At the same time, the community foundation started hosting Chat and Chew sessions: community conversations in the back of a local business called the Coffee Shoppe. Even former segregationists took part in the discussions, alongside long-standing civil rights activists. These conversations have since blossomed into a cross-cultural coalition— one that aims to revitalize Selma's economy by drawing more tourists interested in experiencing civil rights history.

Jackie Smith, the owner of the Coffee Shoppe, is proud that her business has become the backdrop for this movement. In addition to Chat and Chew, Jackie hosts monthly tourism roundtables with people from all sectors of the local community, including faith, business, and education leaders. As she explained in an interview, "We try to put all the ideas, all the challenges, everything on the table, and then find out who at the table can meet those needs. And then, everybody supports everybody."[12]

Like other Black-owned small businesses in Selma, the Coffee

Shoppe not only offers value to the community but also has benefited from bringing people together. The shop has become the go-to stop for many tour groups, providing box lunches for cohorts as large as fifty. And during the fiftieth annual Selma Jubilee—an event held every spring to honor the 1965 march from Selma to Montgomery—Jackie and her team kept the shop open so attendees had a place to eat, sit down, and use the bathroom.

It takes a lot of work to serve that many people. But to Jackie, every second is worth it. "It's because I care and because I love Selma," she said. "I know we have so much to offer; we've done so much for the world. And I finally feel like we're about to cash in on our return." Her colleagues in racial healing efforts have expressed the same optimism.[13]

North of Selma, another Southern community is looking to highlight and build upon a very different aspect of its racial history.

The term *redneck* was originally meant to deride poor White farmers, but beginning in the early twentieth century, some working-class Southerners reclaimed the slight and made it their own. Facing poor wages and dangerous working conditions, Appalachian miners of all different backgrounds banded together to demand a union. Black and White, native-born and immigrant, all wore red scarves as a symbol of "redneck" solidarity.

Almost a century later, Beth Howard, an activist and the daughter of an Eastern Kentucky miner, saw a powerful similarity between the diverse group that stood up for labor rights and the rainbow coalition then marching for justice under the banner of Black Lives Matter. So, she coined the tagline *Rednecks for Black Lives* and encouraged her fellow White Southerners to join the cause.

Beth now works as an organizing director at Showing Up for Racial Justice, or SURJ, a group rallying White Americans to work for equity and unity among races. One of Beth's partners in this work was Greg Reese, a Kentuckian who prior to 2020 sported a Confederate battle flag on the trunk of his car. The murder of George Floyd opened Greg's eyes. He removed the flag, replaced it with a Rednecks for Black Lives sticker, and started a Facebook group to organize fellow White members of his community in support of racial justice. Greg also began working with Southern Crossroads, an SURJ project that brings together multiracial coalitions to organize for social justice.

As Greg puts it, "You can sit back and say, 'Hey, this ain't my fight' . . . [But] it always has been our fight. South, North, White, Black, Brown, Latinos—everyone needs to get in this." And he is exactly right. For just as racism harms every American, so too can everyone benefit from racial healing.

As if to illustrate that point, the Kellogg Foundation recently created a racial healing circle featuring White male CEOs. The circle was designed to consider the role that large employers have historically played in perpetuating inequity. Business leaders typically come into this kind of work as skeptics. One common refrain is that the profit motive is colorblind: Competition to recruit and motivate the best talent, regardless of race, is said to override even unconscious bias. But one of my colleagues led the CEOs on a journey to examine how racism pervades every community and organization—including big corporations—and how businesses might become part of the solution. By the end of it, she had changed more than a few minds.

Shortly after the CEO circle, one of the business leaders wrote to my colleague to thank her for the experience. He noted that he had never before thought about how his organization's culture supported—or failed to support—staff of color, but he had already begun to change his company's practices around investment, hiring, and corporate culture. The healing circle had changed his life and his worldview.

Thankfully, such enthusiastic testimonials are commonplace in the world of racial healing. In my experience, most people who go through a racial healing circle come out of it saying, *I am a better person for it* or *I learned something I never knew before* or—perhaps best of all—*I've connected with another person in a way I've never done until now.*

CHANGING THE NARRATIVE

I have witnessed several such transformations myself, in addition to Chief Blocker's. One of these came in 2017, when I was invited to receive an honorary degree from a prestigious college.

Around the same time that the foundation was developing the TRHT program, a debate was roiling American college campuses, this one included. The debate concerned the provision of safe spaces: refuges on campus where minority students can go to be themselves and escape from the ever-present need to conform to the expectations of the majority—places like the Angela Davis Minority Lounge, which continued to serve as such an oasis for students of color attending the University of Michigan. Some voices, like that of Justice Thomas, opposed such spaces. One administrator at the University of Chicago decried them as places where "individuals can retreat from ideas and perspectives at odds with their own."[14] To me, this argument seemed to stem from a misunderstanding: I knew from personal experience that the students clamoring for safe spaces were seeking temporary respite from prejudice, not permanent exemption from discourse.

At the college giving me the honorary degree, administrators initially resisted the call for safe spaces. But things changed after December 2015, when a dean of the college's music school wrote an article in the campus newspaper expressing his support. At the start of the 2016 school year, the college opened what it called a "multicultural student lounge." But in some quarters, resentment still simmered.

That was the state of play when I arrived on campus to accept an honorary doctorate in May 2017. In my acceptance speech, I planned to say a few words about racial healing. But I had been tipped off ahead of time that some of the college's trustees, still smarting from the debate over safe spaces, didn't approve of my presence or the content of my remarks. Evidently they, too, had noticed the similarities between the principles of racial healing circles and safe spaces.

The college requested that I lead a teach-in on healing circles and safe spaces with the faculty. So on Saturday, the day before the commencement, I made my way to a double-sized classroom. Three rows of chairs were arranged in a circle. Soon, people filled the rows. I have to admit, I was surprised and pleased to see that so many people had shown up on a weekend for a teach-in.

I knew none of these folks personally. But as I began my lecture, I noticed that one participant was becoming increasingly agitated: an older White man who stood up and began walking around the room, scowling. As he leaned against a pole, arms folded, he interrupted me to ask a series of questions, each one more frustrated than the last. "What are you talking about?" he demanded. "What do you mean by 'safe spaces'?"

I calmly explained—using healing methodology—what safe spaces are, why people need them, and how healing circles can offer individuals similar opportunities to tell their own stories and connect with others. Before I could finish advocating for such spaces on campus, the man announced that he had to go. As quickly as he had stood up earlier, he walked out of the room. I didn't know what to make of his departure but assumed that he heard something that he needed to process on his own.

I was shaken, but I continued my presentation. It wasn't until the next day—in the middle of the procession at the commencement—that I learned who that man was. As I walked in a line of professors, administrators, and honorary-degree recipients toward the stage, the same man who had stormed out of my teach-in jumped out from the crowd and stopped me.

"I just want to thank you," he said. "I want you to know that I was totally against safe spaces. I didn't believe in them and didn't know what they were for. But you helped me understand." He then embraced me in a warm hug. "You've changed my life, and I will never be against safe spaces again. Thank you."

After the trustee returned to his seat, I turned to the president of the college, who was right behind me in the procession. He had tears in his eyes.

"Do you know who that is?" the college president asked, looking shocked to his core. "That is one of our most important trustees, and he's been one of our greatest skeptics of our work around safe spaces."

Shortly after the interaction, I accepted my honorary doctorate and spoke about racial healing. The engaged crowd of students applauded—but I knew I had already received the most important honor that day. Sure enough, as I walked offstage, I noticed that same trustee. He wasn't frowning. In fact, he was wearing the biggest smile I had ever seen.

Even as it produces countless personal epiphanies, like this one, racial healing has also helped change narratives and perceptions on a community level.

In Texas, the Dallas Faces Race initiative used racial healing circles as part of an effort to document the city's painful racial history, including deadly violence against Indigenous people and Black and Latinx youth. One result has been a landmark report that tells the truth in stark terms. "Dallas is on stolen land," the report reads, referring to the Indigenous Caddo Nation, who were massacred by federal troops in 1841. It goes on to discuss the city's early reliance on enslaved people under the heading "Dallas was built with stolen labor." But the report ends on a hopeful note, detailing local racial healing circles and calling for more such efforts.[15]

In Los Angeles, California, foundation partners worked to educate the community about historical racism against Asian Americans. As part of this work, they studied underreported events like the Chinese Massacre of 1871, in which a mob of five hundred White and Latino men lynched eighteen Chinese immigrants. TRHT collaborators have also gained recognition for three new public holidays and helped create new monuments to memorialize the victims of LA's tragically racist and violent history.

This work has happened closer to home as well.

The history of Battle Creek—famously known as Cereal City—has long centered around the companies founded by W. K. Kellogg and C. W. Post. But the story of Battle Creek is much more complex than that—for good and for ill. Its very name comes from an 1824 confrontation between two Potawatomi people and a group of White surveyors who had come to aid in their dispossession. Later, Battle Creek became an important hub for the Underground Railroad and home for thirty years to the extraordinary Black abolitionist and civil rights hero Sojourner Truth; the city remains her final resting place.

Alongside racial healing circles, the Battle Creek Coalition for Truth, Racial Healing, and Transformation has created a collaborative timeline. Community members are invited to contribute stories and facts to build a more inclusive view of Battle Creek's history. This, in turn, feeds back into the important conversations happening around race issues across the city.

While our communities work to heal, at the Kellogg Foundation we have also done our best to keep racial healing in the national spotlight. During the 2016 presidential election, the idea for a new project came to me in a vision. I had been trying to figure out how to evolve our racial equity work to meet this divisive moment for our nation. More than anything, I knew we needed solidarity: to show the world, and maybe even to remind ourselves, that people could still work together—that we could still unite communities around the shared goal of racial equity and forge better futures for us all.

So, I called multiple community leaders who were already at the forefront of this work. Out of those conversations came the Solidarity Council on Racial Equity, or SCoRE.

In 2018, the foundation formed the first SCoRE coalition with activists, artists, educators, business leaders, and journalists—individuals uniquely positioned to keep a focus on racial equity and encourage others to do the same. Since then, we've engaged a range of esteemed members, from thought leaders like Michelle Alexander, Maria Hinojosa, Heather McGhee, Tim Ryan, john a. powell, and Rabbi Jonah Pesner to influencers and groundbreakers like Bryan Stevenson, Ava DuVernay, Kerry Washington, and John Legend. Our work has succeeded in raising the profile of grassroots-level activism and the importance of working as a collective to advance change. To this day, SCoRE serves as a crucial reminder: Bringing powerful people into a room together can help us build a powerful, shared future.

My work with Chief Blocker has also grown into something broader—and better. After we came to a better understanding and he initiated racial healing among his officers, the chief invited me to a national meeting of the Police Executive Research Forum (PERF) in New York City. This invitation was a big deal: PERF helps to improve the delivery of police services through strong national leadership, public debate of police and criminal justice, and research and policy development.[16] Chief Blocker wanted me to present to them about the transformative role that racial healing could play in improving community policing.

You might expect a room full of police officers to be less than receptive to that message—the same way Chief Blocker had been when he initially rejected my suggestion that a Black couple trying to stop one of his patrol cars would be unwise. But to their credit, those officers in New York listened. They took it all in. I made friends that day. In fact, several officers invited me to come and talk to their own departments. At least one even used my insights to begin the hard work of racial healing within his own force.

As for Chief Blocker and me, we certainly had our differences, but we became good friends. We have built an entire relationship on truth-telling, intentional listening, and empathy—proof, in itself, that racial healing works.

By the start of 2020, the growing movement of racial healing was going strong. Efforts to bring communities together were expanding around the country. But these efforts were about to face their biggest test to date: a global pandemic combined with a global reckoning around race.

Chapter 6

FACING TWO PANDEMICS

A T THE W. K. KELLOGG FOUNDATION, we started the year 2020 with a sense of hope.

One of the many great ideas to come out of the December 2016 Truth, Racial Healing, and Transformation summit was the call for an annual National Day of Racial Healing. The event would occur each January, slated—with symbolic significance—for the Tuesday after the US federal holiday honoring Dr. Martin Luther King Jr. Racial healing, after all, is an important step toward realizing Dr. King's hopeful vision of a nation where character matters more than color. On the new National Day of Racial Healing, communities would engage in racial healing activities. The Kellogg Foundation would offer a national platform to publicize these activities and inspire further action, as well as provide materials to help spark further healing across the country. Together, we would draw as much attention as possible to the need for racial healing.

As of late 2016, with divisive rhetoric and hate crimes on the rise, we felt there was no time to waste. We held the inaugural National Day of Racial Healing on January 17, 2017, less than six weeks after the TRHT summit. We had to scramble to get everything in place, but it was worth it: In the end, we brought together more than 130 organizations and tens of thousands of Americans.[1]

From there, the National Day of Racial Healing ramped up exponentially in its scope and reach. In 2018, the foundation began marking the occasion with a signature event featuring local leaders, changemakers, and, soon enough, celebrities. By 2020, the governors of six US states had officially acknowledged the day, as had more than sixty local and municipal governments from Selma to Chicago.[2]

The 2020 edition was our biggest yet. On January 21, we took over Washington, DC's world-famous John F. Kennedy Center for the Performing Arts—a short walk from the Lincoln Memorial, where Dr. King had delivered the most famous version of his "I Have a Dream" speech in 1963.

The twin themes of our event were, first, empowering and energizing young people; and second, showing how arts and the media could support racial healing. Accordingly, we brought young movement leaders to the Kennedy Center's hallowed stage alongside well-known figures like actress Storm Reid; food mogul Danielle Chan; and journalist Elaine Welteroth, the first Black editor-in-chief of *Teen Vogue* magazine. All of us sat transfixed by stories of healing from communities across the country, including Indigenous tribes, majority-Black towns, and Latino neighborhoods.

Via livestream on YouTube, the event attracted hundreds of thousands of views. It provoked thousands of conversations among young people on social media, and according to a professional analysis, 99 percent of the comments were positive toward the idea of racial healing. Best of all, people downloaded our racial healing resources more than thirteen thousand times, including our conversation guides and action kits. I knew firsthand the impact of just one racial healing circle. Imagine the power of thirteen thousand of them in communities across the country![3]

Racial healing was hitting the big time.

Amid all the glitz, glamour, and hope, however, storm clouds were gathering. A new infectious disease was spreading with frightening speed. The day before our star-studded event at the Kennedy Center, the Centers for Disease Control and Prevention had confirmed the first case of Covid-19 on US soil.[4] A little over a month later, the White House declared Covid-19 a national emergency.[5] With it, we were about to witness—yet again—the shocking reality of structural racism.

TRANSFORMATION FROM WITHIN

In hindsight, I am particularly grateful for the changes we'd made within the foundation that positioned us to face the daunting challenges that 2020 would soon bring to our doorstep. The team-building operational changes that we had instituted over the previous few years prepared us—at just the right time—to benefit from a new, more flexible approach to running the organization.

For one thing, we were working more efficiently than ever. In partnership with our trustees and executive leadership team, I had fulfilled my promise to change the way the Board of Trustees operated. Under the old system, the board had approved each grant over $400,000 (a low threshold for an $8 billion foundation) and individual board members often issued conflicting instructions to the staff. These practices were meant to apply rigor and care to every investment—a worthy goal. But for us, this approach led instead to micromanagement, inefficiency, and confusion. With the backing and support of countless colleagues, I had replaced this system with a new model of governance—one I'd first heard about a few years before from another nonprofit we partnered with in Mississippi.

Developed by a married couple, both of them psychologists, the Policy Governance model—known as the Carver model, after its creators—was designed to clarify board responsibilities and make organizations run more smoothly. Among other things, the Carver model included two important principles. One: The Board of Trustees should only handle issues and decisions that impact the overall direction of the organization. And two: When the board speaks, it should do so with a single voice.[6]

Once again, the foundation pushed forward. As a result, the division of responsibility became much clearer than before. The board would make big decisions about where we worked and with what purpose. What grants would best serve those declared missions—that was for the staff to decide. In other words, the board focused on the ends, while the staff designed and implemented the means.

To help the staff make those day-to-day calls, I worked hard to break down the invisible walls separating departments and disciplines. I pushed for a flatter and more flexible structure that brought together staff from different fields, all working toward common goals. To realize this vision, I reached for another model that had long proved effective: the networked organizational structure, endorsed by Professor John P. Kotter during my time as an MBA student at Northwestern University. Instead of working in silos, different specialist groups would partner with one another as needed to serve their given project.

The networked organizational model represented an opportunity to practice what we preached. This new structure allowed us to make connections and build relationships across the disciplinary and departmental lines that had once divided us internally. It was a win-win.

Finally, building on my predecessor Sterling Speirn's work as CEO, we created what we called an "authorizing environment."[7] In my three decades at the foundation, this might have been the most meaningful change of all. When I joined, the foundation's top-down organizational culture effectively silenced the voices of most junior staff members. We had to use euphemisms even to talk about "radical" concepts like race-conscious programming. By the start of 2020, however, our culture had transformed. It was the authorizing environment that allowed the foundation to become the anti-racist organization it espoused. The authorization was cascaded down from the board to the CEO to leadership to staff, and everyone felt empowered to act accordingly.

Now, staff throughout the foundation could suggest bold changes and be heard. If the change would help our mission, we would do our best to make it happen, regardless of who had thought of it.

Decades before, Mr. Kellogg had instructed us: "Use the money as you please so long as it promotes the health, happiness, and well-being of children."[8] An authorizing environment brought us closer to fulfilling that fundamental task. I felt a responsibility to Mr. Kellogg to ensure that every dollar spent was for the children.

As I walked the foundation's halls, I did my best to model the kind of organizational leadership I believed we needed. As you might expect, my style differed from the norm. Traditionally, workplace power flows from job titles and hierarchy: The ideas and opinions of people with higher titles matter more than those of people ranked lower in the employer's org chart. While this approach may in theory make decision-making easier, it also has real drawbacks—including making it harder for leaders to hear and act upon new ideas and perspectives. This dynamic is especially true for the ideas and perspectives of women and people of color, who have historically been locked out of higher-ranking positions across organizations, including our own. To be heard, we had to get creative.

I learned very early that a leader's true strength lies not in rank but in what's known as "referent power." This kind of power depends on personal traits and values, such as honesty, integrity, and trustworthiness. Referent power calls for building mutual trust and shared ownership over a mission. It replaces a command-and-control approach with an influence-and-inspire attitude.

This might seem counterintuitive, but—at least for me—humility plays an important role in building referent power. I'm not infallible. Neither is anyone else. By making myself vulnerable, I showed that it was OK for staff to do the same: to go out on a limb, take risks, and do what was necessary to get good ideas heard and implemented.

Not long after creating our famous *It's all about the children* T-shirts,

I went on a retreat with my leadership team to map out the foundation's strategy for the next five years. Everyone on the team would be doing the work to develop this strategy, yet they all looked at me expectantly—waiting for *me* to say what it was. Incredulous, I met their eager gazes one by one. "I won't carry all this water by myself, and I expect every last one of us to be here and stand up when needed to carry this organization," I said. "This isn't a one-person show. It's a team."

As a result of these changes and conversations, information and ideas were flowing through the foundation more freely than ever. Our operations became more streamlined. And with less red tape standing between our funds and the communities that needed them, our grant-making grew more efficient.

When I became CEO, prospective grantees were waiting almost four months, on average, to have their funding requests approved. Incredibly, the longest wait times could stretch to over a year. Meanwhile, the applicant would be left in limbo, not knowing whether their program would get the green light or not. When I came in, I knew we could do better. So I set an ambitious goal: to cut our processing times in half.

Some senior colleagues responded with alarm: "You can't make a grant in one month!" If we compared ourselves with our peers, they had a point: For a large foundation, sixty-day approvals would be the equivalent of warp speed. But I still didn't think that was good enough.

"Banks approve loans even faster," I replied. "We should measure ourselves against the best, no matter what sector they're in."

Some of my colleagues may still have considered this a fruitless quest. But thanks to all of our efficiency measures, it worked. By 2023, we were making grants in less than twenty-three days. Even the longest wait time had dropped, from over a year to under five months.

Meanwhile, we had significantly increased our scores in all the important measures of staff and grantee satisfaction. And best of all, the foundation had dramatically grown the amounts we awarded to grantees of diverse backgrounds. When I took over, we gave forty-two cents out of every dollar to grantees led by people of color. By 2023, that figure was sixty-eight cents on the dollar.

Another benefit of our new, more flexible approach: We were much more ready to face the unpredictability and disruption of the modern world. At the beginning of 2020, we didn't yet know how relevant this resilience would soon become.

"NOTHING LIKE THIS AT ALL, EVER"

In 1966, Dr. King said, "Of all the forms of inequality, injustice in health care is the most shocking and the most inhuman because it often results in physical death." He was talking about the de facto segregation of medical treatment in northern cities like Chicago, but his words might equally apply to the Covid-19 pandemic. By straining society's resources, the disease laid bare how unequally those resources are distributed.

From the very start of the pandemic, Americans of color were getting infected more frequently than their White compatriots. And when they got the disease, they tended to suffer worse complications. The Centers for Disease Control and Prevention has estimated that in many communities, people of color were being hospitalized more than three times as often as White people. Another study found that Black and Hispanic patients—representing about one-third of the population—accounted for more than half of deaths in hospitals.[9]

The toll was especially tragic among the foundation's core constituency: children. In the first year of the pandemic, two-thirds of the American children who died of Covid-19 were Black or Latinx.[10] Low-income children, disproportionately people of color, were more likely to miss preventive care appointments or be unable to access the mental health treatment they needed to deal with the pandemic's emotional toll.[11] Studies show that school districts with higher proportions of Black and Hispanic students experienced larger learning losses.[12] And at least 250,000 children in the United States have lost one or both parents to Covid-19—again, disproportionately in non-White families.[13] It's hard to imagine a more brutal demonstration of the implicit racial hierarchy of human value.

Covid-19 struck close to home for me—twice—as the disease snuck into our lives and began shutting down cities around the world. Within weeks of the Kennedy Center gala, I received a terrible phone call: One of my mentors, Moses Walker, was in the hospital in Kalamazoo. A tremendous community leader, Moses had served as an elected city commissioner, president of a mental health center, and executive director of the Douglass Community Association—one of the first African American–serving organizations in North Kalamazoo. His wise counsel had guided me throughout most of my professional career.

I spared no time in getting to the hospital; I wanted to be by his side just like he had been for me. When I arrived, Moses was hooked up to a ventilator, unable to breathe on his own. The doctor thought he had pneumonia, yet the symptoms his wife described were strikingly similar to those of Covid-19: a cold, a sore throat, and difficulty breathing. Despite being an otherwise healthy man, Moses passed away in the hospital—succumbing to the mystery illness. Along with everyone else who had the pleasure of knowing him, I was devastated.

Two months later, tragedy struck again when Covid-19 took the life of one of our grantees in Detroit: Marlowe Stoudamire, who had spent his entire career giving back to Detroit and restoring the collective memory of the city. Among other achievements, he had served as the project director for the Detroit Historical Society's *Detroit 67: Looking Back to Move Forward*, a nationally acclaimed exhibit highlighting in raw detail the 1967 Detroit Rebellion that had transformed my own life. Over the years, I had become somewhat of a mentor to Marlowe; we had bonded over our shared experiences as fellow Cass Tech alumni, and he would always call me before he made a major career decision.

One day in March, I received a call from Marlowe's office—but Marlowe wasn't on the other end. Instead, the person on the line told me Marlowe had passed away. Once again, I was devastated and confused. Marlowe was only forty-three years old. He was healthy. He had so much left to do in Detroit. His death was surreal; it made me stop and realize for the first time how serious Covid-19 was and how quickly it could take someone's life.

The lives the virus took were disproportionately lives of color. Across the United States, Covid-19 drew attention—in the most stark way possible—to the influence of the social determinants of health.

Thanks to the legacies of segregation and disinvestment, people of color are more likely to be low-income. They are more likely to live in overcrowded homes with poor air quality. They more frequently share space with elderly or otherwise vulnerable family members. They are less likely to have readily available access to the resources and services they need—often having to travel many miles to reach the nearest supermarket or health care provider. They are more likely to live near noxious sites like garbage dumps, industrial plants, and clogged highways, all of them hazardous to lung health.[14] And, worst of all, people of color are much more likely to be homeless or incarcerated—both populations at greater risk of contracting infectious diseases.

As a result of all this, non-White people are more likely to live with exacerbating conditions like diabetes and asthma that make them more susceptible to dangerous illnesses like Covid-19—and with repeated traumatic experiences like hostile encounters with police, which have been shown to increase stress and decrease disease resistance.[15]

Add to this heavy burden an understandable tendency to distrust medical advice and government mandates, born of centuries of mistreatment at the hands of doctors, officials, and scientists—like the researchers at the Tuskegee Institute in the 1930s, who used Black people as guinea pigs in studying syphilis.[16] Many of my own family members, including one of my sons, were skeptical of the Covid-19 vaccine when it became available. They, like many other Black people in the United States, believed the government had ulterior motives behind its Covid-19 response. And given this painful history, it's easy to see why.

The inequities unveiled by the Covid-19 pandemic continued in the workplace, where people of color are overrepresented in frontline, low-paid occupations in hospitality, food service, and similar industries. Not only can these jobs never be done from home—requiring many workers to commute via crowded buses and trains—but they also typically offer zero paid sick days. In 2020, this perfect storm of inequity created one of Covid-19's cruelest ironies: While their jobs were labeled "essential," the people who filled them were too often treated as expendable.

By June 2020, nearly one in three Black Americans knew someone who had died of Covid, compared with fewer than one in ten White Americans. Similar figures haunted other communities of color.[17] The disease robbed families of their breadwinners, compounding poverty and hunger. Some individuals dealt with the added trauma of losing parents, grandparents, extended family members, friends, and neighbors far too soon. Necessary social distancing amplified these tragedies, filling the lives of mourners with unattended deathbeds and online funerals. The death toll emptied pews and even pulpits—in my hometown of Detroit, for example, the traditionally Black church Hartford Memorial Baptist lost nine members in just one month.[18]

Witnessing such losses, as well as the deterioration of communal and cultural networks, some community figures viewed the pandemic as unleashing an even worse impact than the violence that has plagued communities of color for decades. Again in Detroit, the Reverend Horace Sheffield—a renowned civil rights campaigner who mercifully won his own battle with Covid—told PBS News: "We all experience death in urban settings, people who are killed before their time in violence and all that, but nothing like this at all, ever."

Reverend Sheffield's words rang true even in the smaller communities the foundation served—such as those in the Mississippi Delta, where Covid-19 numbers were especially high.[19] Sorely lacking in health care infrastructure, the region saw its challenges deepen as winter turned to spring and summer. I thought about the health care facilities I had visited during my time there and was struck with worry. Although mobile Covid-19 treatment vans were able to reach some of Mississippi's rural communities, many people never got the care they needed.[20] Knowing all this, the death toll in the state weighed more heavily on me as each day passed.

Not all communities of color experienced the pandemic's impact in the same way—though many struggled to access masks, then tests, then vaccines. For example, many Native American tribes were kept in the dark about the disease's progress, both because information was not translated into Indigenous languages and because many reservations have poor internet access.[21]

On top of that, many tribes lost their primary sources of tax revenue when casinos, tourist attractions, and hospitality businesses closed. After the vaccines were invented, the federal government initially made allocations only to federally recognized tribes, leaving unrecognized communities—those left off the US government's list either by accident or by design—to depend on their recognized neighbors for supplies.

Asian American and Pacific Islander (AAPI) communities endured not only the ravages of Covid-19 but also pain of a different kind. Fueled by distorted information about the disease's origins, they were subjected to a tidal wave of hate that brought back memories of the anti-Muslim and anti-Arab vitriol that followed the September 11 attacks.

At the onset of the pandemic, in response to the rise in anti-Asian racism, a group of nonprofits came together to found Stop AAPI Hate, in support of the entire Asian American and Pacific Islander community. I was proud that the foundation provided them with initial funding for this critical organization. Within six weeks of its creation, the coalition had logged almost 1,500 instances of hatred or discrimination, at least 125 of which had involved physical violence.[22] By January 2023, nearly four in ten Chinese Americans—a community more than five million strong—personally knew somebody who had been threatened or attacked because of their race since the pandemic began.[23]

In addition to physical attacks, AAPI people faced open harassment in the street, vandalism of their property, and denial of service from ride-share drivers and others. Understandably, those who got sick often hesitated to venture outside to seek medical treatment, contributing to more severe illness among AAPI communities. Discrimination also upended many AAPI communities' economies: Asian restaurants in the United States lost $7.4 billion in 2020.[24]

Once again, attitudes born from implicit racism wound up hurting White people as well. Researchers at the University of Georgia measured people's opinions of the disease and found that hearing about Covid's disparate effect on communities of color had a domino effect on White Americans: They tended to be less empathetic toward vulnerable people, less fearful of the disease, and more likely to refuse to wear a mask or take other precautions. In doing so, they increased their own exposure to the disease.[25] In other words, racism overrode their own self-preservation. By 2022, death rates among White people matched—and in some places exceeded—those among people of color.[26]

But even here we can see some hearts and minds beginning to change. The University of Georgia team found that a small subset of White Americans surveyed actually showed *increased* empathy—and more fear of the virus—when they were told about racial disparities.[27] What made the difference? It turns out that the people who displayed the most empathy were those who knew the most about structural inequities and systemic racism.

So maybe, just maybe, there was an opportunity—amid the

devastation of Covid-19—to build community and bring people together. Maybe this devastating moment in our nation's history could offer a way to move together from a zero-sum mindset to the recognition that all of us are bound together by a shared fate.

THE BLACK LIVES MATTER MOVEMENT ECHOES NEW VOICES

As if the country had not yet had its fill of injustice and death, on May 25, 2020, yet another national tragedy struck: George Floyd was murdered by a police officer in Minneapolis. He was just forty-six years old.

This time, a bystander caught the violence on camera. Americans could feel Floyd's pain as the cop pressed his face against the concrete. They could hear him plead for mercy—and call out for his mother in a heartbreaking plea—as the pressure crushed his windpipe. They could see the casual cruelty of the arresting officers who snuffed out a human life.

The video that captured those nine minutes and twenty-nine seconds, as chilling as it was to watch, became a lightning rod. Millions of Americans—including me—felt a mother's pain. I imagined Justin or Jordan calling out for me. And just like George's late mother would have, I felt a sharp pain of helplessness! To not be able to answer a cry for help from your child is the worst form of pain a mother can endure. I cried. That video channeled forces that would prove powerful enough to punch through the empathy deficit.

By the beginning of July, tens of millions of Americans had taken to the streets in protest—including my own stepdaughter, Kalynn, who made it her mission to attend as many demonstrations in Detroit as possible. Experts were calling this the biggest mass movement in US history, and the world was watching it unfold in real time. Even the height of the civil rights movement had attracted numbers "only" in the hundreds of thousands.

An independent analysis showed that more than 93 percent of

these protests remained peaceful and led to no property damage.[28] Although there was little indication that the media's reporting bias had shifted—"White protests, Black riots" remained a prevailing view—it did seem that Americans were more aware of this bias now. As early as June 12, less than three weeks after Floyd's death, a Pew poll revealed that half of White Americans felt the nonviolent protests were garnering too little attention, while 44 percent said that isolated, sporadic violence was receiving too much.[29]

Looking at the footage pouring in from demonstrations across the country, I was inspired not just by their sheer scale and peaceful nature, but also by the diversity of the crowds that had turned out. They reminded me of the pictures of Dr. King crossing the Edmund Pettus Bridge in Selma fifty-five years before, an event that had attracted allies from communities well beyond Black America.

Official counts soon confirmed my feeling: One week into July 2020, the Brookings Institution estimated that 54 percent of Black Lives Matter protestors were White.[30] Pew reported that seven in ten Americans had spoken about race in the past month—and that almost three-quarters agreed that "bringing people of different racial backgrounds together to talk about race" would be one effective tactic to achieve equity.[31] A summer that had begun by highlighting the worst of humanity ended up bringing out its best, as people across identities stood in solidarity with the most vulnerable among us.

I realized then that more people understood structural racism than I had previously thought. Our society might lionize the "rugged individual" looking out for no one but themselves, but the horrors of Covid-19 and George Floyd's violent death had made it impossible to keep ignoring the needs of others—even those who did not look like us. To millions of Americans, it was becoming clear that we share a common fate, and that the only way to overcome our twin pandemics was by caring for each other.

Hope glimmered again in my heart. If ever there was a moment for racial healing, it was now.

ENHANCING OUR IMPACT

Fortunately, the foundation was better placed than most to weather the pandemic. Our profession afforded us the privilege of occasionally working via Zoom—a policy we had instated about a year before the pandemic began to give staff more flexibility to work in community alongside our partners. So, despite the disruption, we had the tools and know-how to continue our mission, and we were learning all along the way.

We quickly adapted our racial healing materials for online delivery—and found virtual healing circle sessions almost as powerful as in-person ones. In fact, the technology allowed for racial healing circles that otherwise would not have happened because of physical distance. For example, the American Association of Colleges and Universities brought together participants representing dozens of institutions, from Georgia to Hawai'i, in a circle intended to further racial healing on college campuses. I participated in a few online healing circles around this time and was delighted to find participants' passion undimmed by distance.

This was also a moment when the private sector began awakening to the importance of racial equity and diversity, inclusion, and belonging, at a scale previously unseen. The weeks after George Floyd's death saw many companies make bold commitments to racial equity. By October 2022, these financial promises ballooned to a mind-boggling amount: $340 billion. This was heartening to see, but a question bubbled in the back of my mind: Would these businesses stick to their commitments? At the foundation, we saw an opportunity to support committed companies in taking on internal and external transformations.

We knew from the very beginning that racial healing must extend beyond the nonprofit sector. For years, we had been exploring ways of bringing these vital conversations into corporate America. In 2019, we'd taken a big step in that direction by creating an initiative called Expanding Equity. The idea was to engage with companies that were serious about making genuine, tangible progress in this space—and to help them do so. We partnered with a major consulting firm and paired our human-centered approaches with their best research, tools, and resources, helping participating companies identify where they needed to direct their efforts to make good on their promises.

With my background in accounting, of course, I'm far from naive about the commercial motivation for a company in making such a commitment. Businesses exist to make money, however, and to do that, they need to hire the best staff. By striving for diversity, companies can tap into deep wells of underused talent—and take advantage of the ways diverse teams outperform homogenous ones. For instance, as McKinsey data reveals, the top quartile of companies for ethnic diversity are 36 percent more likely to financially outperform their less diverse peers.[32] Our motives might not align with most companies', but our goals certainly did, because the well-documented business case for equity is clear as day, something we proved in "The Business Case for Racial Equity: A Strategy for Growth," published by the foundation in partnership with the Altarum Institute.[33]

Starting in the summer of 2020, we took the opportunity to supercharge Expanding Equity by forging new partnerships with companies across different industries. One of our anchors in the financial services sector, for example, was based in Minnesota—the state George Floyd had called home.

After an initial call with all our new Expanding Equity participants, this company invited me to do a special session about racial healing with members of its leadership team. The group was all White men who were genuinely interested in how racial healing could pave a path forward from this revealing moment in history. That conversation, alongside many others like it, would once again become foundational to our efforts to advance racial healing on a national scale.

Today, Expanding Equity is going strong. More than eight hundred corporate leaders from more than 170 companies are participants in our network—people well placed to help tear down the enduring structural barriers facing people of color all over the country.

On June 25, exactly one month after the murder of George Floyd, the foundation held a special virtual edition of our National Day of Racial Healing, called Healing in Action. Speakers and performers from the worlds of activism, education, politics, entertainment, and more contributed videos designed to inspire people and give them the tools to carry out racial healing in their own communities.

As the pandemic raged on, we followed that up in January 2021 by producing an online version of our signature event for the annual National Day of Racial Healing. We kept up the focus on racial healing efforts taking place across the nation. We didn't skimp on star power, either. Prominent participants included the singers Camila Cabello and John Legend, the author Ta-Nehisi Coates, and the young poet Amanda Gorman—one day *before* her electrifying reading at President Biden's inauguration.

It was inspiring to see our work continue during such a difficult time. Yet I was determined to use this moment not just to keep going as before, but to transcend "business as usual." I wanted to take the work of racial healing to the next level.

Admittedly, times were tough. The economic maelstrom was buffeting our bottom line as much as anyone else's. Speaking with my accountant's hat on, the prudent course of action for the foundation would have been to hunker down. But it wasn't about us; it was about the children. And they needed us now more than ever.

Some of our frontline grantees were struggling to stay afloat. For example, many nonprofits across the country found it difficult to qualify and apply for emergency federal loans. If these organizations proved unable to supply critical resources and services, children's lives and well-being would be at risk. What we needed was a way to invest in their futures without compromising our own. And we found it.

Alongside four peer foundations—the Ford Foundation, the Doris Duke Charitable Foundation, the John D. and Catherine T. MacArthur Foundation, and the Andrew W. Mellon Foundation—we decided to seek outside investment in 2020 by issuing a "social bond," an idea championed by my friend and longtime colleague Darren Walker, the Ford Foundation's president. Traditionally, social impact bonds, a precursor to our efforts, had been principally issued by governments to pay for projects that drive positive social change—so this was an innovation for private foundations like ours. In the early months of the pandemic, when nonprofit organizations were facing existential peril, it was an urgent means to an urgent end. According to the Nonprofit Finance Fund, three of every four nonprofits were operating with less than six months of cash in reserve, while the federal government directed its interventions toward the private sector.[34] By unlocking some $300 million in additional grants, our specific social bond became a crucial lifeline—particularly for grantees working on racial healing and racial equity.

And our grantees delivered a spectacular return on the investment.

In the Roaring Fork Valley of Colorado, we made a grant to Valley Settlement, a nonprofit serving children and families from Latine immigrant communities that we had worked with before, but, with the help of the resources provided by a social impact bond, we knew we could do even more to meet the needs of children during an extremely difficult time for many families. In a prime example of community-focused programming, the organization began its work by interviewing hundreds of local families and tailoring its services to their needs. For example, it helps parents access jobs and services, support their young children in preschool, and enroll in adult education courses.

Valley Settlement's programs have become the epitome of creative, well-informed community engagement. For instance, in El Busesito Preschool, "little buses" drive up and down the valley providing mobile, bilingual education to preschool-aged children as well as engagement opportunities for their families. The community has warmly embraced El Busesito: Each year, the program graduates fifty children, but graduation ceremonies draw hundreds of friends and family members, proud to support their community's youngest learners.

In more traditional classrooms, Valley Settlement empowers dozens of Latine parents by positioning them as Spanish-speaking aides to teachers whose only language is English. This helps children and families alike. "Volunteering helps me if I'm sad," one parent said. "It's a great way to deal with my feelings." From increasing children's school readiness to reducing their parents' isolation, the results of Valley Settlement's efforts have transformed the Roaring Fork community.

On the other side of the Rocky Mountains, the Kellogg Foundation used our social bond to uplift an Indigenous community and honor the importance of Indigenous-led clean energy solutions in addressing a legacy of energy injustice. Navajo Power, a majority Native-owned public benefit corporation, is helping develop clean energy projects on Tribal lands—a necessary corrective to the generations of environmental and economic exploitation Indigenous Americans have suffered. The corporation also seeks to address inequities that have left fifteen thousand Navajo families without access to electricity.

Navajo Power was working to raise capital for these projects when the foundation saw the corporation's promise and invested $3 million to help get it launched. Since it's been up and running, Navajo Power plans to build more than $3 billion of clean energy infrastructure in Tribal communities by 2030—helping ensure a cleaner climate future while supplying clean power to others in major US cities that will economically benefit Navajo communities.

Brett Isaac, the company's cofounder and executive chairman, told a foundation colleague of mine that the investment was a "game changer." For decades, decisions about infrastructure and natural resources were made in boardrooms and federal government offices far from Navajo land. With Navajo Power, at least some of those decisions will be made by Navajos, for Navajos. "I think we have the expertise," Brett said, referring to his beloved Navajo Nation. "I think we have the talent. We've just been exporting it for years." With the support of the foundation, he continued, "We're not being asked to convert ourselves to something else. We're being supported in the work we're doing in the places we are."[35] Now, that is community-based programming at work just as Dr. Tyrone Baines had imagined it.

We are humbled to partner with incredible communities both in the United States—in fact, we actively support nonprofit organizations in all fifty states as well as sovereign nations—and internationally throughout Mexico and Haiti, and our work with Indigenous peoples has been particularly inspiring and fulfilling for the foundation and those we serve. We have invested in Indigenous communities for decades, and our work with the Navajo Nation is a strong example of the style of partnership we hope to carry into the future. Navajo Nation, the largest Indigenous Tribe in the United States, extends into the states of Arizona, Utah, and New Mexico. We work with our partners across these states to address the ongoing impacts of colonialism, remove barriers to wholeness, and advance equitable outcomes for Indigenous children, families, and communities in the southwestern United States, and in Mexico. Honoring tribal sovereignty is the foundation for these partnerships, and we value their sovereign rights to determine what's most beneficial for Indigenous children to thrive.

Indigenous partnerships have been especially critical in New Mexico, a state that exemplifies the importance of long-term, community-led change. New Mexico, already a priority for us, was one of the geographic areas where my predecessor, Sterling Speirn, chose to prioritize part of the foundation's portfolio on place-based grantmaking in select geographic areas—and with good reason. The state's children—most of whom were, and are, children of color—had for years languished among our nation's most underserved. The state moved to establish increased minimum wages for childcare workers. Before the raises, employees were earning more working in fast food than providing childcare. The children, families, and childcare providers of New Mexico are only beginning to see the positive effects of the hard work of so many advocates. Thanks to the foundation's focus on community-led programming through our grant-making strategy in the state for over two decades, organizations from Albuquerque to Las Cruces were primed to make even more meaningful change in the lives of children.

One example comes from a Native community that also happens to be a UNESCO World Heritage Site: Taos Pueblo, where adobe houses are stacked in clusters up to five stories high. Justly famous around the globe, the oldest of these structures predate the arrival of European colonizers by well over a century, but the community still preserves them with loving care, replastering their sand-colored walls as needed.

Beyond these stunning facades, however, the young children of the Taos Pueblo, like so many children in New Mexico, were growing up with uneven access to crucial services. Among other things, when children did go to school, some were showing up so hungry that they couldn't properly focus on classes.[36]

Enter Taos Pueblo Head Start, where teachers lead the little ones through lessons tailored to their age group: one-year-olds (whom the program calls "Storytellers"), two-year-olds ("Dream Catchers"), three-year-olds ("Stars"), and four-year-olds ("Moons"). Throughout the school day, each Storyteller, Dream Catcher, Star, and Moon also receives breakfast, lunch, and a nutritious snack.

The food is just as important as the learning, according to Bettina

Sandoval, the Taos Pueblo's education director. As Bettina shared in 2023, "Education involves not just schools or administrators. It's about the health, well-being, safety, and food security that our families have so that they can access education."[37]

Alongside these endeavors, the Taos Pueblo is taking steps to preserve their culture and, in particular, the Tiwa language. Today, the Taos Pueblo people offer everyone from babies and elementary schoolers to adults the opportunity to learn their ancestral language. Those who become proficient in Tiwa are empowered to further engage with their history, celebrate their culture, and participate more fully with ancestral traditions rooted in language, like song and storytelling. Just as important, they gain the opportunity to become teachers for the next generation, helping to keep tribal culture alive well into the future.

This is vital work—and I'm overjoyed to say it continues to pay dividends for the children and families in our nation's communities. In 2022, New Mexico became the first state to create a permanent fund for childcare, approved by more than 70 percent of voters. Childcare is now a constitutional right in the state, with nearly $150 million allocated each year for early learning. By supporting efforts like the ones led by Taos Pueblo, we not only help preserve cultures and traditions that might otherwise be lost. We also honor the great debt we owe to the Indigenous communities that continue to champion the work of racial healing.

Other grants from the foundation's social bond are helping communities far and wide. For example, in the wake of George Floyd's murder, an Oakland-based organization called the Teaching Well used the foundation's support to establish Racial Healing Affinity Groups to help teachers across the United States and Canada work through the ways race and racism have affected their lives. In turn, these groups also have equipped educators to discuss racial and other social issues responsibly with their students. Reflecting our country's diversity, the groups served educators from a multitude of backgrounds: Black, Latino, White, multiracial, Asian American and Pacific Islander, Middle Eastern, North African, Southwest Asian, and Indigenous.

Customized to its participants, each group helped educators safely reprocess traumatic experiences and deepen their understanding of systemic issues. The Teaching Well expanded the program in the 2022–2023 school year, adding a three-day, multiracial event that brought affinity groups together to discuss their experiences. As it so often does, racial healing produced personal epiphanies among the teachers who took part in these circles. One participant said, "This group answered so many questions in my heart that I didn't even know were there." Another lauded the "big breakthroughs" the program had led to, saying that it had "exceeded my expectations tenfold."

I've been equal parts proud and moved to see the impact of the foundation's social bond over just two years. Using that $300 million in additional grant-making, we've been able to fund hundreds of effective grassroots organizations to support, for example, increased testing and vaccination for Covid-19 in cities like Detroit. We've been able to materially improve conditions for children across the country and provide rare but necessary moments of hope. And I'm especially proud of the way our team at the foundation stepped up to do it, essentially increasing our grantmaking by 50 percent without adding staff, in the midst of a global pandemic when so many were themselves struggling to care for children and other family members and grieve loved ones. It wasn't easy work, but our communities needed us, and we responded to that need in the most robust way we could.

The tribulations of 2020 produced hardship, but also stories of courage and solidarity in the face of adversity. For me, some of the most inspiring stories came out of a town that has become familiar to Americans for all the wrong reasons: Flint, Michigan.

REFRAMING FLINT'S NARRATIVE

I've known Flint since I was a kid. The city is only about an hour's drive from my childhood home in Detroit. My brother Greg's traveling baseball team often played games in the area, and the whole family would travel to support him. When I was growing up, my mother also had a cousin there. Every so often, Mom would decide to visit her cousin, and I would tag along, excited to go on a "long" drive. Back in the 1960s and 1970s, when the auto industry was still strong, I remember Flint as quiet and pleasant. It was a treat to travel there, not least because we so rarely got to go on even short road trips.

Many years after my joyful childhood visits to the city—I visited Flint again, this time on behalf of the foundation. I saw inspiring projects led by local communities, but I also saw neighborhoods ravaged by decades of neglect—a city in agonizing decline pockmarked with deserts of all kinds: food deserts, hospital deserts, playground deserts, and more. I also saw more bottled water in Flint than I had ever seen anywhere else. Piles of bottles either sat idle or filled the beds of trucks. Needless to say, Flint was no longer the thriving place I remembered.

Most Americans are aware now of the city's notorious water crisis that started in 2014, a public health emergency in which lead from corroded pipes leached into the drinking water, putting nearly one hundred thousand people at risk of severe poisoning. City and state officials had brushed aside complaints about the water's color, smell, and taste, telling Flint's majority-Black community to "relax."[38] The event was a spectacular failure of public officials to look after their constituents, and a powerful example of structural inequity at work.

Covid-19 made contemporary segregation in Flint even more impossible to ignore. During March 2020, the city's Black residents—a little more than half the population—accounted for more than 80 percent of infections and more than 90 percent of deaths.[39] The following month, Black residents of Flint were seventy-three times more likely than their White neighbors to die of Covid.[40] By June 2020, Genesee

County (where Flint is the biggest city) had suffered more deaths than several entire states.[41]

Perhaps nowhere else in the United States was the confluence of these twin pandemics—Covid-19 and structural racism—more evident than in the city of Flint.

Flint's plight has deep roots in systemic racism. Between 1919 and 1933, General Motors built three beautiful neighborhoods in the city, aiming to attract skilled workers. But GM put in place racially restrictive covenants to ensure that these neighborhoods would be exclusively White. Meanwhile, Flint's neighborhoods of color were left to crumble. A 1934 study found that 98 percent of the housing in majority-White areas was in good repair, while in majority-Black neighborhoods, one in four homes lacked hot water. More than one in eight lacked toilets.[42]

Three years later, the federal authorities redlined Flint. By labeling neighborhoods of color "hazardous," they made those areas no-go zones for mortgage lenders.[43] This move denied residents of color the opportunity to build equity in their homes—something I've seen afflict far too many of my own friends and family members.

The indignities accumulated from there, in a pattern that is familiar by now. By 1940, Flint had become one of the United States' most segregated cities. In the 1950s, White opposition doomed Flint's plan to incorporate wealthier suburbs into the city, a tax base that would have funded critical city infrastructure and other urban development. And efforts to integrate Flint's neighborhoods just a decade later met with a vigorous campaign of blockbusting, in which realtors, hungry to snap up houses at bargain prices, fed White residents dire warnings of what integration would do to the value of their homes. A mass exodus from the city followed. As a local Flint activist once quipped, integration was only "the period between the moving in of the first Negro in a neighborhood and the exit of the last White."[44]

Today, these events might seem like relics of the distant past. But they aren't fragments of our history; they're the building blocks of our present. That's especially true in Flint. As a Michigan State University study showed, Flint's families of color in 2019 still overwhelmingly lived in the neighborhoods to which the federal government had confined them in 1937. Concentrated poverty and the collapse of Flint's tax base precipitated the water crisis—a catastrophe that exposed thousands of citizens, mostly people of color, to lead and legionella. The former can profoundly impair a child's development; the latter can be fatal. For at least twelve Flint residents, it was.[45]

When I heard about this devastation, I thought of my beloved family in Flint. I thought of the health issues that communities of color already experienced disproportionately and worked hard to mitigate. I thought of how similar crises, when left unaddressed, had impacted communities for generations—robbing families of their potential, stealing children's chances to grow and succeed. At the Kellogg Foundation, our mantra was as clear as ever: *It's not about me. It's not about you. It's about the children.*

We had to help Flint.

In August 2016, at the height of the water crisis, the foundation awarded $7.1 million in grants to more than a dozen organizations on the ground, each of which was helping alleviate the immediate risk. Months later, recognizing that the crisis was only the most acute symptom of a much greater disease—structural racism—we included Flint on the list of the initial fourteen communities to pilot the Truth, Racial Healing, and Transformation framework. It was time for systemic change.

To lead the work, we selected one of our 2016 grantees, the Community Foundation of Greater Flint. But when Gail Christopher first proposed racial healing to the Community Foundation's incoming president and CEO, Isaiah Oliver, he politely but firmly refused. Isaiah, a leader of color who had been working on the ground in Flint for years, told Gail that his organization was already working to help people through the water crisis. They didn't have time to worry about a "nice to have" like racial healing.

Now, anyone who knows Gail knows she does not take no for an answer. Isaiah Oliver was about to find that out himself. Gail sat down with Isaiah and set out for him all the ways that structural racism had produced the crisis—and the fact that, until it was dealt with, it would obstruct any solution. She made the foundation's case: Equity does not last long without healing. And she changed his mind.

Flint's TRHT efforts were born.

As with TRHT efforts elsewhere, one of the first orders of business was speaking the truth: allowing the community to tell its story, sparing no painful details. Alongside healing circles and a local Day of Racial Healing, the Community Foundation held several visioning sessions. Flint residents used these to imagine a better future for their city—and to begin working together toward that collective vision. At the same time, the Community Foundation commissioned researchers from the University of Michigan and the city's Sloan Museum of Discovery to shed light on Flint's Indigenous history.

Given Flint's distressing record of racist housing policies, it was perhaps inevitable that housing would become a major theme of the community's racial healing efforts. And the Community Foundation would come to focus its attention on one neighborhood in particular: Atherton East.

In the mid-1960s, as Flint's integration efforts fell to blockbusting, the federal government announced a plan for "urban renewal"—a euphemism masking forced displacement, mostly affecting families of color, to make way for a highway. Residents of the destroyed neighborhoods would be relocated to a new public housing development called Atherton East. Opened in 1967, Atherton East was built hastily, cheaply, and in the middle of a floodplain. From the beginning, residents were plagued by cockroaches. When it rained, their basements flooded. As the community's fortunes sank, gun violence erupted, and Atherton East became notorious as a symbol of Flint's tragic decline.

It took half a century and a water crisis for the federal government to start righting the wrongs it had done to these families. But at last, in 2018, the Department of Housing and Urban Development made a $30 million grant that would tear down Atherton East. It planned a replacement development, Clark Commons Choice Neighborhood, and offered residents the option to move there.

This time, at least, the relocation was being done for a good reason. A move to Clark Commons promised better access to stores, buses, jobs, and good schools. But being forced to leave your home is traumatic under any circumstances. Besides, Clark Commons was to be built between existing neighborhoods, creating an area of mixed-income housing. Without careful handling, there was a very real risk that Flint might see a rerun of the failed integration efforts in the years before Atherton East was built: Fearful of the new development, higher-income residents might flee the same way White families had fled my Detroit neighborhood when I was a kid.

The Community Foundation recognized this as another opportunity to use the empathy-building techniques of TRHT. In partnership with the City of Flint, they first held racial healing circles with the residents of Atherton East, giving them the space to tell stories of the trauma caused by forced displacement over generations. Next, they invited residents of the two neighborhoods flanking Clark Commons to racial healing circles of their own. Here, in keeping with the core philosophy of TRHT, they were able to express their hopes and misgivings free from judgment. Finally, the Community Foundation merged the three sets of circles, fostering empathy and trust between residents of the three affected neighborhoods.

Without racial healing, well-intentioned efforts to shine a spotlight on disinvestment and even to fund solutions could have accidentally reinforced some of the very narratives—of runaway blight, of needy communities, of problems that need to be "fixed"—that contributed to disinvestment in the first place. Instead, community partners came together to speak honestly about historical wrongs and begin to make them right. This was a powerful reframing of Flint's story, and the first step on a long journey toward lasting change.

In an article penned in January 2020, Isaiah Oliver summed up his hopes for his organization's ongoing racial healing work: "For my children to experience a just, equitable world, we must come together to heal. We must explore and unravel the deeply held racial biases of the past—the biases that hold us back from unleashing our collective energy and potential."[46]

Two months later, the pandemic hit. For Flint, it would be the first big test of racial healing in action.

"WALK WITH US!"

With the effects of the water crisis still lingering, Flint Mayor Sheldon Neeley described the situation in March 2020 as "a crisis on top of a crisis with a side of crisis." Fears built upon fears, and trust in government crumbled even further. On May 1, tensions boiled over into tragedy when three people, all from the same family, murdered a store security guard following a dispute over the store's mask mandate.[47]

I'll admit it: I was worried. That incident was shocking, especially on top of the staggering death tolls in Flint. Miles away in Battle Creek, as I adjusted to mask-wearing and virtual meetings, I couldn't help but wonder: Would our years of supporting racial healing work in Flint stand strong against these calamities? The pressures of fear and insecurity had doomed other communities. Would the people of Flint be able to weather them?

The answer to both questions was a resounding *yes*. Thanks to his experience with TRHT, Isaiah Oliver knew from the beginning that historical and systemic racism would bring greater suffering to communities of color during the pandemic. On a flight back to Flint from a conference, Isaiah sketched out his design for an organization that would bring together representatives from community groups, faith congregations, local business, city government, and more to help transform Flint's experience of the pandemic: the Greater Flint Coronavirus Taskforce on Racial Inequalities.

In the face of the false hierarchy of human value that still plagues systems like medicine and housing, Isaiah's Taskforce would seek to combat inequities in access to testing, treatment, and economic aid. Racial healing was in its DNA from the start. Its mission statement quoted Gail Christopher when it committed to "jettison the hierarchy of human value." Like I said, she never takes no for an answer.

By April 21—less than six weeks after Mayor Neeley declared a municipal emergency around the pandemic—the Taskforce was ready to roll. At its first meeting, Taskforce members heard a presentation from Flint resident Dr. Debra Furr-Holden, an epidemiologist at Michigan State University. As she recounted later in an interview with *Mother Jones* magazine, Dr. Furr-Holden spoke about the social determinants of health, urging her fellow Greater Flint Coronavirus Taskforce on Racial Inequalities members to "look further upstream and identify what are the systems and structures that give rise to these disparities, and . . . have a lot of our actions happen at that level." Around the table, she saw light bulbs coming on over people's heads. The seed had been planted.

In accordance with Dr. Furr-Holden's advice, one of the first things the Taskforce did was break down practical obstacles standing between people of color and Covid testing. These included economic barriers, like the cost of tests; administrative ones, like requiring IDs or prescriptions; and geographic ones, like having to take more than one bus to reach a testing site.[48] Shiloh Missionary Baptist Church, previously a hub for distributing bottled water during the water crisis, now became a Covid testing site. Later, the church would transform itself again, becoming a center for vaccination.

Throughout the pandemic, the Taskforce held public consultations with the local community to ensure its needs were being met and its concerns addressed. In addition to maintaining an advisory committee of local leaders, the Taskforce held regular consultations to which everyone was invited. Meanwhile, it also worked to keep the role of systemic racism in the spotlight, successfully lobbying for local government at the city and county levels to declare racism a public health crisis in its own right—thereby helping to restore some of the trust lost.

Thanks to these efforts, Flint's residents of color were being tested for Covid-19 in ever-increasing numbers. Because they learned they had the disease early, infected people were able to support their own recovery and avoid infecting others. By the end of September 2020, the race gap in Flint had not only shrunk; it had reversed. Black residents of Flint represented just 38 percent of the city's Covid cases and half of its deaths—an underrepresentation on both counts, in proportion to population.[49]

The thoughtful approach grounded in racial healing had paid off. The Greater Flint Coronavirus Taskforce on Racial Inequalities had saved lives.

Given Flint's harrowing history of segregation, displacement, and disparities in the initial wave of Covid, one might have expected the inequity to continue through the pandemic—or worse. To be honest, my fears about Flint grew in the days following the murder of George Floyd, when I felt a disturbing sense of déjà vu. Once again, law enforcement in several US cities met protests with a heavy hand. In Minneapolis, where Floyd was killed, the violence had begun within a day of his death. In Detroit, police used tear gas and rubber bullets against demonstrators,[50] which brought back potent memories of the Rebellion decades earlier. But instead of exploding into frustration, destruction, and violence, the city of Flint showed how radically a mindset of racial healing had transformed the community.

On the Saturday evening after Floyd's death, a crowd of demonstrators converged on the Flint Township Police Department, a low brick building southwest of downtown. They found it ringed by police officers and sheriff's deputies clad in riot gear. But instead of charging the protestors or ordering them to disperse, the officers present began to engage them in peaceful conversation. One report from the scene described an exchange of "high-fives, hugs, and fist-bumps."

Finally, Christopher Swanson, the sheriff of Genesee County, took off his helmet, set down his baton, and walked into the thick of the protest. A video shows Swanson—a White man—addressing the crowd: "We want to be with you all for real," he said. "So you tell us what you need us to do."[51]

A cry went up from the protestors: "Walk with us! Walk with us!"

"Let's walk," Sheriff Swanson said. He and many officers and deputies then joined the march.

It was one of the most powerful demonstrations I had ever seen: police and protestors side by side, in solidarity with those who needed it most. At the end of the demonstration, Swanson spoke to the protestors. "This is the way it's supposed to be. The police working with the community," he said. "The cops in this community, we condemn what happened." He described Officer Derek Chauvin, George Floyd's murderer, as "not one of us," before concluding, "I love you guys. The police love you."[52]

In Flint that night, no one set fires. No one got arrested. No one sustained injuries.

This peaceful incident was like a master class in healing: a community in solidarity with those sworn to protect it. The participants looked each other in the eye. They spoke civilly, finding common ground. They spoke the truth about injustice and outrage. They fostered empathy—even love.

"I believe we saved lives last night," Sheriff Swanson told the news media the next day. Despite the turmoil engulfing the rest of the country, I could have jumped for joy. This was how it was supposed to be.

Years before, Gail Christopher had told my colleagues and me that we needed to call people *into* the work of healing, not just call them out. In 2020, in Flint, we saw the effectiveness of that approach over the long term. With every opportunity to drive each other away, the people of Flint instead found a way to call each other in. And every community in the city benefited from it.

For me, the experience of Flint and other communities during Covid-19 and the racial reckoning showed three things above all: First, communities with TRHT infrastructure in place—such as Flint and Battle Creek, tend to see less violence at demonstrations and to be more open to demands for healing and peaceful dialogue. Second, that amid the many failures of 2020, sparks of hope still exist when communities commit to a healing journey. And third, even in difficult times, racial healing can create concrete steps toward racial equity.

In fact, it's already happening—all around the world.

Chapter 7

THE PURSUIT OF EQUITY

RACIAL HEALING AFFIRMS everyone's common humanity. It generates empathy. It fosters authentic relationships. It creates community. Person by person, heart by human heart, it breaks down our unconscious belief in a false hierarchy of human value. This is a worthy ambition, in and of itself. Even more important, however, racial healing is also a path to racial equity.

That's what's behind the second *T* in the Kellogg Foundation's TRHT initiative: Truth, Racial Healing, and *Transformation*. TRHT efforts seek to challenge the systems and structures that keep our communities apart. This work aims to eliminate the bias and discrimination built into our public policy, and to tear down the barriers to opportunity that still plague communities of color.

By creating trust across racial lines, racial healing helps build a broad constituency in favor of measures to address these intersecting forces of inequality over time. But the connection between healing and equity can be much more immediate and close to home. In fact, local, grassroots progress against injustices of all kinds can grow directly from racial healing. The transformative experience of the Flint community shows what is possible. And Flint is by no means alone.

I've been moved to see the impact of racial healing in communities across the world and right here in the United States—including three that exemplify the systemic challenges and personal pain that racial healing is uniquely equipped to address.

KALAMAZOO: TAKING A BIG-PICTURE APPROACH

Kalamazoo will always hold a special place in my heart. The city was my home for almost thirty years. My family and I found a vibrant, diverse, and welcoming community there. We enjoyed the parks and nature as well as all the culture connected to Western Michigan University, the region's anchor institution. The city was the site of my reunion with my high school sweetheart, Avery, whom I later married in 2009—a love story nearly two decades in the making! And by and large, it was an amazing place to raise children.

Yet even as someone who loves Kalamazoo, I found it hard to ignore the challenges in certain neighborhoods: Vacant lots with grass growing through rubble. Abandoned homes decaying. Unhoused people forced to camp out in the city's central park.

By now, we are familiar with the reasons for concentrated poverty. The federal government redlined Kalamazoo in 1937, the same year as Flint. And as in Flint, the redlining was explicitly racist, condemning neighborhoods with "Negro homes" and "aliens" while praising those with racially restrictive covenants that kept populations of color out. This segregation was deliberate and nearly total: Of all Kalamazoo's Black families, just seventeen lived outside areas marked "hazardous" to investors. And the families who escaped this designation did not fare much better: All seventeen lived in neighborhoods deemed "declining," the next-lowest category.

Decades later, researchers from Michigan State University over-laid the 1937 redline map with demographic data from 2019. They found an uncanny correlation. Uncanny, but unsurprising: The scars of segregation are long-lasting.

The practices of redlining, blockbusting, and racial covenants are all illegal today, but housing discrimination persists. Across the United States, for example, people of color are less likely to be approved for mortgages, according to the Urban Institute. In Kalamazoo County specifically, Second Wave Southwest Michigan found county data indicating that banks reject around half of Black mortgage applicants, compared with only around one-quarter of White applicants.[1]

Discrimination still has an impact even when it is not direct. When landlords make a policy of refusing to rent to certain categories of people—like those with previous evictions or convictions, or those eligible for federal housing vouchers—they disproportionately exclude people of color.[2]

Still more insidious is the practice of racial "steering," in which realtors and landlords attempt to direct people to particular neighborhoods, buildings, or units based on race. Whether it is done consciously or not, steering is illegal—but it still happens. In the city of Kalamazoo, a comprehensive 2021 study called the Housing Equity Report found that more than one-third of survey respondents said they had experienced housing discrimination themselves or knew someone who had. And of those who said previous evictions or convictions had become barriers to housing, almost two-thirds were Black.[3]

Perhaps the most disturbing consequence of housing discrimination is the "color-coding" of homelessness. As a mother in Kalamazoo, I often took my young sons to play with other children in Bronson Park, the oldest park in the city, with more than three acres of grass, trees, benches, tables, and artwork—always home to the best Christmas decorations in town. Bronson Park is an idyllic place, welcoming enough to earn its local nickname: Kalamazoo's "front porch." But in August 2018, unhoused people began to set up camp on the park's lush lawns.[4] These people were not the problem: If Bronson Park is Kalamazoo's front porch, they were knocking on the city's door, asking for help. Yet city officials did not listen. Instead, the following month, they bulldozed the encampment and arrested ten unhoused people.[5]

Since then, encampments have also been raised—and razed—along the Kalamazoo River. And in the summer of 2023, the city's department of public safety issued a sharp spike in tickets to unhoused people in public parks, including Bronson. Those tattered makeshift tents in Bronson Park and elsewhere were disproportionately populated by people who look like me. In Kalamazoo County as a whole, where only around one in ten residents is Black, the unhoused population is almost two-thirds Black.

Housing discrimination creates additional inequity superimposed on the deep layer of structural racism in communities like Kalamazoo. The resulting segregation further confines families of color to neighborhoods with polluted air and poor access to healthy food; concentrates their children in underfunded schools; and opens the door to selective over-policing, an injustice that has resulted too often in tragedy. Yet even in a community facing as fraught and complex a challenge as housing discrimination, racial healing can be a part of the solution—as Kalamazoo itself has shown.

Kalamazoo, along with the cities of Flint and Selma, and the state of Alaska, was one of the first fourteen communities the Kellogg Foundation selected for the launch of TRHT in 2017. In its first three years, TRHT Kalamazoo took the city by storm. The organization held dozens of community racial healing circles, as well as thirty-two TRutH Talks, offering one hundred panelists from all kinds of backgrounds a public platform to tell their stories.

In 2018, TRHT Kalamazoo created a book club for teens and young adults, featuring deep discussions of literature like *March*, Congressman John Lewis's autobiography in graphic novel form. The following year, TRHT's Law Design team—led by Kalamazoo's first Black female police captain, Stacey Randolph Ledbetter—established racial healing circles at the Kalamazoo Valley Community College

Police Academy, helping cadets recognize and address racial tensions from the very start of their career in law enforcement.

These public endeavors earned TRHT Kalamazoo dozens of appearances in the local and statewide news media—further fueling its efforts to bring the community together.

Behind the scenes, the whirlwind of activity was no less intense. TRHT is by its nature expansive, and in Kalamazoo it brought community leaders together like never before. TRHT Kalamazoo initially consisted of fewer than ten partners who came together at our first TRHT summit in Carlsbad, California. Less than a year later, in November 2017, the group had grown to more than 180 partners. By 2021, it could boast more than six hundred with experience—and valuable networks of contacts—in education, criminal justice, small business, and many more fields.[6]

This broad-based approach enabled local TRHT leaders to think big. For the first time, they could connect the dots among the needs they had previously addressed as individuals. By putting those pieces together, they were able to see—and tackle—the community's challenges on a grand scale.

One of those challenges, naturally, was housing. In 2018, TRHT Kalamazoo partnered with another local group, an interfaith network called the Interfaith Strategy for Advocacy & Action in the Community—or ISAAC—to create a Housing Task Force.[7] In keeping with the tenets of racial healing, the task force started by bringing to light the truth: At the beginning of 2019, they invited city officials, landlords, and residents to a workshop about Kalamazoo's history and persistent reality of discrimination.

The workshop delved deep into the city's troubled past, with presentations from historians, housing advocates, and a senior representative of the Gun Lake Band of Pottawatomi, whose ancestors the federal government had expelled from their land to make way for Kalamazoo and other settlements. Taking place just months after the city had removed a fountain from Bronson Park that showed a White settler facing down an Indigenous American in a headdress, this truth-telling was long overdue.

Racial healing depends on understanding our history, but personal stories are no less vital. And one of the advocates who spoke at the 2019 workshop, Patrese Griffin—a professional property manager as well as then–vice chair of the Fair Housing Center of Southwest Michigan—came with firsthand experience of housing discrimination. Just two years before the Housing Task Force formed, the home Patrese had been renting was condemned—an all-too-common occurrence in neighborhoods of color, where the housing stock is disproportionately likely to be both poorly built and neglected.

Patrese and her husband, Ed, began to look for a new home. But after submitting several applications and spending around $350 in fees, they found themselves rebuffed. This left them unhoused for over a year, bouncing between hotels and the homes of generous friends while their three children were in school. As a mother who raised two sons in Kalamazoo, my heart went out to Patrese and Ed. Still, it's tough for anyone not in their situation to imagine the full extent of their anguish and frustration.

The landlords who rejected Patrese and Ed were not required to explain their decisions. But the couple had more than an inkling about why they were repeatedly denied housing: Ed had a history of felony convictions—albeit a record that had been spotless for over sixteen years. This past was now coming back to haunt not just Ed and his wife, but also the next generation. This, too, is a distressingly common experience among people of color, who are much more likely than White Americans to be incarcerated.

It was this ordeal that drove Patrese Griffin to become an activist for fairer housing policy with the Housing Task Force. And her dogged advocacy, in turn, brought her to the attention of city officials—including Commissioner David Anderson. In June 2019, after the early resignation of one city commissioner, the remaining members of the Kalamazoo City Commission selected Griffin to fill the vacancy. That November, Griffin not only won election as a commissioner in her own right but garnered enough votes to become vice mayor of Kalamazoo, alongside newly minted Mayor David Anderson. Thanks to Patrese's efforts and the Housing Task Force's determined network-building, TRHT Kalamazoo now had a powerful elected advocate.

Meanwhile, TRHT Kalamazoo carried out a survey and a series of community listening sessions to determine Kalamazoo's most serious barriers to fair housing.[8] Alongside affordability, the results included steep application fees and blanket policies excluding those with criminal histories—both scenarios that had hindered the dream of home ownership for Griffin and her family. Other identified hurdles included having previously been evicted, relying on government assistance as payment, and even being a victim of domestic violence. To add to the frustration and heartache, as Patrese and Ed had also discovered, landlords were fully entitled to keep prospective tenants in the dark about why they had been denied housing.

Based on these results, Griffin and other advocates began drafting local legislation to amend the city's Code of Ordinances and remove many of the barriers disproportionately affecting people of color. No longer would housing providers be allowed to discriminate based on a prospective tenant's prior convictions, lack of a driver's license, history as a survivor of domestic abuse, or entitlement to housing vouchers. When setting application fees, landlords would not be allowed to charge more than the cost of the background check. Those who did choose to reject an applicant would be required to provide their reasons in writing. And those who discriminated would face a fine.[9]

Importantly, the bill also included an enforcement mechanism in the shape of a new Civil Rights Board, empowered to investigate alleged violations and make official recommendations to the city. As Griffin has said, "We intend for the board to have teeth."[10]

At the beginning of 2020, Griffin introduced her bill with the aim of securing a final vote in September. The Housing Task Force went about campaigning for the bill's passage with its usual zest: It hosted workshops and racial healing circles focused on fair housing. It held meetings with renters and landlords to explain the bill's provisions. Advocates fanned out across the city, knocking on no fewer than 1,700 doors in an effort to get the word out.[11]

After the onset of Covid-19—which worsened homelessness and housing instability in communities across the United States—the Housing Task Force shifted some of its campaigning work online with a series of virtual community engagements. Once again, the scale of this campaign was made possible by TRHT Kalamazoo's broad-based, expansive approach.

And it worked.

On September 8, 2020, Patrese Griffin's bill came up for its final vote at a hearing of the city commission. A few dissenters showed up to protest. One, calling the measure "absurd" and himself "appalled," threatened to cease purchasing rental properties if the bill passed. He predicted that many city landlords would do the same.

As we know by now, this kind of zero-sum logic is a disturbingly common thought pattern in race relations. But to his credit, Commissioner Chris Praedel, a White man, immediately pushed against it. Calling the landlord's objection "shortsighted," he said, "We don't have to lose something to give other people more rights." In the end, more expansive thinking prevailed, and the commission passed the fair housing bill unanimously.

TRHT Kalamazoo's work is far from over. Now aptly renamed the Michigan Transformation Collective, the group continues to pursue racial healing, having trained more than sixty local advocates to serve as cofacilitators and created a permanent endowment to support this work indefinitely.[12] Among other transformation efforts, the collective is tackling gun violence by seeking to implement a prevention model successfully deployed across Lake Michigan in Milwaukee, Wisconsin. And another community-based organization, the Campaign for Criminal Justice Transparency, is pushing for the county to make its arrest statistics public. This transparency would reveal the whole truth about disparities in policing—and empower the community to start addressing them.

My husband and I moved to Battle Creek in 2014, so I haven't experienced all of these changes personally. But the cities are close enough to share a local news station—so when the Housing Task Force began to amend the city's Code of Ordinances, I found myself glued to local coverage every night, cheering on Patrese and her colleagues.

I heard the debates around the issue. I saw how hard the task force worked to push and adapt its initiative. Most important, I saw this source of strife—one of the greatest plagues in our society—become a cause for celebration. People in the community came together, across backgrounds and experiences, to advocate for the most vulnerable among us.

Racial healing doesn't happen overnight; for many, it's a lifelong effort. But in TRutH Talks and book clubs, in community circles and one-on-one conversations, the people of Kalamazoo came to better understand each other. They uncovered the goals they share for their city. And they turned talk into action to make a real and lasting difference.

BUFFALO: TURNING BUSINESS LEADERS INTO EQUITY ALLIES

This kind of success is by no means confined to Michigan. Hundreds of miles from Kalamazoo, on the shores of Lake Erie, racial healing has helped another city even in the direst of circumstances. Kalamazoo exemplifies the long-term effects of systemic inequities in policy and infrastructure. Buffalo, New York, shares many of these historical obstacles—and recently experienced a further tragedy no community should have to endure.

Just off Lake Erie, Buffalo has played an important role in US history. The city spent decades feeding the nation as a hub for the grain industry. In the 1840s, abolitionists made Buffalo a way station on the Underground Railroad. The city's steel industry was a major contributor to the United States' economic growth for much of the twentieth century. Yet Buffalo's racial history follows a depressingly familiar pattern.

As in Flint and Kalamazoo, the federal government redlined the city in 1930s. Later, Buffalo joined Flint as a city subjected to "urban renewal"—a cloak for federal destruction of neighborhoods of color by building highways and pursuing other harmful infrastructure projects.[13] And as in Flint, Kalamazoo, Detroit, and so many other communities, de facto segregation was enforced via municipal boundaries and housing bias.

By the 2020s, little had changed for the better. Buffalo still ranked among the worst cities in the United States for segregation between Black and White residents. A 2021 study by the University at Buffalo's Center for Urban Studies found that among Black Buffalonians, the average wage—along with rates of poverty, unemployment, and home ownership—had remained stagnant since 1990.[14]

I've had the pleasure of visiting Buffalo to meet with some of the advocates working to create more opportunities—starting with the Greater Buffalo Racial Equity Roundtable. In 2015, the Community Foundation for Greater Buffalo, then led by Clotilde Perez-Bode Dedecker, began convening the roundtable to bring together thirty-two community leaders from a variety of fields. As in Kalamazoo, the aim was to aggregate experiences, see the bigger picture, and begin to address the community's needs on the widest level.

Racial healing and truth-telling have long been at the forefront of the roundtable's efforts. With support from the Kellogg Foundation, it has partnered with local faith congregations to bring racial healing circles to Buffalo and the Western New York region. Since 2017, the roundtable and its partners have held dozens of these circles.

To provide a more public platform, the Greater Buffalo Racial Equity Roundtable has partnered with the local NPR affiliate, WBFO, to air frank conversations and personal stories about racial equity, inspired in part by the phenomenally popular StoryCorps series on NPR. Reporting from the WBFO Racial Equity Project has included personal experiences of incarceration, Covid-19, and mental health challenges; no-holds-barred conversations between local White leaders and their counterparts of color in faith, business, and other fields; and wider investigations into racist violence, food insecurity, and prison reform.

Yet I've been most impressed by the roundtable's efforts to empower Buffalonians of color, particularly Black men. In recent years, the roundtable conducted a series of listening exercises to identify the main barriers facing communities of color. One major theme that emerged was a lack of economic opportunity—a key concern for a city where, according to the 2021 Center for Urban Studies report mentioned earlier, the median Black household earns an income that amounts to approximately 57 percent of the median White household's income, with Latino and Indigenous households trailing behind at about 43 percent and 50 percent, respectively.[15]

Drawing on its members' community connections, the Greater Buffalo Racial Equity Roundtable put together a Business Leaders Task Force with leaders from fourteen major employers in the Western New York region. Participants included hospitals, banks, colleges, manufacturers, and retailers. These businesses might operate in wildly different fields, but the CEOs quickly realized they had one thing in common: Whether they were buying surgical supplies or security services, computer parts or construction equipment, food ingredients or facilities management, they all spent a lot of money in Western

New York's economy. If steered in a positive direction, that collective purchasing power could be very potent indeed.

In 2019, the business leaders formed the Buffalo Purchasing Initiative (BPI) with the aim of directing more of that spending toward businesses owned by people of color. Among other things, participating employers took a hard look at their own practices and procedures to figure out where they could be more inclusive. Then they worked to identify and reach out to diverse businesses and held local networking and matchmaking sessions to get to know these suppliers.

By the beginning of 2024, the participating employers had already doubled the amount they were spending with local businesses of color. And they had laid the groundwork to do even more by nearly tripling their business relationships with owners of color.

BPI's beneficiaries hail from a range of backgrounds. For example, Rodriguez Construction, a participating company, has been hired as a prime contractor by no fewer than five members of the initiative, enabling the business to expand and create more jobs. Rubens Mukunzi, an entrepreneur who found refuge in the United States following the genocide in his native country of Rwanda, received a landmark janitorial contract with the Wegmans chain of grocery stores, enabling him to continue employing his workforce, most of whom are also former refugees. Wegmans has also begun stocking coffee from the Black-owned, Buffalo-based firm Golden Cup Coffee, allowing the company to upgrade its equipment. Golden Cup Coffee's co-owner, Larry Stitts, celebrated the name recognition this has brought, saying, "It's like being in the Super Bowl of grocery markets!"

At the other end of the spectrum of opportunity, people returning to society from prison often find themselves unable to get a job or to access basic services like education, housing assistance, and health care. Because of structural bias in our criminal justice system, these reentrants are disproportionately people of color. The stigma of having served time can cling to ex-offenders for years—as Patrese Griffin,

Kalamazoo's vice mayor, found when her husband's long-distant record trapped her family in a cycle of homelessness. Left hopeless and desperate, reentrants sometimes find it all too easy to slip back into crime.

When the Greater Buffalo Racial Equity Roundtable considered barriers to economic progress, one statistic that jumped out was Buffalo's recidivism rate. More than eight in ten formerly incarcerated Buffalonians were becoming trapped again in a cycle of crime following their release.[16] Clearly, something had to be done to help these folks reintegrate after serving their time.

Again, the roundtable's diverse roster of contacts became useful. They brought together a Reentry Coalition featuring more than fifty partners from government, law enforcement, and the community—including residents who had experienced the criminal justice system. With all these players pooling knowledge, experience, and data, one major impediment soon became clear: the confusing array of agencies that reentrants needed to contact to access support.

In partnership with the local mental health department and the sheriff's office, the Reentry Coalition created the Service Link Stop. Located near the local jail, the Service Link Stop is a place free from judgment where reentrants are welcomed and can find many of the services they might need, all in one place: health insurance, food stamps, legal aid, assistance with housing, mental health and addiction services, and much more. The tagline for the Service Link Stop is *No matter where you've come from, it matters where you're going.* Since opening in 2020, it has helped hundreds of Buffalonians reenter society safely and productively every year.[17]

Tragically, no community of color is safe from the United States' pandemic of racial violence. On May 14, 2022, a white supremacist terrorist opened fire at the Tops Friendly Market in the Masten Park neighborhood of Buffalo's East Side. He killed ten Black American men and women whose ages ranged from thirty-two to eighty-six.[18] Alongside grief and righteous anger, the attack unearthed harsh memories. In

1980, a white supremacist terrorist went on a murderous, racist rampage in Buffalo. Over the course of a few weeks, he killed six Black males, one of them just fourteen years old. At the height of the massacre, the terrorist underlined his racist motives by erecting a ten-foot burning cross in a majority-Black neighborhood.[19]

Four decades later, the 2022 attack typified the most recent turn of white supremacy's vicious cycle. The shooter had written a manifesto referring to the "great replacement" conspiracy theory and claiming inspiration from other acts of white supremacist violence, including the 2019 El Paso Walmart shootings that targeted Latino Americans. He had traveled two hundred miles across the state from Binghamton specifically to find a high concentration of Black victims—a demographic likelihood he had confirmed online, searching census data by zip code.

Tragically, it was because decades of racist policy and practice had segregated Buffalo and other cities that the murderer was able to find a disproportionate density of Black Americans. These practices deliberately—and successfully—ensured the continuation of white supremacy across generations.

The killings highlighted other consequences of segregation, too. Tops Friendly Market was the only large grocery in the neighborhood, and its opening in 2003 had come after a decade-long campaign by local residents. After the shootings, its closure as a crime scene immediately turned Masten Park back into a "food desert"—an area without local access to fresh, healthy, and affordable food. This phenomenon is disproportionately likely to afflict neighborhoods of color: The Center for Urban Studies report found that Black Buffalonians were six times more likely than White residents to live in a food desert, a statistical similarity among many cities and towns across the United States.

The murders at Tops made painfully clear—specifically in Buffalo but truly all around the United States—the unfinished business of racial healing and racial equity. Fortunately, years of TRHT had given the city a strong foundation to undertake the hard work of healing.

After the Tops shooting, Clotilde Perez-Bode Dedecker, president and CEO of the Community Foundation for Greater Buffalo, said something that surprised me: "La June, it could've been worse."

Worse? I wondered. *How?*

The tragedy was horrific, and nothing could change or fix that. But Clotilde explained that Buffalo's previous work in racial healing had eased the aftermath. Communities leaned on preexisting relationships. People from different backgrounds already trusted each other. In another city, a similar event could have torn residents apart; instead, in Buffalo, healing held. The community came together.

And they worked together. After the Tops shooting, local organizations coordinated to provide fresh fruits and vegetables to the community. Another nonprofit, Breaking Barriers Buffalo, set up racial healing circles to give Black men a chance to express their feelings, practice and share the burden of resilience, and begin to learn and grow together. This is critical and ongoing work.

Perhaps most important, Buffalo residents of all races and backgrounds stood up for their city. Like Clotilde, Dr. Henry Louis Taylor Jr., the founding director of the Center for Urban Studies at the University at Buffalo, saw this unity as evidence of a brighter future—one that healing had enabled. As he told one journalist, "Racial healing is simply about rebuilding the society based on equity and social justice."[20] Buffalo's ongoing progress is evidence of that.

THE DESCENDANTS: TALKING (AND LIVING) MERCY

Racial healing is not just for cities, towns, or neighborhoods. Its practices can help any community, whether geographic or not—even one torn apart by tragedy.

Not all communities are defined by where they live. Some are bound together by shared experiences and histories—and sometimes, those histories stretch far into the past. Indeed, one of the most powerful ongoing stories of racial healing I've encountered began alongside our republic's founding.

In 1789, three months before George Washington took his first oath of office, the Jesuits of Maryland—the local branch of a powerful Catholic religious order—founded, on the banks of the Potomac River, the institution we know today as Georgetown University. The Jesuits had grown rich through tobacco plantations throughout the colony, and later the state, of Maryland. These plantations, of course, operated on forced labor from hundreds of enslaved Black Americans. To some, it may come as a surprise to find ordained men of God openly claiming to own their fellow human beings, but slavery was disturbingly common for Catholic organizations in the antebellum United States.

By the late 1830s, however, Georgetown University was in dire financial straits. In less than a decade, the college had built too quickly and too grandly. Now, it struggled under debt. To escape these financial straits, local Jesuit leaders decided to sell some of the people they had enslaved. Starting in 1838, they sold at least 314 men, women, and children in one of the largest mass sales of human beings in US history. Out of these dealings, the Jesuits received the equivalent of about $4 million today, saving Georgetown from bankruptcy and allowing it to grow into the world-renowned institution it has since become.

The human cost was horrific.

As documented by the GU272 Memory Project, named after the term used globally to refer to the enslaved people sold by the Jesuits, most of the enslaved people were sold to Louisiana slavers who put them to work in sugar plantations near Baton Rouge. At the time, the area was notorious: a mosquito-infested swamp where working conditions were harsh even by the brutal standards of nineteenth-century slavery. For the enslaved people, it was a time of misery and panic. When the boat came, several people had to be forcibly dragged to it. In an 1838 letter, the Reverend Peter Havermans described one enslaved person, a pregnant woman, asking a priest, "If ever someone should have reason for despair, do I not now have it?"[21]

At the request of Jesuit leaders in the Vatican, the contracts of sale specified that families must not be split up. They further required that the needs of the elderly and infirm be met. The local Jesuits agreed, knowing full well that these clauses were unenforceable and almost certain to be ignored—which they were, compounding the misery of dozens of people.

As the Vatican's stipulations suggest, some members of the Catholic Church were uncomfortable with what they considered the excessive brutality of the Louisiana sale. A year after the sales, Pope Gregory XVI formally condemned the transatlantic slave trade—but he did not bar Catholics from the private dealings that perpetuated it, including owning and selling enslaved people. This allowed Georgetown to continue its grim transactions into the 1840s. Moreover, slavery apparently remained popular among the Georgetown community: Of its alumni who served in the Civil War, more than four-fifths were Confederates.

Following emancipation, the failure of Reconstruction, and the beginning of the Jim Crow era, many of the formerly enslaved and their descendants began to spread across the United States in much the same way my family did: through successive waves of the Great Migration. As time went on, many of these families, understandably, were unable to share stories of their ancestors' enslavement, as few had reliable records or even family heirlooms. Their descendants grew up knowing little about this part of their past. Not until the early twenty-first century were American universities finally forced to reckon with their shameful entanglement in slavery.

For Georgetown, the flashpoint was the 2015 reopening of Mulledy Hall, one of the two buildings named for the college presidents who had concocted the 1838 sale. After protests, both Georgetown and the Jesuit order apologized for the school's participation in enslavement.

The university renamed both buildings—one of them in honor of Isaac Hawkins, the first enslaved person named on the bill of sale.

Symbolic gestures like apology and renaming are necessary: They help to highlight the truth and correct false narratives, two of the primary aims of racial healing. But by themselves, such measures are by no means sufficient. Knowing this, a group of Georgetown alumni, friends, and allies joined forces to fund an effort to trace descendants of the people who had been sold. They would eventually identify thousands of individuals.

One descendant who discovered this connection turned out to be someone I knew very well: the Kellogg Foundation's former board chair and the man who had championed my bid for president and CEO, Joe Stewart.

Joe was raised Catholic, and his faith remains dear to him to this day. He grew up in Louisiana, not far from the site of the plantations to which the Georgetown Jesuits had sold so many people. Other than that, he knew little about his ancestry until Richard Cellini, founder of the Georgetown Memory Project, a genealogy research group, reached out to him in 2016. It turns out that Joe is the great-great-great-grandson of Isaac Hawkins, the formerly enslaved person whose name now graces one of the refurbished dorms at Georgetown.

At first, Joe didn't know how to feel. On the one hand, he had found out about his family's origins for the first time, and it was enlightening to know the story. On the other hand, he had also learned that the church he so loved had enslaved his ancestors—and finally, betrayed them to a still more brutal fate. Joe's distress reminded me of a time in my youth when I had struggled to understand how God could allow slavery to happen. I couldn't find easy answers then; nor could Joe find them now. True to form, however, he soon converted this swirl of emotions into action.

Joe started by helping organize many of his fellow descendants into the GU272 Descendants' Association. When the association first met in August 2016, emotions were understandably high among those whose ancestors had been so wronged. The idea had surfaced of suing the Jesuit order for damages. But Joe knew from a quarter century of racial healing work that anger and confrontation would meet only defensiveness and retrenchment. In the process, the wider quest for racial equity would be lost.

Accordingly, Joe advocated with his usual passion and persuasiveness that the descendants seek reconciliation—maybe even ways of working with the Jesuits to address the wider challenges of racial injustice. It was a broader, longer-term approach than seeking individual payments. As Joe told me later, "If we don't invest in eliminating the remnants of slavery and reducing the impact of racism that continues to stand between the haves and the have-nots, then we are wasting our time. We will never get a full return on the investments we make."

Right away, Joe—along with three top Jesuits and five other descendants—sought to open a dialogue with the Jesuit order. Unfortunately, its branches covering Maryland and Louisiana ignored his overtures. Never one to give up, Joe and some of his fellow descendants went all the way to the top, petitioning the worldwide head of the Jesuit order at the Vatican.[22] In keeping with the philosophy of healing, they asked not for retribution but for truth. They requested that the order face up to its own misconduct; document the compounding harm inflicted over the years; and consider, in light of Catholic beliefs, its moral obligations to present and future generations.

Joe and his fellow descendants closed their petition by quoting none other than Pope Francis: "It is one thing to talk mercy . . . yet another to live mercy."[23] This proved sufficient. The order reached out, and the necessary conversation began at last.

Despite having been initially ignored by local Jesuits, Joe remained committed to working alongside them. In 2018, he reached out to Father Timothy Kesicki—the president of the Jesuit Conference of Canada and the United States, as well as an inaugural member of the

Kellogg Foundation's Solidarity Council on Racial Equity—who later visited Joe's house in Battle Creek.

Upon opening the door, Joe greeted Father Kesicki not with resentment or mistrust, but with a container of holy water. "Father," Joe asked, holding out the container, "will you bless our home?"

After that meeting, Joe called me to ask if I would help lead the descendants and the Jesuits through healing circles. I told him that nothing would make me happier.[24]

By sheer coincidence, the foundation had just launched TRHT Louisiana, not far from the plantations where Joe's ancestors had been enslaved. I called Flozell Daniels Jr., the CEO of our local grantee, the Foundation for Louisiana. "You know that healing methodology we've spoken about?" I asked.

Flozell did, of course. He had seen the impact of racial healing elsewhere and was enthusiastic about the Truth, Racial Healing, and Transformation initiative.

"Well," I replied, "how would you like to put these ideas into practice?"

To lead the work, I called on a stellar pair of facilitators. One was Monica Haslip, a visionary Black leader in the arts, education, and social justice, and protégée of Gail Christopher. Not only had Monica been cofacilitating racial healing circles for years; she had also trained hundreds of other practitioners to do the same. The other facilitator was Jerry Tello, a legendary figure in racial justice and racial healing, particularly in the Latino and Indigenous communities, both of which count him as a member. Monica and Jerry were among a handful of extraordinary individuals honored by President Obama as "Champions of Change." Importantly, they also brought a diverse and complementary range of perspectives, built on the foundation of their cultural and professional backgrounds. If anyone could help heal the festering wounds of enslavement and betrayal that divided the GU272 descendants and the Jesuits, it was them.

Our healing circles in Flint involved three distinct communities: the families moving into Clark Commons and those living in the two neighborhoods surrounding it. Here, there were only two groups seeking to heal—descendants and Jesuits—but the approach we designed was similar. Monica, Jerry, and their team met with each community separately at first, to explain the process of racial healing and explore each community's expectations and aspirations. Only when each was comfortable did they merge the circles.

Attending some of the early circles in Baton Rouge, I found that the descendants were still divided on how to proceed. Some wanted to sue the Jesuits and already had lawyers working on their case. They didn't see the value or possibility of healing. The Jesuits, meanwhile, had similar misgivings. They had tried to ignore the descendants, only to be effectively ordered to engage in the wake of Joe and his fellow descendants' powerful missive to the head of their order at the Vatican. They were far from enthusiastic about taking part in the circles, and many believed they had more pressing priorities.

At each of the sessions, I served as a sort of keynote speaker, testifying from my personal experience to the power of healing. I emphasized how healing could go beyond the individual to address the systems that allowed racism to persist. Meanwhile, the cofacilitators led descendants and Jesuits alike through the hard work of understanding what healing was about and how it could help them. In the end, Joe, Monica, Jerry, and Father Tim Kesicki—the Jesuit leader who had blessed Joe's home—got the Jesuits and a majority of the descendants on board with the healing process. It was a remarkable achievement, especially in such fraught circumstances.

Later, I heard about some of the blended healing circles. As in previous circles I had joined, the atmosphere sometimes became heated. The Jesuits were highly learned members of a nearly five-hundred-year-old order known for its support of higher education; some seemed to think that their degrees and pedigree meant they automatically knew best. My mind replayed the patrician attitudes I had encountered in philanthropy when I had started out in the 1980s. Meanwhile, many of the descendants—including Joe himself—were feisty, no-frills people who would call a chicken a chicken without hesitation. This personality clash, together with the sheer difficulty of the topics under discussion, gave rise to tensions.

Indeed, throughout the healing process, relationships remained rocky—but interactions became more and more productive as the hours passed. Joe told me about some of his "in-your-face" communication with the Jesuits. "There were times that we got mad as hell," he recounted in an interview on public radio, "and we were not afraid to express that."[25]

This, too, is part of racial healing, as Joe knew well from the sessions he had first hosted a quarter century earlier in his backyard with local Battle Creek leaders. Participants must feel free to speak their minds—and commit to listening when others do the same. This is how we heal. As I often say, racial healing is not about blaming and shaming. It's about finding common humanity with your fellow participants. Or as Joe put it in that same public radio interview: "You look for the positive thing that can help you move forward toward a bigger goal. And our goal is to heal."

In time, these truth and healing conversations turned to the more tangible question of transformation: What could the Jesuits do now to redress the evils their order had inflicted? Again, Joe had an idea: Create a foundation, modeled after—what else?—the W. K. Kellogg Foundation.

This was more than just a convenient and familiar model for Joe; it fit with his aspiration toward long-term healing. The organization that Mr. Kellogg had created back in 1930, now centered on an enduring belief in the power of racial healing, had amply stood the test of time. "That is the purpose of having Mr. Kellogg's model," Joe told me, explaining that the dialogue would need to last for "one hundred years. It can sustain the efforts. Because we can't change much in only a few years."

For Joe, the confluence of his philanthropic experience and his descendant background was no mere coincidence—it was providence. Referring to his time as a trustee of the foundation, he told me, "It came out of the fact that God had blessed me to be in the Kellogg Foundation and to live that for fourteen, fifteen years."

Inspired once again by TRHT, Joe called the new organization the Descendants Truth & Reconciliation Foundation (DTRF). Georgetown University donated $1 million to get it off the ground. I was flattered and delighted to serve as one of the first trustees, working alongside Joe and four other descendants of Jesuits' enslavement, three top Jesuits in the United States, a catholic Bishop, an HBCU chancellor, the chief of staff at Georgetown, and a nationally recognized TRHT facilitator. Here was an opportunity to transform a horrific evil into a positive legacy for future generations.

The new foundation would have three pillars: One, it would address the needs of today's descendants who were elderly or infirm, delivering at last on one of the promises made disingenuously in 1838. Two, it would provide for the aspirations of the next generation by supporting their education, from early childhood to college. And three, it would contribute to the expansion of racial healing programming across the United States. After all, the Descendants Truth & Reconciliation Foundation would not have been possible without racial healing and its impacts.

What could have been a fractious relationship has instead borne lifelong friendships. Racial healing has made it possible for Joe and his fellow descendants to find personal fulfillment and justice. The work continues, as healing always does. But its successes for Joe and his fellow descendants speak for themselves. In March 2021, the Jesuit order announced that it would donate $100 million to the new foundation within five years. By September 2023, thanks to further prompting from Joe in his usual irrepressible style, the order was on track to meet this commitment, having pledged a total of $42 million.

Bolstered by these successes, in July 2023 DTRF announced its first formal program. Working with the nationally renowned Thurgood Marshall College Fund, it created a need-based scholarship for descendants to attend college—with a focus on those planning to go to historically Black colleges and universities. And today, the Descendants Truth & Reconciliation Foundation, with a board that consists of both Jesuits and descendants, continues to raise money to repair harms and fund wider collective healing work. In this way, it is helping to turn a vicious cycle into a virtuous one.

A GLOBAL MOVEMENT: RACIAL HEALING IS FOR EVERYONE

The Kellogg Foundation's support of healing work is by no means limited to the United States. I receive updates from each of the groundbreaking organizations we serve and eagerly look forward to learning about the heights their projects reach. This work fills me with a profound sense of hope that, together, humanity can tackle inequity everywhere.

One of the most inspiring places we have worked is South Africa. Even before the fall of apartheid in the 1990s, the foundation was providing scholarships to help educate future Black leaders. And indeed, President Nelson Mandela would go on to hire some Kellogg Fellows and bursary recipients into his administration.

Later, South Africa's Truth and Reconciliation Commission formed one of the major inspirations for TRHT. The chair of that commission, Nobel Peace Prize laureate Archbishop Desmond Tutu, spoke at the foundation's seventy-fifth anniversary celebration in Battle Creek. There, Archbishop Tutu charted South Africa's journey out of apartheid. "The repulsive caterpillar metamorphosed into a glorious multicolored butterfly," he told a rapt audience at the Kellogg Arena. How had this miracle come about? Because, he said, South Africa's new democratic leaders had focused not on "revenge and retribution but [on] reconciliation and forgiveness."[26]

In light of this history together, it has been especially meaningful for the foundation to work in partnership with—and to continue the legacy of—the man who led South Africa out of apartheid: Nelson Mandela.

Late in his life, Mandela began raising funds to build a new children's hospital in Johannesburg, South Africa's largest city. I saw for myself why South Africans needed the facility when I visited the government hospital: The levels of destitution would make you cry. The foundation was only too happy to help fund an alternative—a state-of-the-art facility that would offer two hundred beds to treat children's most pressing medical needs.

Mandela, who passed away in 2013 at the age of ninety-five, didn't live to see his vision for the hospital become a reality. But when it launched in 2016, the Nelson Mandela Children's Hospital was fittingly named in his honor.

Thousands of miles away, Haiti faces a different set of challenges. Following the devastating earthquake there in 2010, the foundation made a commitment to the children of Haiti, designed to last at least a generation. Based on advice from our grantees, we realized that one of the problems Haiti faced was fragmentation in its elementary education system. Some schools were public whereas others were private. Others were run by the Catholic Church. Still others were part of nonprofit school networks. These systems didn't communicate, leading to inefficiency and confusion. So, starting in 2013, we used the methodology of collective healing to bring them all together and get them talking.

This work has since evolved into the Model School Network, which pools knowledge, expertise, and resources for a common cause: serving

Haitian children. In 2019, the network completed a survey of rural school buildings and developed comprehensive guidelines to fund and carry out repairs, rebuilding, and expansion—all based on need, not on the school's sector. Inevitably, the work has been set back by the pandemic and an uptick in local political unrest. But with the level of determination I see on display in Haiti, I have no doubt that the Model School Network will realize the transformative change it seeks.

We've done a great deal of work in Mexico as well—specifically, in the states of Chiapas and Yucatán. Indigenous peoples of Mexico, including Mayans, suffer from the lingering effects of colonialism and structural racism in similar ways to Indigenous people in the United States and elsewhere. They endure disproportionate rates of poverty, poor housing, and violence. And even today, their land is taken from them with disturbing frequency. The Mexican government, like others around the world, has too often failed to protect Indigenous people and their homes.

In Chiapas, the foundation's grantees have used collective healing methods to introduce themselves to these communities and figure out their most pressing needs. These circles brought people together by honoring existing traditions such as communal rituals and group dances. And the message from the communities was clear: *Before you do anything else, help us get safe drinking water.* This need, too, grew from structural racism—in this case, from systems that denied Indigenous communities equal public services. As of 2016, for example, 86 percent of Indigenous schools in Mexico lacked access to safe, reliable drinking water for their students.

Enter our grantee Fundación Cántaro Azul, which works to address this situation by advocating for a better water supply across the highlands of Chiapas. Cántaro Azul has so far brought safe drinking water to six hundred thousand people. That's a meaningful improvement in the quality of life of 150 communities across the state.

Unfortunately, as the histories of South Africa, Haiti, and Mexico amply demonstrate, racial inequity is a global phenomenon—a legacy of colonial systems, practices, and beliefs that Europeans exported for centuries. Recognizing this, in 2020 the foundation launched Racial Equity 2030: a program providing $90 million (in honor of our ninetieth anniversary) to enhance equity. In addition to honoring the foundation's centennial in the year 2030, the program aligns with the United Nations' Sustainable Development Goals at the core of its 2030 Agenda for Sustainable Development.

In 2021, the program awarded $1 million each to ten finalists. And in 2022, we split the remaining $80 million across just five recipients, offering each organization a transformative amount of money across a long grant term. These projects reflect not just the international nature of racial inequity, but also the determination today of people around the world to address it. ActionAid Brazil aims to create the world's first anti-racist education system. In Chicago, Communities United calls on young people to step up and lead community healing. In Latin America, the Indian Law Resource Center is providing legal and technical assistance to communities looking to enforce their land rights. The Partners in Development Foundation, and its local partners in Hawai'i, aim to replace mass youth incarceration with Indigenous-inspired restorative programs. And in Kenya, Sierra Leone, and the United States, the organization known as Namati—a Sanskrit word for "to shape into a curve," a reference to Dr. King's "arc of the moral universe"—empowers communities of color to overcome centuries of environmental exploitation.[27]

In 2023, we brought our Racial Equity 2030 awardees together for the first time—along with members of the Solidarity Council on Racial Equity (SCoRE) and WKKF Global Fellows Network—for our inaugural Global Leadership Forum. When we decided where to host this gathering, there was only one place to do so: South Africa. In Johannesburg, we convened multigenerational leaders from around the globe to strengthen our collective pursuit of racial healing and racial equity. One of our headline speakers was a hero of the struggle, the nearly ninety-year-old Justice Albie Sachs.

Sachs began campaigning against apartheid as a teenager in the 1950s and later became an attorney representing his fellow dissidents, many of whom faced imprisonment and murder at the hands of the regime. Sachs himself was imprisoned for speaking out and spent months languishing in solitary confinement. Then, in 1988, South African intelligence attempted to assassinate him with a car bomb that destroyed his right arm and his vision in one eye—and almost took his life.

Through all of this, Sachs never gave up the struggle. And when apartheid finally ended, the nascent democracy called on him to help draft its constitution and to serve on its constitutional court.

I was honored to join Sachs in conversation at our Global Leadership Forum, where he discussed his approach to reconciliation and healing, which he said was inspired by the Zulu philosophy of *ubuntu*. "I'm a person because you're a person," he said, explaining this concept in simple terms. "I can't separate my humanity from acknowledging your humanity.... That means, however atrocious the behavior of your fellow human being, he's still a person."[28]

Sachs told me about this vision for Constitution Hill, the site of the Constitutional Court as well as a human rights museum built around the former prison where Nelson Mandela, Mahatma Gandhi, and tens of thousands of inmates were held. "You don't destroy the past," he told me. "You surround the past with the present. You contest the past. And in that sense, you overwhelm the past with the positivity of the present."[29]

What better motto for the truth-telling and narrative-building inherent in racial healing?

If South Africa can dismantle apartheid with love and compassion, any community can tackle its own racism by the same means. As Archbishop Tutu told us at the Kellogg Arena in 2005, his country became a beacon of hope so that "nowhere in the world can we ever again say, 'Ours is an intractable problem.' If it could happen in South Africa, it can happen any- and everywhere."[30]

On the surface, the residents of Kalamazoo, those in Buffalo, and the descendants of people enslaved by the Jesuits of Maryland—let alone the inhabitants of South Africa, Haiti, and Mexico—may seem like radically different communities. They have different backgrounds. They are located in different parts of the world. They face different and wide-ranging challenges. But all these communities have suffered from the reverberations of racial inequity. That's why each of them needed racial healing. And racial healing, for each of our communities and partners, has so far worked.

On a person-to-person level, racial healing taps into our deep desire to connect with our fellow human beings. To tell stories about our own experiences. To understand others and have them understand us. People who know each other on that level are better able to work together, exchanging ideas and pursuing projects.

Racial healing empowers people to share their visions of a better future, and to light the path leading toward that better future for their community. And when they reach that stage, it's almost inevitable that they will work together to foster equity.

Any community—no matter its shape or size—can take part in this movement. And every community should.

Conclusion

OUR SHARED FATE

L ESS THAN ONE HUNDRED MILES from Mound Bayou, Mississippi—some sixty miles from Clarksdale where, in 1954, my parents began their journey to Detroit—is the town of Oxford, home to the University of Mississippi, also known as Ole Miss. In 1844, Ole Miss was established by the state's legislature (which ardently supported the institution of slavery) for children of the elite, who were mostly slaveholders. During the four years that followed, the university was constructed by the hands of enslaved people—women and men whose names remain lost to history.

On the day of my birth—October 4, 1962—Oxford and all of Mississippi were reeling. A few weeks earlier, the United States Supreme Court had held that Ole Miss must enroll its first Black student, James Meredith, a veteran from rural Mississippi like my dad. But when he arrived on campus to register, an armed, white-supremacist mob of 2,500 greeted him, fomenting a violent insurrection. Within hours, President John F. Kennedy mobilized more than thirty thousand troops—to that point, the largest force ever assembled to quell a domestic disturbance. When the dust settled, the riot left two dead and hundreds wounded.

Later that month, Dr. Martin Luther King Jr. visited with students at Cornell College in Mount Vernon, Iowa. He was there to organize support among young people in the north for the gathering civil rights movement in the south.[1] And as he reflected on the events in Mississippi—on the evolving, accelerating struggle for justice across the United States—he pleaded not for vengeance or reprisal, but for empathy.

He was convinced, he said, that people "hate each other because they fear each other. They fear each other because they don't know each other. They don't know each other because they don't communicate with each other. They don't communicate with each other because they are separated from each other."

Dr. King continued, "God grant that something will happen to open channels of communication."[2]

Today, across the United States and around the world, that "something"—engaged, empathetic conversation—is happening. From disparate community roots reaching back millennia, racial healing has blossomed into an international movement.

I believe that philanthropy has played a catalytic role in supporting it. We test and pilot and learn. We find and scale what works, most effectively when we work in proximity and partnership with the very communities already doing the work. But, the truth is, you do not need a Kellogg Foundation grant to get started. In fact, some of the most inspiring stories out there have come from the groups that started practicing racial healing on their own.

A few years ago, a colleague of mine was attending a conference. Skimming through the program, he noticed an upcoming presentation about race and child welfare in Cincinnati, Ohio. He thought that sounded interesting, so he dropped in.[3] The presenter was Dr. Wendy Ellis, a Cincinnati native and the founder of the Center for Community Resilience. She described an impressive array of community enrichment and empowerment activities. Among other things, the center had been working hard to highlight the trauma caused by historical and present-day racism, to offer residents an outlet to tell their stories, and to activate local partners across several sectors.

Wait a minute, my colleague thought as Dr. Ellis spoke. *This sounds a lot like Truth, Racial Healing, and Transformation.* But if there was any connection between Dr. Ellis's center and the foundation, my colleague wasn't aware of it.

After the session, he introduced himself to Dr. Ellis and got the whole story. It turned out that Dr. Ellis had applied for TRHT funding from the foundation. Sadly, hers was one of the hundreds of worthy proposals we were forced to turn down in the face of overwhelming demand.

Undeterred, Dr. Ellis went ahead anyway.

She downloaded the TRHT Implementation Guide from our website and created a racial healing program from scratch. Since then, the Center for Community Resilience has teamed up with other non-profits as well as the University of Cincinnati's own TRHT initiative to build a coalition for truth and healing in the city. The center has also produced a documentary, *America's Truth: Cincinnati*, spotlighting the effects of structural racism on the city's communities of color.

Dr. Ellis and her center are by no means alone. Each year, in fact, tens of thousands of people download our racial healing materials. And racial healing activities are springing up all over the United States.

In Clinton, Missouri, two residents—a Black man and a White woman—decided to start a racial healing circle at their local library.

In Tulsa, Oklahoma, the Mayor's Office of Resilience and Equity has held more than fifty racial healing dialogues since 2018.

In Cocoa, Florida, residents started an interfaith racial healing group featuring leaders from Jewish and Christian congregations as well as a retired major from the local police department.

The historic town of Williamsburg, Virginia, has brought people together for racial healing dialogues intended to broaden the historical narrative about race while addressing the injustices perpetuated by our incomplete narrative.

The University of Hawai'i held racial healing events marking both the National Day of Racial Healing and the annual commemoration of the United States' unlawful overthrow of Native rule in Hawai'i.

Dozens of higher education institutions have created on-campus Truth, Racial Healing, and Transformation Campus Centers through a program led by the American Association of Colleges and Universities.

People across the country are hosting their own racial healing events in homes, schools, and community centers.

Each of these events carries us one step closer to the "open channels of communication" Dr. King hoped to create.[4]

From my perspective, I've been gratified to watch this movement grow, with numbers that swell with each passing year. We can see the scale it has reached by looking at the overwhelming public response to the National Day of Racial Healing: In 2024, millions of people tuned in to coverage of the day's events across NBCUniversal News Group platforms. Commemorations around the world generated more than one thousand stories in media outlets from Florida to Hawai'i and from Bermuda to Japan. During and immediately after the event, our racial healing implementation materials were downloaded more than eighty-four thousand times.

That's a lot of racial healing circles.

○ ○ ○

On a personal level, it takes courage to begin racial healing.

We must be willing to confront and communicate painful truths about our society and about our own unexamined beliefs. That's why first-time circle members often find themselves deep in their own heads. Through the process, though, they wind up instead in the heads—and hearts—of everyone present. Suddenly, they realize that they are not just individuals: They are part of a whole. They are participants in a shared fate.

In April 1963, two months before he visited Detroit, Dr. King described his concept of shared fate from his jail cell in Birmingham, Alabama. On scraps of newspaper and notepads, he wrote, "We are caught in an inescapable network of mutuality, tied in a single garment of destiny." Never have truer words been written about our imperfect American experiment—or about the unequal American experience that it has engendered.

For better or worse, we are tied together by a shared fate, and when that fate is confined by hatred, by division, we are all diminished. As history affirms, when we choose to ignore our interconnection and interdependence with one another, we fail to grow stronger together. But when we embrace what we share—our humanity, our values, our aspirations—we can build better futures for our children, families, and communities.

We saw the impact of our shared fate starkly during the pandemic. Even as many of us sheltered in our homes to stay safe from a deadly virus, we all relied on doctors and nurses to care for us when we were sick, grocery store workers to ensure we could get the food our families needed, and first responders of all kinds to keep us safe. And when we tried to reopen our workplaces and restart the economy, we saw the powerful role that care work, especially childcare, plays in the functioning of our economy. As they struggled to get employees—especially women—to return to work, corporate America saw the impact of our shared fate directly, and because of that experience, more and more segments of the business community have become allies in the struggle to build an economy that works for all working families. The simple fact is that only when we allow for healing and connection can we realize the promise of our common humanity, of *ubuntu*: "I'm a person because you're a person."

That is what my story shows—and what the story of the W. K. Kellogg Foundation and our work to promote racial healing proves. Whenever I have participated in racial healing efforts, I have witnessed people uncovering what links their fates to the fates of others, and vice versa. These epiphanies—these precious *aha!* moments—change lives, and the experience is open to anyone with the courage to take part.

Still, some people remain skeptical. When I speak about racial healing, I often hear the cynical retort, "You're not going to end racism." In the minds of some, it's as if racism were as natural as the wind.

It is not.

Racism is a system created by people. Perpetuated by people. And it can be dismantled by people, too. Just think about the stories I have told in this book, the accounts from communities everywhere. These stories, these people, show what healing can achieve.

So does my own story: the story of one little Black girl from the East Side of Detroit, not all that different from any other little Black girl. But this little girl benefited from love, and education, and the opportunities to pursue her passions and dreams—the very things so many others are denied, through no fault of their own—simply because they are ensnarled in systems and structures that people have created.

Systems and structures that people, together, can change.

Not long after I started as president and CEO of the Kellogg Foundation, I received a letter from one of my girlfriends from Cass Tech, now an educator overseeing several schools in Detroit. To celebrate Black History Month, she told me, one of her second-grade teachers had asked her class to draw and give a presentation about a Black leader of their choice. As I slid a second piece of paper out of the envelope, I realized with delight that one little girl in that class had drawn . . . me.

I was surprised, of course, and flattered, too. I have always tried to serve children above all, but it never occurred to me that one of them might put me in the same category as the Black American heroes I have revered since I was a girl. When this eight-year-old girl thought of a leader, the person she thought of didn't need to have "gravitas"—that undefined quality I'd been told was necessary to steward a philanthropy. For her, perhaps a leader just needed to have heart and to be working toward something worthwhile.

That cute stick-figure portrait of me provoked a deeper realization: The children are watching us. They see the need for healing. They know it's vital to their future. And they are judging us based on the work we are doing to realize the best version of our shared fate.

While we may struggle to carry the baggage of the past, young people come to this work with fresh eyes and fresh minds. They bring optimism and energy. They bring a new way of being in community that we haven't experienced because of limitations imposed by America's history and ideology of racial inequality.

All those years ago, W. K. Kellogg insisted that "one of the most beneficial services that could be bestowed upon civilization is to make the lives of little children happier, healthier, and more promising."[5] He was exactly right, and this unwavering commitment informs our work every single day. But one thing I've learned is that the inverse is true, too: We can benefit from the children, particularly from their abiding sense of hope—as I do from my grandchildren, Marley, Avery, and Charles Jr., for whom I wish a better, fairer, more just world.

Building that world together starts with conversation—honest, ongoing conversation. It starts with the hard truths that can provoke mutual understanding, mutual respect, and mutual recognition—with each of us seeing ourselves in each other. And it starts with the humility and the humanity to see that the path to repair and transformation runs through empathy and action.

This is how we heal.

ACKNOWLEDGMENTS

WRITING A BOOK and building a meaningful life and career are collaborative efforts. Nobody does these things alone. I am grateful for—blessed by—the love and support of so many.

Given the focus of the journey I've shared, I want to start by thanking the movement of racial healing practitioners and local leaders, including many grantees and partners, who are committed to building relationships, bringing people together, and making transformational change possible in communities, large and small, in every corner of our world. Healing is hard, often underappreciated work, but the work you do as your heart's calling is improving the lives of children and families today and for generations to come. Thank you for letting my colleagues and me learn from your triumphs and challenges, welcoming us into your healing circles, and motivating us every single day.

The W. K. Kellogg Foundation, my professional community and home for nearly four decades, has inspired and energized me, beginning with our founder. Where some in his position might have preserved wealth for their own children and grandchildren, Mr. Kellogg insisted that his legacy benefit *all* children. His actions set a high bar for generosity, integrity, and impact—a standard to which I always have aspired.

Crucial to this mission were my many mentors, and during my time at the foundation I have benefited from three above all: Dr. Norm

Brown, Dr. Bill Richardson, and Dr. Gloria Smith. All, sadly, have passed on, but their legacies live within me and all of us at WKKF. Likewise, I am profoundly grateful for all the CEOs, board members, and leadership team colleagues who came before me and whom I have been honored to serve alongside. The Kellogg Foundation would not be the institution it is today without everything you have given to it.

Throughout my career, I have treasured my working relationships across our institution and across the decades. To my colleagues: Thank you for your extraordinary advocacy on behalf of children, families, and communities. It has been a privilege and a joy to serve the mission of this institution that we love, together. In our work to promote racial healing and racial equity, community engagement, and leadership, you have been a model of solidarity and allyship—and in our work beyond, you have been a model for twenty-first-century philanthropy. I will forever cherish the partnerships and friendships that have enriched our days and enhanced our impact.

Capturing a life's journey is no easy task, especially when drawing from decades of memory and history—and when exploring complex, thorny topics. This book would not exist without the many people who gave their time and shared their experiences and expertise: My sisters Rita Fay Hicks and Brenda Montgomery Williams; my husband, Avery Tabron; my son Justin Talley; my high school friends (members of "The Gang," or as our parents called us, "a bunch of loud, cackling hens") Michelle Coleman, Dr. Tracy Joshua, Sharon Norris-Shelton, and Tiffany Taylor Tait; my college friends Cheryl Cook and Susie Gibson; and my current and former colleagues Dr. Tyrone Baines, Annette Beecham, Roslyn Brock, Laura Burr, Dr. Gail Christopher, Dr. Arelis Diaz, Stephanie Dukes, Janet Evans, Dianna Langenburg, Dr. Paul Martinez, Dr. Marvin McKinney, Leslie Murphy, Dr. Carla D. Thompson Payton, Dr. Icela Pelayo, Carlos Rangel, Dr. Barbara Sabol, Alicia Shaver, Annie Sherzer, Sterling Speirn, Joe Stewart, Ska-xjeing-ga/Vicky Stott, Dr. Henrie Treadwell, Howard Walters,

Dr. Alandra Washington, Kahlil Williams, and Don Williamson. Special thanks to Barbara Sabol's daughter, Frankie Foster-Davis, for her patience and tech support.

My special gratitude to the foundation's inspired communications team, which shepherded this project from start to finish, particularly Michael Murphy, Neil Sroka, and Kathy Reincke; to the talented team at West Wing Writers, Annie Farber, Caleb Gibson, Jonas Kieffer, Abby White, and Brianna Willis, who brought this story alive with invaluable support from collaborator A.J. Wilson; and to the outstanding professionals at Disruption Books, Kris Pauls, Janet Potter, and Alli Shapiro, who helped me navigate the complexities of publishing.

At the heart of everything in my life and story is family. Herbert and Mary Louise Montgomery were the first leaders I knew, and to this day, I count them among the strongest. They uprooted their own lives, met adversity with grace, and worked for decades so that my siblings and I would enjoy more and better opportunities. "If at first you don't succeed, try, try again!" Thank you, Mom and Dad.

No less important, our parents taught me and my nine brothers and sisters to love and support each other. That lesson has never wavered through the decades. Avaloyne, Herbert Jr., Sylvester, Louis, Marian, Dorothy, Gregory, Rita, Brenda, and I have always been among each other's most passionate cheerleaders. Thank you for making me laugh, lifting me up, and teaching me everything about everything—how to dance, how to write, how to dream, how to lead.

Of course, during the past sixteen years (and counting), I have also enjoyed the love and support of my husband, Avery Tabron. From championing my leadership at the foundation to helping raise the children and now grandchildren who are the light of our lives, Avery has been by my side at every step, all while building his own successful and fulfilling career. Thank you for our life, my love.

To my sons, Justin and Jordan, I'm so proud of what you have become. As young boys and now men of color, I sheltered you, just as

I had been sheltered, from the brutal reality of the risks you faced in a racist world. You were naive and didn't believe that anything would block the path to your dreams. You persevered, you overcame obstacles, and you actually listened to the wise counsel of your parents, Julius, Avery, and me. And for your commitment and hard work, the promise of your pursuit is in front of you. To my stepdaughters, Lauren and Kalynn; and three grandchildren, Marley, Avery, and Charles Jr., it's hard to imagine my life being what it is today without you. Thank you for teaching me so much and bringing into my life the joy, pride, love, and hope that every parent and community deserves to have in the generations that follow them.

I have always believed that we—all of us—stand on the shoulders of giants. To my family, on whose shoulders I stand, I dedicate this book.

ABOUT THE AUTHOR

L A JUNE MONTGOMERY TABRON is both the first woman and
the first African American to serve as president and CEO of
the W. K. Kellogg Foundation, one of the largest philanthropic foundations in the world. For more than twenty years, La June has been a
leader in the foundation's racial equity work, including its landmark
commitment to Truth, Racial Healing, and Transformation.

La June joined the foundation in 1987 and has served in a variety
of roles across the organization, including chief operating officer and
chief financial officer. Starting in 2011, she led the foundation's place-
based grant-making in Mississippi and New Orleans, and in 2013,
she launched a significant effort to help set young males of color on
the path to success.

A committed community and civic leader, La June is a member of
the Kalamazoo Chapter of The Links, Incorporated. She also serves
on the boards of Battle Creek Community Health Partners, Bronson
Healthcare Group, Kellanova, the Descendants Truth & Reconciliation Foundation, the Michigan Economic Development Corporation
(MEDC), the Upjohn Institute, the Detroit Regional Partnership, and
the Teachers Insurance and Annuity Association of America-College
Retirement Equities Fund (TIAA). She also chairs the W. K. Kellogg
Foundation Trust.

An international thought leader, La June has appeared at and participated in discussion on stages around the world, such as the Aspen Ideas Festival, the Clinton Global Initiative, the ESSENCE Festival of Culture, and the World Economic Forum.

La June has also received many accolades, including the 2020 Bynum Tudor Fellowship at Kellogg College in Oxford, England, and the 2022 Louis E. Martin Great American Award, the highest honor granted by the Joint Center for Political and Economic Studies. In 2023, *Inside Philanthropy* included her in its list of the 50 Most Powerful Women in US Philanthropy. The same year, *The New York Times* named her a Groundbreaker at its annual DealBook Summit, while in 2024, *Worth* magazine named her to its list of 100 Groundbreaking Women and *Forbes* named her to its 50 Over 50 list.

ABOUT THE W. K. KELLOGG FOUNDATION

THE W. K. KELLOGG FOUNDATION exists to support thriving children, working families, and equitable communities. Created in 1930 by breakfast cereal innovator and entrepreneur Will Keith Kellogg, the foundation ranks among the largest philanthropic entities in the world.

Guided by the belief that all children should enjoy an equal opportunity to thrive, the foundation works in partnership with communities to create conditions to ensure that every child can realize their full potential in school, work, and life.

The foundation works throughout the United States, internationally, and with sovereign tribes. In carrying out its mission, the foundation pays special attention to priority places where it has made generational commitments to children, families, and communities including Michigan, Mississippi, New Mexico, and Louisiana in the United States, as well as Mexico and Haiti.

In 2017, the foundation established the National Day of Racial Healing as part of its work toward Truth, Racial Healing, and Transformation. Every January, on the day after Martin Luther King Jr. Day, communities come together to discuss how we can challenge our attitudes and assumptions about people who are different from us, how we can heal from the effects of racism, and how we can inspire collective action toward racial equity.

Visit www.dayofracialhealing.org to find out how to start and sustain these vital conversations with family, friends, and colleagues. If you'd like to learn more about the W. K. Kellogg Foundation, visit www.wkkf.org.

GETTING STARTED WITH RACIAL HEALING

DEAR READER,

If this book does one thing, I hope it inspires you to pursue racial healing in your own community—be it in your home, a neighborhood, a town, a workplace, a school, a place of worship, an affinity group, or any other place where people come together. As these pages make clear, any and every community can benefit from racial healing.

To help you start this journey, I have included an excerpt below from the foundation's *Racial Healing Conversation Guide*. By now, you should find this material familiar—and that's by design. This is the same essential process being used to transform communities around the world.

As you would expect from such a broad global movement, the *Conversation Guide* is just one of dozens, if not hundreds, of terrific racial healing resources out there. When you are ready to learn more, I recommend perusing the following:

- Dr. Gail Christopher's book *Rx Racial Healing*, published by the American Association of Colleges & Universities in 2022 and available wherever books are sold.

- The National Day of Racial Healing website, www.dayof-racialhealing.org, which includes the full *Racial Healing Conversation Guide* as well as suggestions for hosting or participating in a National Day event.

Good luck in your journey toward racial healing. I hope you will find it as transformative as I have.

Sincerely,
La June

RACIAL HEALING
CONVERSATION GUIDE:
AN EXCERPT

CREATING A BRAVE SPACE involves a number of steps. You may want to reach out to friends and colleagues who have facilitated meaningful conversations. It may also be useful to explore online resources. But here are some basic suggestions.

Before you begin, you may want to have (or ask participants to have) refreshments available. Encourage people to introduce themselves to one another. From there, follow these five steps:

1. **Reinforce the Purpose.** This first conversation should be to explore, to listen, and to learn from each other. As facilitator, you should steer participants away from blaming or belittling statements. Participants do not need to all agree or find an antidote to racism.

2. **Set Agreements.** Encourage dialogue, mutual respect, and deep listening to what fellow participants share. Post these agreements—such as "Practice Active Listening" and "Don't Interrupt"—in a visible place in your meeting room or as your virtual background.

- Encourage participants to be relaxed and comfortable with one another, especially as differences in beliefs and experiences emerge. A key for successful discussion is to be interested and deeply listen to what fellow participants have experienced, to hear what they think.

- Consider saying, "I've never thought of that before—could you explain why you think that?" rather than "I don't believe that; it's never happened to me."

- Recognize that people with good intentions misspeak or make statements that can hurt or offend. Letting individuals know how their words affect you or might be misunderstood is useful, but ascribing intent can be counterproductive.

  › Consider saying, "I feel frustrated (or I feel disrespected) when people say . . . because . . ." rather than "That pisses me off; that's such a stupid (or racist) thing to say."

- Establish strategies for everyone to participate and to be heard. For instance, you might invite quieter participants to share their thoughts and/or questions, and you might actively encourage more talkative guests to give space for other voices. (Perhaps include use of something like a talking stick or a virtual talking stick.)

- Announce a strategy for brief "breather breaks" or for "hitting the restart button" if the conversation veers into spaces that are too conflicted or unproductive. Select discussion moderator(s)—folks whom everyone will acknowledge and respect—who will be responsible for helping everyone abide by the ground rules.

3. **Open the Conversation.** Begin with a conversation starter to help everyone get to know one another. Begin with one or two of the following prompts:

   • Tell about a place that makes you feel good.

   • Tell a story about something that you have lost or found.

   • Tell a story about a surprise.

   • Tell a story about a time you were generous.

   • Tell a story about a time you got angry.

   • Tell about someone you miss.

   • Tell something about how you played as a child.

4. **Deepen the Conversation.** Once everyone is more comfortable, get serious and deepen the conversation using one or more of the following prompts:

   • How often do you think about your racial or ethnic identity?

   • What aspect of your racial or ethnic identity makes you the proudest?

   • In what ways does being African American/Black/ Latino/Hispanic/American Indian/Alaska Native/Asian/ Pacific Islander/White impact your personal life? Your professional life?

   • Have you ever experienced a situation where your racial or ethnic identity seemed to contribute to a problem or an uncomfortable situation?

   • Does racial or ethnic identity enter in your process of making important or daily decisions? If so, how?

- Have you ever felt "different" in a group setting because of your race/ethnicity? How did this affect you? How often/ deeply do you interact with people of a different racial/ethnic identity other than your own? What is the nature of these relationships and interactions?

- Have you ever witnessed someone being treated unfairly because of their racial or ethnic identity? If so, how did you respond? How did it make you feel? What would you do differently today?

After two or three people have shared, ask other participants to reflect on what they've heard and share what they related to or what stood out to them, without blaming, shaming, or rescuing. Then ask a few more people to share. Repeat the process.

5. **Bring the Conversation to a Close.** As you reach a point where you feel it is time to close the conversation, consider doing any of the following:

- Extend gratitude to everyone for their courage and willingness to participate.

- Share how this experience impacted you as the host, and offer space for participants to share how the conversation impacted them. This can be as simple as sharing one word to summarize their feelings about the experience.

- Encourage guests to share an appreciation for the group process or for someone in the group.

- Encourage group members to follow up with someone from the conversation for deeper dialogue to continue learning and personal discovery.

- Ask people to share what they learned about themselves or their one takeaway from the conversation.

- Inquire whether there are any actions people are inspired to take as a result of the conversation.

- Schedule another conversation?

REMEMBER . . .

Racial healing is an ongoing process, supportive of wholeness in individuals, communities, and societies. It benefits all people because, regardless of background, we live in and are impacted by the narratives and conditions present throughout this increasingly interconnected world. This process provides opportunities to acknowledge the tremendous damage inflicted by individual and systemic racism. When we choose to ground ourselves in respectful truth and empathy and orient our efforts toward racial equity, we give ourselves an incredibly restorative opportunity—an opportunity to affirm the inherent value of all people.

Thank you for taking this journey toward truth, racial healing, and community transformation.

"I AM FROM" POEM

BY LA JUNE MONTGOMERY TABRON

First delivered at WKKF New Mexico Grantee Convening, July 22–23, 2014

I am from the D, from the Motown sound
and big, fancy cars.
You know, diamond in the back, sunroof top,
Digging the scene with a gangster lean . . .

I am from the big white house on Cadillac Boulevard,
where there was much laughter and many visitors.
I am from honeysuckle bushes and beautiful lawns,
where neighbors competed to grow the greenest grass.

I am from singing and dancing and listening to music.
From ten children and two loving parents,
from playing school, family chores, and watching *Soul Train*
on Saturdays.

I am from "Do as you are told,"
and "Do unto others as you would wish them to do unto you,"
with the reminder that "It's all about love."

I am from Detroit, Michigan, by way of Clarksdale, Mississippi,
from fried chicken and banana pudding,
from my dad, Herbert Montgomery,
who knew that opportunities awaited in the North,
where he landed employment at Chrysler Corporation,
and worked there for twenty-five years.

I am from family dinners at Christmastime that appeared to look
very similar year after year, as you flip through the family photo album.

And I am from the pictures that I have added,
of my husband and four children,
as we create holiday traditions for the future.

NOTES

INTRODUCTION

1   I have a dream: Martin Luther King Jr., "Speech at the Great March on Detroit" (speech, Detroit, June 23, 1963), Mesa Arts Center, https://www.mesaartscenter.com/download.php/engagement/jazz-a-to-z/resources/archive/2016-2017/teacher-resources/speech-at-the-great-march-detroit.

2   In response to this incident, he later wrote: "W. K. Kellogg," Philanthropy Roundtable, https://www.philanthropyroundtable.org/hall-of-fame/w-k-kellogg/.

3   Its roots reach back: Julena Jumbe Gabagambi, "A Comparative Analysis of Restorative Justice Practices in Africa," Hauser Global Law School Program, October 2018, https://www.nyulawglobal.org/globalex/Restorative_Justice_Africa.html#_3._Restorative_Justice; Beverly Jacobs, "Indigenous Justice in Oceania and North America," *Oxford Research Encyclopedia of Criminology*, August 31, 2021, https://oxfordre.com/criminology/display/10.1093/acrefore/9780190264079.001.0001/acrefore-9780190264079-e-627.

4   I will show you how my ancestors: Walker Bray, "Preservation and Public History in Mound Bayou, Mississippi" (undergraduate thesis, Sally McDonnell Barksdale Honors College, 2022), https://egrove.olemiss.edu/cgi/viewcontent.cgi?article=3537&context=hon_thesis.

5   Healing is a necessary stage: Frederick Douglass, "A Composite Nation" (speech, Boston, MA, 1869), Library of Congress, https://www.loc.gov/resource/mss11879.22017/?sp=8&st=image.

CHAPTER 1

1   By the mid-1980s: Isabel Wilkerson, "Urban Homicide Rates in US Up Sharply in 1986," *New York Times*, January 15, 1987, https://www.nytimes.com/1987/01/15/us/urban-homicide-rates-in-us-up-sharply-in-1986.html.

2   In 2013, it earned a dubious distinction: Brad Plumer, "Detroit Isn't Alone. The US Cities That Have Gone Bankrupt, in One Map," *Washington Post*, July 18, 2013, https://www.washingtonpost.com/news/wonk/wp/2013/07/18/detroit-isnt-alone-the-u-s-cities-that-have-gone-bankrupt-in-one-map/.

3   Over the course of the Great Migration: Craig Wesley Carpenter, "Detroit," Redlining in Michigan, https://www.canr.msu.edu/redlining/detroit.

4   White Detroiters: "City Snapshots: Detroit," Othering & Belonging Institute, accessed May 6, 2024, https://belonging.berkeley.edu/city-snapshot-detroit#:~:text=In%20the%20two%20years%20following,to%20a%20majority%20Black%20city.

5   Despite this, the Detroit Police Department: History.com Editors, "1967 Detroit Riots," History.com, September 27, 2017, https://www.history.com/topics/1960s/1967-detroit-riots.

6   By 1967, the entire force: Detroit Historical Society, "Uprising of 1967," Encyclopedia of Detroit, https://detroithistorical.org/learn/encyclopedia-of-detroit/uprising-1967.

7   Tellingly, the injuries suffered: Heather Ann Thompson, "Rethinking the Politics of White Flight in the Postwar City Detroit, 1945-1980," *Journal of Urban History* 25, no. 2 (January 1999), https://lsa.umich.edu/sid/detroiters-speak/detroiters-speak-archive/_jcr_content/par/download_2135375176/file.res/Journal%20of%20Urban%20History%20by%20Heather%20Thompson.

8   Newspaper accounts revealed: Lorraine Boissoneault, "Understanding Detroit's 1967 Upheaval 50 Years Later," *Smithsonian*, July 26, 2017, https://www.smithsonianmag.com/history/understanding-detroits-1967-upheaval-50-years-later-180964212/.

9   But to paraphrase: Langston Hughes, "Harlem," Poetry Foundation, https://www.poetryfoundation.org/poems/46548/harlem.

10   The unrest came: My sister Rita Fay remembers that night differently: She doesn't think we took cover. This isn't an unusual discrepancy. With "memory amplification," trauma survivors often remember events as having been even more distressing than they were in real life. Yet the trauma is still real—and it lasts.

11   Stunned, my mother: Author interview with Rita Fay Hicks, August 29, 2023.

12   A 1930s Federal Housing Administration manual, "FDR and Housing Legislation," Franklin D. Roosevelt Presidential Library and Museum, accessed May 6, 2024, https://www.fdrlibrary.org/housing#:~:text=As%20the%20Manual%20noted%2C%20%E2%80%9Cincompatible,generational%20wealth%20through%20home%20ownership.

13   They moved to Harper Woods: US Census Bureau, *1970 Census of Population: Vol. I Characteristics of the Population Part 24, Michigan* (Washington: Government Printing Office, 1973).

14   In 1967, that figure doubled: Bill McGraw, "Detroit 67: The Deep Scars the City Still Feels Today," *Detroit Free Press*, July 29, 2017, https://www.freep.com/story/news/detroitriot/2017/07/30/detroit-67-riot-race/512977001/.

15   In the aftermath: IBW21, "Worlds of Color by W. E. B. Du Bois (April 1925)," Institute of the Black World 21st Century, March 15, 2022, https://ibw21.org/editors-choice/worlds-of-color-by-w-e-b-du-bois-april-1925/.

16   We sought to embody: James Brown, "Say It Loud – I'm Black and I'm Proud (Pts. 1 & 2)," Universal Music Group, posted December 13, 2018, YouTube video, https://www.youtube.com/watch?v=fpLpqpniRi4.

17   Irene McCabe, a local resident: "A History of Busing in Metro Detroit," *Detroit News*, July 21, 2019, https://www.detroitnews.com/picture-gallery/news/local/oakland-county/2019/07/22/history-busing-segregation-metro-detroit/1791862001/.

18   Justice Thurgood Marshall, dissenting: Milliken v. Bradley, 418 U.S. 717 (1974).

19   The racial gap: "QuickFacts: Detroit, City, Michigan," US Census Bureau, July 2022, https://www.census.gov/quickfacts/fact/table/detroitcitymichigan,MI/PST045222; "Detroit Public Schools Community District's 2023 Graduation Rates Showcase Significant Post-Pandemic Recovery," Detroit Public Schools Community District, accessed May 6, 2024, https://www.detroitk12.org/site/default.aspx?PageType=3&DomainID=4&ModuleInstanceID=4585&ViewID=6446EE88-D30C-497E-9316-3F8874B3E108&RenderLoc=0&FlexDataID=87829&PageID=1.

20   In Grosse Pointe: "QuickFacts: Grosse Pointe city, Michigan," US Census Bureau, July 2023, https://
      www.census.gov/quickfacts/fact/table/grossepointecitymichigan/PST045223#PST045223; Scott
      Levin, "Michigan High School Graduation Rates Bounce Back: See Your School's Rate," Michigan
      Live, March 10, 2024, https://www.mlive.com/data/2024/03/michigan-high-school-graduation-rates-
      bounce-back-see-your-schools-rate.html.

21   After Barack Obama was elected: Daniel Schorr, "A New, 'Post-Racial' Political Era in America," NPR,
      January 28, 2008, https://www.npr.org/templates/story/story.php?storyId=18489466.

22   This misguided concept suggests: Simon Clark, "How White Supremacy Returned to Mainstream
      Politics," Center for American Progress, July 1, 2020, https://www.americanprogress.org/article/
      white-supremacy-returned-mainstream-politics/.

23   At the Unite the Right rally: Adam Gabbatt, "'Jews Will Not Replace Us': Vice Film Lays Bare
      Horror of Neo-Nazis in America," *The Guardian*, August 16, 2017, https://www.theguardian.com/
      us-news/2017/aug/16/charlottesville-neo-nazis-vice-news-hbo.

24   Again, White anxiety: Brandon Mulder, "Arkansas Residents Make a Case for Reparations 100 Years
      After the Elaine Massacre," *The American Prospect*, September 30, 2019, https://prospect.org/justice/
      arkansas-reparations-elaine-race-massacre/.

25   Greenwood was prosperous: Yuliya Parshina-Kottas et al., "What The Tulsa Race Massacre Destroyed,"
      The New York Times, May 24, 2021, https://www.nytimes.com/interactive/2021/05/24/us/tulsa-race-
      massacre.html.

26   A White mob descended: Parshina-Kottas et al., "What The Tulsa Race Massacre Destroyed."

27   A report by the United States Department of Justice: German Lopez, "What
      Did the Justice Department's Investigation into the Ferguson Police Department
      Find?," Vox, January 27, 2016, https://www.vox.com/2015/5/31/17937860/
      justice-department-ferguson-police-michael-brown-shooting.

28   Two in five have been stopped: "Poll: 7 in 10 Black Americans Say They Have Experienced
      Incidents of Discrimination or Police Mistreatment in Their Lifetime, Including Nearly Half
      Who Felt Their Lives Were in Danger," news release, KFF, June 18, 2020, https://www.kff.org/
      racial-equity-and-health-policy/press-release/poll-7-in-10-black-americans-say-they-have-
      experienced-incidents-of-discrimination-or-police-mistreatment-in-lifetime-including-nearly-half-
      who-felt-lives-were-in-danger/.

29   An uptick in prominent incidents: Alaska Advisory Committee to the U.S. Commission on Civil
      Rights, "Racism's Frontier: The Untold Story of Discrimination and Division in Alaska," April 1, 2002,
      https://www.usccr.gov/files/pubs/sac/ak0402/ch1.htm.

CHAPTER 2

1   Fewer than 2,000 were Black: The Office of Academic Affairs, "A Report to the Regents on Minority
      Recruitment, Enrollment, Retention and Graduation at The University of Michigan Fall, 1979," The
      University of Michigan, February 1980, https://ro.umich.edu/sites/default/files/reports/Historic-
      Minority/1979-1980.pdf.

2   The founding of dedicated spaces: "Asubuhi Minority Lounge," University of Michigan, accessed June
      18, 2024, https://housing.umich.edu/cultural-lounge/asubuhi-lounge/.

3   Until we destroy the idea: Heather McGhee, *The Sum of Us: What Racism Costs Everyone and How We
      Can Prosper Together* (London: One World, 2021), 15.

4   This businessman, Vikas Narula: Angela Davis, "Two Friends. One Stranger. And a Chance Encounter on a Sailboat," MPR News, August 19, 2020, https://www.mprnews.org/episode/2020/08/19/davis-two-friends-one-stranger-and-a-chance-encounter-on-a-sailboat.

5   "That's one person's opinion": Holly Bailey, "Derek Chauvin Defends Restraint of George Floyd in Newly Disclosed Body-cam Video, Saying He Was 'Probably on Something,'" *Washington Post*, March 31, 2021, https://www.washingtonpost.com/nation/2021/03/31/derek-chauvin-trial/.

6   The very layout: Front page, *New York Times*, New York print edition, August 25, 2014, https://archive.nytimes.com/www.nytimes.com/indexes/2014/08/25/todayspaper/index.html.

7   Because of this focus: Summer Harlow, "There's a Double Standard In How News Media Cover Liberal and Conservative Protests," *Washington Post*, January 13, 2021, https://www.washingtonpost.com/politics/2021/01/13/theres-double-standard-how-news-media-cover-liberal-conservative-protests/.

8   The media company Vox: German Lopez, "Media Coverage of Protests Sure Looks Different When Demonstrators Are White," Vox, January 4, 2016, https://www.vox.com/2016/1/3/10705610/oregon-terrorists-racism-race.

9   Black and Latinx suspects: Scott W. Duxbury et al., "Mental Illness, the Media, and the Moral Politics of Mass Violence: The Role of Race in Mass Shootings Coverage," *Journal of Research in Crime and Delinquency* 55, no. 6 (November 2018), https://journals.sagepub.com/doi/abs/10.1177/0022427818787225.

10 A 2019 study by scholars: Danielle K. Brown et al., "Protests, Media Coverage, and a Hierarchy of Social Struggle," *The International Journal of Press/Politics* 24, no. 4 (October 2019), https://journals.sagepub.com/doi/10.1177/1940161219853517.

11 The title of another study: Heather Yarrish, "White Protests, Black Riots: Racialized Representation in American Media," *Young Scholars in Writing* 16 (2019), https://youngscholarsinwriting.org/index.php/ysiw/article/view/271/295.

12 Or, as they put it: Matthew D. Lassiter and the Policing and Social Justice HistoryLab, "Detroit Under Fire: Police Violence, Crime Politics, and the Struggle for Racial Justice in the Civil Rights Era," University of Michigan Carceral State Project, 2021, https://policing.umhistorylabs.lsa.umich.edu/s/detroitunderfire/page/kerner-commission.

13 When the skin shown was Black: Jason Silverstein, "I Don't Feel Your Pain," Slate, June 27, 2013, https://slate.com/technology/2013/06/racial-empathy-gap-people-dont-perceive-pain-in-other-races.html.

14 The researchers behind a similar study: Sophie Trawalter et al., "Racial Bias in Perceptions of Others' Pain," *PLoS ONE* 7, no. 11 (November 2012), https://www.ncbi.nlm.nih.gov/pmc/articles/PMC3498378/.

15 In this latter study: Trawalter, "Racial Bias."

16 For example, on visits: Trevor Thompson et al., "White Patients Are More Likely Than Black Patients to be prescribed Opioids for Pain in US Emergency Departments. Here's Why It Matters," Fortune Well, October 29, 2023, https://fortune.com/well/2023/10/29/why-white-patients-prescribed-opioids-more-than-black-united-states-emergency-rooms/.

17 In 2016, the National Academy of Sciences: Joseph Losavio, "What Racism Costs Us All," *Finance & Development* (September 2020), https://www.imf.org/en/Publications/fandd/issues/2020/09/the-economic-cost-of-racism-losavio.

18 But over the years: Wilson Sim et al., "The Perspectives of Health Professionals and Patients on Racism in Healthcare: A Qualitative Systematic Review," *PLoS ONE* 16, no. 8 (August 2021), https://www.ncbi.nlm.nih.gov/pmc/articles/PMC8407537/.

19   But over the years: M.C. Smith, "Rates of Hip and Knee Joint Replacement Amongst Different Ethnic Groups in England: an Analysis of National Joint Registry Data," *Osteoarthritis and Cartilage* 25, no. 4 (April 2017), https://www.sciencedirect.com/science/article/pii/ S1063458417300432.

20   But over the years: Samantha M. Meints, "Racial and Ethnic Differences in the Experience and Treatment of Noncancer Pain," *Pain Management* 9, no. 3 (May 2019), https://www.ncbi.nlm .nih.gov/pmc/articles/PMC6587104/.

21   Teachers, for example: Patrick B. McGrady and John R. Reynolds, "Racial Mismatch in the Classroom: Beyond Black-white Differences," *Sociology of Education* 86, no. 1 (January 2013), https://journals.sagepub.com/doi/full/10.1177/0038040712444857#: ~:text=Thus%2C%20the%20generally%20accepted%20explanation,academic%20potential %20than%20white%20students.

22   Infrastructure problems that threaten: Erika M. Kitzmiller and Akira Drake Rodriguez, "The Link Between Educational Inequality And Infrastructure," *Washington Post*, August 6, 2021, https://www.washingtonpost.com/outlook/2021/08/06/school-buildings -black-neighborhoods-are-health-hazards-bad-learning/.

23   Native Hawaiian, Pacific Islander: "Infant Mortality and African Americans," US Department of Health and Human Services Office of Minority Health, accessed May 7, 2024, https://minorityhealth. hhs.gov/infant-mortality-and-african-americans#:~:text=How%20Does%20Infant%20Mortality%20 Affect,rate%20as%20non%2DHispanic%20whites.

24   During the COVID-19 pandemic: "Impact of Racism on our Nation's Health," Centers for Disease Control and Prevention, last modified August 16, 2023, https://www.cdc.gov/minorityhealth/racism- disparities/impact-of-racism.html.

25   During the COVID-19 pandemic: Wei Li, "Racial Disparities in COVID-19," Science in the News, October 24, 2020, https://sitn.hms.harvard.edu/flash/2020/racial-disparities-in-covid-19/.

26   Children of color: Olivia Sanchez and Meredith Kolodner, "Why White Students Are 250% More Likely to Graduate Than Black Students at Public Universities," *The Hechinger Report*, October 10, 2021, https://hechingerreport.org/%E2%80%8B%E2%80%8Bwhy-white -students-are-250-more-likely-to-graduate-than-black-students-at-public-universities/.

27   Children of color: Rakesh Kochhar and Stella Sechopoulos, "Black and Hispanic Americans, Those With Less Education Are More Likely to Fall Out of the Middle Class Each Year," Pew Research Center, May 10, 2022, https://www.pewresearch.org/short-reads/2022/ 05/10/black-and-hispanic-americans-those-with-less-education-are-more-likely-to-fall -out-of-the-middle-class-each-year/.

28   And they are much more likely: "Black Preschoolers Far More Likely to Be Suspended," Code Switch, NPR, March 21, 2014, https://www.npr.org/sections/codeswitch/2014/03/21/292456211/black- preschoolers-far-more-likely-to-be-suspended#:~:text=Across%20age%20groups%2C%20black%20 students,Native%20American%20girls%20are%20suspended.

29   In Hawai'i, Native Hawaiians: Annabelle Le Jeune, "How Hawai'i Is Ending Youth Incarceration After More Than a Century of Colonization," *Nonprofit Quarterly*, January 19, 2023, https://nonprofitquarterly.org/how-hawai%CA%BBi-is-ending-youth-incarceration-after -more-than-a-century-of-colonization/.

30   That same year: Alexi Jones and Wendy Sawyer, "Not Just 'A Few Bad Apples': US Police Kill Civilians at Much Higher Rates Than Other Countries," Prison Policy Initiative, June 5, 2020, https://www.prisonpolicy.org/blog/2020/06/05/policekillings/.

CHAPTER 3

1   Its grantees established: "Kellogg Makes Practical Nurse Education Grants to Five States," *American Journal of Nursing* 52, no. 1 (January 1952), https://journals.lww.com/ajnonline/citation/1952/01000/kellogg_makes_practical_nurse_education_grants_to.54.aspx.

2   Given this impressive theory: W. K. Kellogg, "The Life & Legacy of W. K. Kellogg," W. K. Kellogg Foundation, posted March 8, 2023, YouTube video, 8:20, https://youtu.be/ADW9yC_-9PQ?si=CvnzSFBC7u-TZLk9&t=500.

3   Reading about the foundation's: "Who We Are," W. K. Kellogg Foundation, accessed May 7, 2024, https://www.wkkf.org/who-we-are/.

4   At that time: Author name redacted, "Federal Research and Development Funding at Historically Black Colleges and Universities," Congressional Research Service, November 10, 2011, https://www.everycrsreport.com/files/20111110_RL34435_acbcccd5c0d382bec3cd87763ad8061e6945941c.pdf.

5   A White man born: "Norman Brown," Legacy.com, obituary, reprinted from *Kalamazoo Gazette*, September 27, 2012, https://obits.mlive.com/us/obituaries/kalamazoo/name/norman-brown-obituary?id=20406815.

6   A lack of diversity: Sylvia Ann Hewlet et al., "How Diversity Can Drive Innovation," *Harvard Business Review*, December 2013, https://hbr.org/2013/12/how-diversity-can-drive-innovation.

7   Decrying the notion: Students For Fair Admissions, Inc. v. President and Fellows of Harvard College, 600 U.S. 20-1199 (2023): 29, https://www.supremecourt.gov/opinions/22pdf/20-1199_hgdj.pdf.

8   "These trends increasingly encourage: Students v. President, 46.

9   "It will take longer: Students v. President. (Jackson, J., dissenting), 25.

10   Dr. Henrie Monteith Treadwell: Treadwell interview.

11   Dr. Tyrone Baines: Tyrone Baines, interview with the author, September 28, 2023.

12   Tyrone Baines continued: Marvin McKinney, interview with the author, October 6, 2023.

13   Gloria Smith hired: Barbara Sabol, interview with the author, September 19, 2023

14   A 2002 study found: Susan Hassmiller, "Turning Point: the Robert Wood Johnson Foundation's Effort to Revitalize Public Health at the State Level," *Journal of Public Health Management and Practice* 8, no. 1 (January 2002), https://pubmed.ncbi.nlm.nih.gov/11789031/.

15   Knowing how impossible it is: Joe Stewart, interview with the author, September 19, 2023.

16   Knowing how impossible it is: Joe Stewart, interview with the author, September 26, 2023.

17   That year, a new CEO, Sterling Speirn: Sterling Speirn, interview with the author, September 6, 2023.

18   Our commitment to anti-racism: Rock Cohen, "A Foundation Changes Course," Youth Today, October 1, 2008, https://youthtoday.org/2008/10/a-foundation-changes-course/.

CHAPTER 4

1   The doctors told Gail and her husband: Gail C. Christopher, *Rx Racial Healing: A Guide to Embracing Our Humanity* (Washington, DC: American Association of Colleges and Universities, 2022), 25–26.

2   This holistic understanding evolved: Christopher, *Rx Racial Healing*, 26–27.

3   She realized that most of the factors: Christopher, *Rx Racial Healing*, 27.

4   And just as stress poisons a body, Gail realized: Christopher, *Rx Racial Healing*, 28.

5   Discouraged, she soon switched: Gail C. Christopher, interview with the author, October 3, 2023

6   Tyrone and Joe held sessions: Joe Stewart, interview with the author, September 26, 2023.

7   I don't believe you: Joe Stewart, interview with the author, September 26, 2023.

8   Nothing good is likely to come from this: Stephan Thernstrom, "Kellogg's Bet on 'Racial Healing,'" *Wall Street Journal*, May 21, 2010, https://www.wsj.com/articles/SB1000142405274870331540457525 0643359879372.

9   And if we're going to address it: W. K. Kellogg Foundation, "Scholars Address Wide Impact of Unconscious Bias at America Healing Conference," news release, April 25, 2012, https://www.wkkf.org/news-and-media/article/2012/04/ scholars-address-wide-impact-of-unconscious-bias-at-america-healing-conference/.

10 Turning to potential remedies: Cheryl Staats, "Implicit Racial Bias and School Discipline Disparities," Kirwan Institute Special Report, May 2014, https://kirwaninstitute.osu.edu/sites/default/files/ documents/ki-ib-argument-piece03.pdf.

11 The study found: Ani Turner, "The Business Case For Racial Equity: A Strategy For Growth," *Altarum*, April 24, 2018, https://altarum.org/news-and-insights/business-case-racial-equity-strategy-growth.

12 By 2050, in fact, we could increase the GDP: Bureau of Economic Analysis, "Gross Domestic Product, 4th Quarter and Annual 2018 (third estimate); Corporate Profits, 4th Quarter and Annual 2018," news release, March 28, 2019, https://www.bea.gov/news/2019/ gross-domestic-product-4th-quarter-and-annual-2018-third-estimate-corporate-profits-4th.

13 By 2050, in fact, we could increase the GDP: "How Much Has the US Government Spent This Year?," US Treasury Fiscal Data, accessed May 8, 2024, https://fiscaldata.treasury.gov/americas-finance-guide/ federal-spending/.

14 For example, whenever Gail Christopher published: Gail Christopher, "US Truth, Racial Healing, and Transformation Funders' Briefing Program, January 19, 2021: Opening Remarks," *Health Equity* 5, no. 1 (September 2021), https://www.ncbi.nlm.nih.gov/pmc/articles/PMC8665781/.

15 He concluded: W. K. Kellogg Foundation, *W. K. Kellogg Foundation: The First Eleven Years* (Battle Creek, MI: The Trustees of the W. K. Kellogg Foundation, 1942).

16 When filing, the state-appointed city manager: "Timeline: A History of Detroit's Fiscal Problems," *Reuters*, December 10, 2014, https://www.reuters.com/article/idUSKBN0JO1YW/#:~:text=%2D%20 Detroit%20defaulted%20on%20more%20than,finances%20and%20%2418%20billion%20debt.

17 That was why he had told his staff: "Who We Are," Kellogg Foundation.

CHAPTER 5

1   By 2014, Battle Creek's population: Jessica Pizarek, "An Equity Profile of Battle Creek," PolicyLink and PERE, 2017, https://www.michigan.gov/-/media/Project/Websites/mdcr/racial-equity/equity-profile-battle-creek-region.pdf?rev=c1940dffd47247a0a833c3ebc06fabae.

2   In Battle Creek, these were the districts: "Explore Battle Creek, Michigan," Facing Whiteness, Columbia University, accessed May 8, 2024, https://www.facingwhiteness.incite.columbia.edu/ battlecreek-explore-2.

3   The report concluded: David A. Harris, "Driving While Black: Racial Profiling On Our Nation's Highways," American Civil Liberties Union, June 7, 1999, https://www.aclu.org/publications/driving-while-black-racial-profiling-our-nations-highways.

4   Mr. Kellogg had come to this same conclusion: W. K. Kellogg Foundation, First Eleven Years.

5   For example, commissions in Guatemala: Commission for Historical Clarification, "Truth Commission: Guatemala," United States Institute of Peace, February 1, 1997, https://www.usip.org/publications/1997/02/truth-commission-guatemala; Commission for Historical Clarification, "Truth Commission: Timor-Leste (East Timor)," United States Institute of Peace, February 7, 2002, https://www.usip.org/publications/2002/02/truth-commission-timor-leste-east-timor.

6   Many Native American tribes follow similar practices: Steve Yeong and Elizabeth Moore, "Circle Sentencing, Incarceration and Recidivism," Crime and Justice Bulletin 226 (April 2020), https://www.bocsar.nsw.gov.au/Pages/bocsar_publication/Pub_Summary/CJB/CJB226-Circle-Sentencing-Summary.aspx; Suvi Hynynen Lambson, Peacemaking Circles: Evaluating a Native American Restorative Justice Practice in a State Criminal Court Setting in Brooklyn (New York, NY: Center for Court Innovation, 2015), https://www.innovatingjustice.org/sites/default/files/documents/Peacemaking%20Circles%20Final.pdf; Julena Jumbe Gabagambi, "A Comparative Analysis of Restorative Justice Practices in Africa," GlobaLex, New York University, October 2018, https://www.nyulawglobal.org/globalex/Restorative_Justice_Africa.html#_3._Restorative_Justice.

7   The Center for Courage and Renewal: "Center for Courage & Renewal," accessed June 18, 2024, www.couragerenewal.org.

8   To quote the Reverend Alvin Herring: W. K. Kellogg Foundation, "Truth, Racial Healing, & Transformation Summit – Closing Video," YouTube, January 16, 2017, https://www.youtube.com/watch?v=xwtnanuRrrc&t=274s.

9   The foundation gave the Battle Creek Police Department a grant: Battle Creek Police Department, "Battle Creek Police Department 2014 Annual Report," Battle Creek Police Department, August 2015, https://www.battlecreekmi.gov/ArchiveCenter/ViewFile/Item/170.

10   Speaking at a Foundation event in 2021: Gail Christopher et al., "U.S. Truth, Racial Healing, and Transformation Funders' Briefing Program, January 19, 2021: Panel on Local Insights," Health Equity 5, no. 1 (September 2021), https://www.ncbi.nlm.nih.gov/pmc/articles/PMC8665781/.

11   Today, Selma is one of the poorest cities: Emmanuel Felton, "Selma Is Tired of Being Just a Symbol—It Wants Change," Washington Post, April 11, 2022, https://www.washingtonpost.com/nation/2022/04/11/selma-struggles-economic-justice/.

12   As she explained in an interview: Claretta Bellamy, "Selma's Black businesses build 'unity and community' nearly 60 years since Bloody Sunday," NBC News, January 11, 2023, https://www.nbcnews.com/video/selma-s-black-businesses-build-unity-and-community-nearly-60-years-since-bloody-sunday-159705157567.

13   Her colleagues in racial healing efforts: Claretta Bellamy, "Selma's Black businesses build 'unity and community' nearly 60 years since Bloody Sunday;" Kari Carlson, "Selma: Building on History to Change the Future," Every Child Thrives, W. K. Kellogg Foundation, January 13, 2023, https://everychildthrives.com/selma-building-on-history-to-change-the-future/.

14   One administrator at the University of Chicago: Scott Jaschik, "U Chicago to Freshmen: Don't Expect Safe Spaces," Inside Higher Ed, August 24, 2016, https://www.insidehighered.com/news/2016/08/25/u-chicago-warns-incoming-students-not-expect-safe-spaces-or-trigger-warnings.

15   But the report ends on a hopeful note: Jerry Hawkins et al., "A New Community Vision for Dallas," annual report, Dallas Truth, Racial Healing & Transformation, 2019, https://dallastrht.org/wp-content/uploads/2019/05/DTRHT-Report.pdf.

16   This invitation was a big deal: "About PERF," Police Executive Research Forum, accessed August 8, 2024, https://www.policeforum.org/about-us.

CHAPTER 6

1   We brought together more than 130 organizations: "National Day of Racial Healing – Jan. 17," W. K. Kellogg Foundation, January 6, 2017, https://www.wkkf.org/news-and-media/article/2017/01/national-day-of-racial-healing-jan-17/#:~:text=17,-Jan%206%2C%202017&text=The%20W.K.,of%20Racial%20Healing%20on%20Jan; Gail Christopher, "Truth, Racial Healing, and Transformation: Creating Public Sentiment," *Health Equity* 5, no. 1 (September 2021), https://www.ncbi.nlm.nih.gov/pmc/articles/PMC8665795/.

2   By 2020, the governors: W. K. Kellogg Foundation, "Racial Healing Takes Center Stage at Kennedy Center and Across the Country," *PR Newswire*, January 21, 2020, https://www.prnewswire.com/news-releases/racial-healing-takes-center-stage-at-kennedy-center-and-across-the-country-300990760.html.

3   Thirteen thousand of them: "National Day of Racial Healing," Propper Daley, accessed June 18, 2024, https://www.propperdaley.com/case-study/national-day-of-racial-healing/.

4   The day before our star-studded event: Benjamin Mueller, "When Was the First U.S. Covid Death? CDC Investigates 4 Early Cases," *The New York Times*, September 9, 2021, https://www.nytimes.com/2021/09/09/health/first-covid-deaths.html.

5   The White House declared Covid-19: Joseph R. Biden Jr., "Notice on the Continuation of the National Emergency Concerning the Coronavirus Disease 2019 (COVID-19) Pandemic," The White House, February 10, 2023, https://www.whitehouse.gov/briefing-room/presidential-actions/2023/02/10/notice-on-the-continuation-of-the-national-emergency-concerning-the-coronavirus-disease-2019-covid-19-pandemic-3/#:~:text=On%20March%2013%2C%202020%2C%20by,(COVID%2D19)%20pandemic.

6   And two: When the board speaks: "The Policy Governance® Model," John Carver's Policy Governance Model, last modified April 4, 2016, http://www.carvergovernance.com/model.htm.

7   Finally, building on my predecessor: Denver Frederick, "W. K. Kellogg Foundation CEO Shares Insights on Becoming an Anti-Racist Organization," The Business of Giving, December 28, 2022, https://denver-frederick.com/2022/12/28/w-k-kellogg-foundation-ceo-shares-insights-on-becoming-an-anti-racist-organization/.

8   Decades before, Mr. Kellogg had instructed us: "Who We Are," Kellogg Foundation.

9   Another study found: Maritza Vasquez Reyes, "The Disproportional Impact of COVID-19 on African Americans," *Health and Human Rights Journal* 22, no. 2 (December 2020): 299–307, https://www.ncbi.nlm.nih.gov/pmc/articles/PMC7762908/.

10 In the first year of the pandemic: Arielle Mitropoulos, "Children of Color Disproportionately Impacted by Severe COVID-19 and Related Illness, Data Reveals," *ABC News*, February 25, 2021, https://abcnews.go.com/Health/children-color-disproportionately-impacted-covid-19-data-reveals/story?id=76063845.

11 Low-income children: Reyes, "The Disproportional Impact."

12 Studies showed school districts: Kevin A. Gee et al., "Educational Impacts of the COVID-19 Pandemic in the United States: Inequities by Race, Ethnicity, and Socioeconomic Status," *Current Opinion in Psychology* 52 (August 2023), https://www.sciencedirect.com/science/article/pii/S2352250X2300088X#:~:text=Also%2C%20disparities%20in%20math%20between,gains%20in%20math%20and%20reading.

13 At least 250,000 children: COVID-19 Response Team, "COVID-19-Associated Orphanhood and Caregiver Death in the United States," Imperial College London, accessed May 9, 2024, https://imperialcollegelondon.github.io/orphanhood_USA/.

14 They are more likely to live: Hiroko Tabuchi and Nadja Popovich, "People of Color Breathe More Hazardous Air. The Sources Are Everywhere," *The New York Times*, April 28, 2021, https://www.nytimes.com/2021/04/28/climate/air-pollution-minorities.html.

15   As a result of all this, non-White people: Michael Esposito et al., "Aggressive Policing, Health, and Health Equity," *Health Affairs*, April 30, 2021, https://www.healthaffairs.org/do/10.1377/ hpb20210412.997570/.

16   Add to this an understandable tendency to distrust: Darcell P. Scharff et al., "More than Tuskegee: Understanding Mistrust about Research Participation," *Journal of Health Care for the Poor and Underserved* 21, no. 3 (August 1010): 879–897, https://www.ncbi.nlm.nih.gov/pmc/articles/ PMC4354806/#:~:text=Mistrust%20stems%20from%20historical%20events,research%20 participation%20or%20socioeconomic%20status; "The Untreated Syphilis Study at Tuskegee Timeline," Centers for Disease Control and Prevention, last modified December 5, 2022, https://www.cdc.gov/ tuskegee/timeline.htm.

17   Similar figures haunted other communities of color: Amy Goldstein and Emily Guskin, "Almost One-Third of Black Americans Know Someone Who Died of COVID-19, Survey Shows," *Washington Post*, June 26, 2020, https://www.washingtonpost.com/health/ almost-one-third-of-black-americans-know-someone-who-died-of-covid-19-survey- shows/2020/06/25/3ec1d4b2-b563-11ea-aca5-ebb63d27e1ff_story.html.

18   The death toll emptied pews: Martina Guzmán, "On Easter Weekend, Detroit Churches Mourn the COVID-19 Dead from Afar," *Bridge Michigan*, April 11, 2020, https://www.bridgemi.com/ urban-affairs/easter-weekend-detroit-churches-mourn-covid-19-dead-afar.

19   Reverend Sheffield's words rang true: Rachel Treisman, "As Cases Rise Fast, Mississippi Governor Mandates Masks and Delays Start of School," NPR, August 4, 2020, https://www.npr.org/sections/coronavirus-live-updates/2020/08/04/899167480/ as-cases-rise-fast-mississippi-governor-mandates-masks-and-delays-start-of-schoo.

20   Mobile Covid-19 treatment vans: Ruth Cummins, "UMMC takes COVID-19 Vaccine on the road," University of Mississippi Medical Center, October 18, 2021, https://www.umc.edu/news/News_ Articles/2021/10/Grenada-mobile-vaccine-clinic.html.

21   For example, many Native American tribes: Randall Akee, "How COVID-19 Is Impacting Indigenous Peoples in the US," *NewsHour*, PBS, May 13, 2020, https://www.pbs.org/newshour/nation/ how-covid-19-is-impacting-indigenous-peoples-in-the-u-s.

22   Within six weeks of its creation: "In One Month, STOP AAPI HATE Receives Almost 1,500 Incident Reports of Verbal Harassment, Shunning, and Physical Assaults," Asian Pacific Policy and Planning Council and Chinese for Affirmative Action, joint news release, April 24, 2020, https://www. asianpacificpolicyandplanningcouncil.org/wp-content/uploads/Press_Release_4_23_20.pdf.

23   By January 2023, nearly four in ten Chinese Americans: Neil G. Ruiz et al., "Discrimination Experiences Shape Most Asian Americans' Lives: Methodology: 2022–23 survey of Asian Americans," Pew Research Center, November 30, 2023, https://www.pewresearch.org/race-ethnicity/2023/11/30/ methodology-2022-23-survey-of-asian-americans/.

24   This discrimination also upended: Justin T. Huang, "The Cost of Anti-Asian Racism During the COVID-19 Pandemic," *Nature Human Behavior* 7 (May 2023): 682–695, https://www.nature.com/ articles/s41562-022-01493-6.

25   In doing so, they increased: Allison L. Skinner-Dorkenoo et al., "Highlighting COVID-19 Racial Disparities Can Reduce Support for Safety Precautions Among White US Residents," *Social Science & Medicine* 301 (May 2022), https://www.sciencedirect.com/science/article/pii/S027795362200257X

26   By 2022, death rates among White people matched: David Leonhardt, "Covid and Race," *The New York Times*, June 9, 2022, https://www.nytimes.com/2022/06/09/briefing/covid-race-deaths-america.html.

27   The University of Georgia team found: Skinner-Dorkenoo et al., "Highlighting COVID-19 racial disparities."

28 An independent analysis showed: Roudabeh Kishi and Sam Jones, "Demonstrations and Political Violence in America: New Data for Summer 2020," Armed Conflict Location & Event Data Project, September 3, 2020, https://acleddata.com/2020/09/03/demonstrations-political-violence-in-america-new-data-for-summer-2020/.

29 As early as June 12, a Pew poll revealed: Amy Mitchell et al., "Majorities of Americans Say News Coverage of George Floyd Protests Has Been Good, Trump's Public Message Wrong," Pew Research Center, June 12, 2020, https://www.pewresearch.org/journalism/2020/06/12/majorities-of-americans-say-news-coverage-of-george-floyd-protests-has-been-good-trumps-public-message-wrong/.

30 Official counts soon confirmed my feeling: Dana R. Fisher, "The Diversity of the Recent Black Lives Matter Protests is a Good Sign for Racial Equity," Brookings Institution, July 8, 2020, https://www.brookings.edu/articles/the-diversity-of-the-recent-black-lives-matter-protests-is-a-good-sign-for-racial-equity/.

31 Pew reported: Kim Parker et al., "Amid Protests, Majorities Across Racial and Ethnic Groups Express Support for Black Lives Matter Movement," Pew Research Center, June 12, 2020, https://www.pewresearch.org/social-trends/2020/06/12/amid-protests-majorities-across-racial-and-ethnic-groups-express-support-for-the-black-lives-matter-movement/#most-americans-say-theyve-had-conversations-about-race-or-racial-equality-in-the-last-month.

32 As McKinsey data reveals: Sundiatu Dixon-Fyle, "Diversity wins: How inclusion matters," McKinsey, May 19, 2020, https://www.mckinsey.com/featured-insights/diversity-and-inclusion/diversity-wins-how-inclusion-matters.

33 For more on this: "The Business Case for Racial Equity: A Strategy for Growth," W. K. Kellogg Foundation, accessed June 18, 2024, https://www.businesscaseforracialequity.org/.

34 According to the Nonprofit Finance Fund: Ines Marino-Torres and Avichai Scher, "COVID-19 & Cash Reserves: How Government Funding Practices Left Nonprofits Unprepared," National Finance Fund, June 15, 2020, https://nff.org/blog/covid-19-government-funding-nonprofits-unprepared.

35 With the support of the foundation: Alana Tomasita Martínez Moriarty, "Providing energy with an Indigenous lens: Q&A with Navajo Power co-founder Brett Isaac," Every Child Thrives, April 7, 2023, https://everychildthrives.com/providing-energy-with-an-indigenous-lens/.

36 Among other things, when children did go to school: Tribal Home Visiting Program, "Taos Pueblo," Administration for Children & Families, accessed May 9, 2024, https://www.acf.hhs.gov/sites/default/files/documents/ecd/taos_pueblo_profile.pdf.

37 As Bettina shared: "New Mexico: A Journey of Education, Culture, and Equity," W. K. Kellogg Foundation, YouTube, August 10, 2023, https://www.youtube.com/watch?v=adT3Z_psPpg&ab_channel=W.K.KelloggFoundation&themeRefresh=1.

38 City and state officials had brushed aside: Merrit Kennedy, "Lead-Laced Water in Flint: A Step-By-Step Look at the Makings of a Crisis," NPR, April 20, 2016, https://www.npr.org/sections/thetwo-way/2016/04/20/465545378/lead-laced-water-in-flint-a-step-by-step-look-at-the-makings-of-a-crisis.

39 During March 2020, the city's Black residents: Elisse Ramey, "Flint Eliminates COVID-19 Disparity Among African Americans," ABC 12, November 14, 2020, https://www.abc12.com/news/health/flint-eliminates-covid-19-disparity-among-african-americans/article_08149e22-234b-53fe-bad7-7a0b8d4209ad.html; "Flint Eliminates COVID-19 Disparity Among African Americans," Michigan State University, last accessed June 18, 2024, https://mph.chm.msu.edu/news-items/covid-19/flint-and-covid-19/386-flint-eliminates-covid-19-disparity-among-african-americans.

40 The following month: Edwin Rios, "How Flint Closed the Gap Between Black and White Suffering Under COVID," Mother Jones, September/October 2021, https://www.motherjones.com/politics/2021/07/how-flint-closed-the-gap-between-black-and-white-suffering-under-covid/.

41   By June 2020, Genesee County: Leonard N. Fleming, "COVID-19 Compounds Flint's Woes After Contaminated Water Crisis," *Detroit News*, June 2, 2020, https://www.detroitnews.com/story/news/local/michigan/2020/06/02/covid-19-compounds-flints-woes-after-contaminated-water-crisis/5221851002/.

42   More than one in eight lacked toilets: Dan Levy, "The Flint Water Crisis: Systemic Racism Through the Lens of Flint," report of the Michigan Civil Rights Commission, February 17, 2017, https://www.michigan.gov/-/media/Project/Websites/mdcr/mcrc/reports/2017/flint-crisis-report-edited.pdf?rev=4601519b3af345cfb9d468ae6ece9141.

43   By labeling neighborhoods of color: Craig Wesley Carpenter, "Flint," Redlining in Michigan, Michigan State University, accessed May 9, 2024, https://www.canr.msu.edu/redlining/flint#:~:text=The%20federal%20government%20redlined%20Flint,even%20near%20residents%20of%20color.

44   *Flint Journal*, February 8, 1963.

45   For at least 12 Flint residents: "Flint Water Prosecution Team Response to Michigan Supreme Court's Decision on the Felony Flint Water Crisis Charges," Michigan Department of Attorney General, news release, September 20, 2023, https://www.michigan.gov/ag/news/press-releases/2023/09/20/flint-water-prosecution-team-response-to-michigan-supreme-court-decision-on-the-felony-charges.

46   Isaiah Oliver summed up: Isaiah M. Oliver, "What if all our children could live in a just, equitable world?", Medium, January 17, 2020, https://cfgf.medium.com/by-isaiah-m-oliver-1d1cd9ff29bf.

47   On May 1: Khushbu Shah, "For vulnerable black communities, the pandemic is a 'crisis on top of a crisis,'" Vox, March 27, 2020, https://www.vox.com/2020/3/27/21196983/coronavirus-black-communities-flint.

48   These included economic barriers: Michigan Coronavirus Racial Disparities Task Force, "Interim Report," Michigan Department of Health and Human Services, November 2020, https://www.michigan.gov/mdhhs/-/media/Project/Websites/coronavirus/Folder33/interim_report_final_mar_2021.pdf?rev=1d9013b1dff1465e8bb3aaa2dcb1bb18&hash=C5323440CE684343D92B49519640FE15.

49   Black residents of Flint represented: Ramey, "Flint Eliminates COVID-19 Disparity."

50   Police used tear gas: Gus Burns, "Detroit George Floyd police brutality protest turns violent as police fire tear gas, rubber bullets," MLive, May 31, 2020, https://www.mlive.com/public-interest/2020/05/detroit-george-floyd-police-brutality-protest-turns-violent-as-police-fire-tear-gas-rubber-bullets.html.

51   A video shows Swanson: Mariel Padilla, "Michigan Sheriff Took Off His Helmet and Marched With Protesters," *The New York Times*, May 31, 2020, https://www.nytimes.com/2020/05/31/us/flint-sheriff-protestors-camden-police-ferguson.html.

52   He described Officer Derek Chauvin: Mariel Padilla, "Michigan Sheriff Took Off His Helmet and Marched With Protesters."

CHAPTER 7

1   In Kalamazoo County specifically: Mark Wedel, "Kalamazoo's Systemic Inequities in Housing and Efforts to Correct Them," *Southwest Michigan's Second Wave*, June 18, 2020, https://www.secondwavemedia.com/southwest-michigan/features/Kalamazoo-s-systemic-inequities-in-housing-and-efforts-to-correct-them-061820.aspx.

2   When landlords make a policy: Nichole Nelson, "Tenant Screening Systems Are Unfair to Black and Brown People. Here's What Our Government Should Do About It," National Community Reinvestment Coalition, June 27, 2023, https://ncrc.org/tenant-screening-systems-are-unfair-to-black-and-brown-people-heres-what-our-government-should-do-about-it/#:~:text=Although%20denying%20someone%20housing%20based,practice%20still%20generates%20discriminatory%20effects.

3   And of those who said: "Art: General Provisions, Chapter 18," eCode360, City of Kalamazoo, MI law code, https://ecode360.com/36972084.

4   But in August 2018: Adam Reyes, "Homeless Say They Feel Safe and Supported in Downtown Kalamazoo Camp," WMUK News, September 10, 2018, https://www.wmuk.org/wmuk-news/2018-09-10/homeless-say-they-feel-safe-and-supported-in-downtown-kalamazoo-camp.

5   They bulldozed the encampment: Franque Thompson, "10 who refused to leave Bronson Park encampment arraigned Wednesday in Kalamazoo court," WWMT Newschannel 3, October 3, 2018, https://wwmt.com/news/local/10-who-refused-to-leave-bronson-park-encampment-arraigned-wednesday-in-kalamazoo-court.

6   By 2021, it could boast: Kalamazoo Community Foundation. "TRHT Kalamazoo Impact Report" October 20, 2021, 89, https://issuu.com/kalfound/docs/executive_summary_trht_impact_report_for_print.

7   TRHT Kalamazoo partnered with another local group: Kalamazoo Community Foundation, "TRHT Kalamazoo Impact Report," 55.

8   A survey: Kalamazoo Community Foundation, "TRHT Kalamazoo Impact Report," 55.

9   And those who discriminated: "Art: General Provisions, Chapter 18," eCode360, City of Kalamazoo, MI law code, https://ecode360.com/36972084.

10   As Griffin has said: Public Media Network, https://www.publicmedianet.org/blog/kalamazoos-fair-housing-ordinance-step-right-direction-after-years-racist-housing-policies.

11   Advocates fanned out: Kalamazoo Community Foundation, "TRHT Kalamazoo Impact Report," 57.

12   The group continues: Kalamazoo Community Foundation. "Executive Summary: TRHT Kalamazoo Impact Report" October 20, 2021, 7, https://issuu.com/kalfound/docs/executive_summary_trht_impact_report_for_print.

13   Later, Buffalo joined Flint: "Urban Renewal," The Inclusive Historian's Handbook, November 12, 2019, https://inclusivehistorian.com/urban-renewal/.

14   A 2021 study: Henry-Louis Taylor Jr. et al., "The Harder We Run: The State of Black Buffalo in 1990 and the Present," University at Buffalo Center for Urban Studies, September 2021, 6–10, https://www.investigativepost.org/wp-content/uploads/2021/10/TaylorHL-The-Harder-We-Run.pdf.

15   One major theme that emerged: Taylor Jr., "The Harder We Run."

16   More than eight in ten: Erica Brecher, "New Grant-funded Program in Erie Co. Aims to Reduce Recidivism," *WIBV-TV*, July 28, 2019, https://www.wivb.com/news/local-news/erie-county/new-grant-funded-program-in-erie-co-aims-to-reduce-recidivism/.

17   Since opening in 2020: "Service Link Stop," Erie County Department of Mental Health, accessed May 10, 2024, https://www3.erie.gov/mentalhealth/sites/www3.erie.gov.mentalhealth/files/2021-07/sls-brochure_v5.pdf.

18   He killed ten Black American men and women: Bill Chappell, "Here are the 10 people killed and 3 hurt in the Buffalo shooting," National Public Radio, May 16, 2022, https://www.npr.org/2022/05/16/1099124755/buffalo-shooting-victims-names.

19   The terrorist underlined his racist motives: Keeanga-Yamahtta Taylor, "Hiding Buffalo's History of Racism Behind a Cloak of Unity, *The New Yorker*, June 9, 2022, https://www.newyorker.com/news/our-columnists/hiding-buffalos-history-of-racism-behind-a-cloak-of-unity.

20   As he told one journalist: Claretta Bellamy, "Historic systemic racism plagues East Buffalo's growth," W. K. Kellogg Foundation, last accessed June 18, 2024, https://healourcommunities.org/watch/buffalo/.

21 In an 1838 letter, the Rev. Peter Havermans: "What Will Become of Me?": Fr. Havermans Reports on the Anguish of the Slaves," The Georgetown Slavery Archive, October 20, 1838 and November 12, 1838, http://slaveryarchive.georgetown.edu/items/show/226.

22 Never one to give up, Joe: Rupa Shenoy, "'Our Goal is to Heal': Jesuits and Descendants of the Enslaved Reflect on Landmark Agreement," *The World*, March 22, 2021, https://theworld.org/stories/2021-03-22/our-goal-heal-jesuits-and-descendants-enslaved-reflect-landmark-agreement.

23 Joe and his fellow descendants: "Pope at Audience: 'it's one thing to talk mercy, another to live it,'" Archdiocese of Malta, January 7, 2016 https://church.mt/pope-at-audience-its-one-thing-to-talk-mercy-another-to-live-it/.

24 After that meeting, Joe called me to ask: Author interview with Joe Stewart, September 19, 2023; author interview with Joe Stewart, September 26, 2023.

25 As Joe recounted in an interview: Shenoy, "'Our Goal Is to Heal'."

26 Because, he said, South Africa's new democratic leaders: "Kellogg Foundation—75th anniversary," address by Desmond Tutu in Battle Creek, Michigan, August 5, 2005, https://archive.tutuiptrust.org/Documents/Detail/kellogg-foundation-75th-anniversary-battle-creek-michigan-5-august-2005/4211.

27 And in Kenya, Sierra Leone, and the United States: "Who We Are: Our Name," Namati, https://namati.org/who-we-are/#:~:text=Namati%20is%20a%20Sanskrit%20word,dedicated%20to%20bending%20that%20curve.

28 Sachs discussed his approach: Albie Sachs, Remarks at 2023 Global Leadership Forum, W. K. Kellogg Foundation, accessed June 18, 2024.

29 Sachs told me about this vision: Albie Sachs, Remarks at 2023 Global Leadership Forum, W. K. Kellogg Foundation.

30 As Archbishop Tutu told us: Desmond Tutu, Address given on the 75th anniversary of the Kellogg Foundation in Battle Creek, August 5, 2005, https://www.unitus.org/FULL/tutu.PDF.

CONCLUSION

1 He was there to organize support: "Dr. Martin Luther King's Visit to Cornell College," *Cornell College News Center*, https://news.cornellcollege.edu/dr-martin-luther-kings-visit-to-cornell-college/.

2 Dr. King continued, "God grant": "Dr. Martin Luther King's Visit to Cornell College."

3 He thought that sounded interesting: Author interview with Howard Walters, February 29, 2024.

4 Each of these events carries us: "The King Philosophy," The King Center, https://thekingcenter.org/about-tkc/the-king-philosophy/#:~:text=In%20a%201957%20speech%2C%20Birth,aftermath%20of%20nonviolence%20is%20reconciliation.

5 All those years ago, W. K. Kellogg: Kellogg Company. "Nourishing Families So They Can Flourish and Thrive," 2014 Corporate Responsibility Report, April 23, 2015, 74, https://filecache.mediaroom.com/mr5mr_kellogs_cr/181041/KelloggCompany_CRReport_2014.pdf.